a miserable antagonist

By
Reid Matthias

Copyright © Reid Matthias 2024

All rights reserved. Other than for the purposes and subject to the conditions prescribed under the *Copyright Act*, no part of this publication may be reproduced, stored in a retrieval system, or transmitted in any form or by any means, electronic, mechanical, photocopying, recording or otherwise, without the prior permission of the publisher.

ISBN paperback: 978-0-6456882-2-1
     ebook: 978-0-6456882-3-8

This edition first published by A 13 in May 2024

Typesetting by Ben Morton

Publication assistance from Immortalise

Front and back cover images by Josephine Matthias.

Acknowledgments

A long time ago, I submitted my first manuscript to a professional editor who predictably, in working with an unknown writer and his amateurish skill, unsheathed her powerful red pen, and stabbed my story to death. The red whorls and slashes were not only wounds on the pages, but I felt them personally, as if the pen had severed the jugular of my literary creativity. As I leafed through the 'I-don't-like-this' and 'Have-you-been-curling-up-with-a-thesaurus-at-night' and a few 'I-can't-read-any-more-of-this,' I almost hurled my computer into the digital compost heap and decided to stick with *reading* books rather than *writing* them.

Why is it that criticism feels so much like a miniature death?

My personal author's resurrection came shortly after the editor's post-mortem, when my friend Keith read the manuscript and said, in spite of the need for more editing, 'I loved it!' Curiously, at his exclamation, something changed in my perspective – could it have been hope? Happiness? – and it suddenly dawned on me that the purpose for my writing was all wonky. Just like the rest of humanity and its senseless addiction to erect thumbs, love-hearts, emojis, and all that, I was writing for people I didn't know, and I didn't care about. Worst of all, I was writing for editors and critics, and their vacuous comments of adoration or abhorrence, whose opinions, though professionally sterile, didn't matter one whit to my own sense of value.

Instead, after finishing my first novels, I handed them with trembling hands to editors who mattered. Though they don't have the 'credentials' of professional editors, they have the same eye, the same reading knowledge, and the same passion for books, as the countless benumbed proofreaders in the 'real world' of literature. What my personal editors have, though, is my trust. They are people like my sister, Vikki, whose meticulous eye for detail has been so appreciated.

Like Bonnie, a re-acquainted friend from high school, who spots textual deficiencies and relays them openly and with careful critique. Like Ben and his work with typesetting and cover art. As always, Christine, Elsa, Josephine and Greta have read and re-read this story to make it as aesthetically pleasing as possible. My appreciation cannot be overstated. I could go on endlessly, but I'm sure you'd like to turn your eyes to this joyful work titled *A Miserable Antagonist*.

A long time ago, while at college, I encountered a professor who shall not be named (not in Voldemortian aversion, but in the general sense that time has cleansed the wounds leaving only scars) with whom I struggled mightily. My feelings toward the professor have mellowed, yet I have found a certain desire to, as Brian Helgeland wrote in his screenplay of *A Knight's Tale*, '…eviscerate you in fiction. Every pimple, every character flaw. I was naked for a day; you will be naked for eternity.' Though I do not wish eternal nudity on my professor, I wrote this story cathartically to spite my memories of that time; I found a malevolent glee, something very freeing, writing in such a way. There is no better methodology of revenge, if it can be called that, than turning misery into humor.

This book is dedicated to nine college friends who affectionately entered into a cooperative of mirth called the Warm Fuzzies. As we've aged, our laughter has turned to fine wine, or vinegar, depending on the day. Even though apart, we remain together.

For Ryan, Raber, Dettmer, Albright, Curtis, Maassen, Thul, Hageman, Neil.

Chapter 1

"The protagonist always, always, always has a character flaw."

These words came on the fourth Wednesday night of class, the night when Baxter Burnside truly began his new life as an author. Professor Mangall kicked off his Creative Writing 102 class by lifting his green whiteboard marker to point at individual students, marking them for life or death, like a literary medic in authorial triage.

And so it was that when Mangall pointed in the general vicinity of Baxter Burnside and continued his blathering, Baxter found himself completely adrift in nouns, verbs and an assortment of worthless adjectives.

"It's one of the great truths of effective literature, people. The author, the reader, and all other characters recognize the protagonist's pride, or his greed, or his lack of empathy, or any selection from the menu of sins, deadly or otherwise, and see that the protagonist is always, always, always! blind to said flaw." With each successive *always*, Professor Mangall rapped the palm of his hand with the green marker.

Baxter squirmed uncomfortably in his cushioned seat and snuck an unobtrusive glance at the beautiful woman sitting next to him. Her name was Hana. She was from Austria. And she had a delightful accent that Baxter loved. Hana was the reason he had registered for the class. As he watched her from the corner of his eye, he was mesmerized by the way she restlessly curled a tendril of lovely hair near her temple. Until, that is, Professor Mangall dropped his next pearl of wisdom. She paused her tendrilling to scrawl the professor's next words in majestic cursive.

"The good guys of literature have selective vision regarding their flaws. They choose to believe that they float above the horrible things in which the common masses swim."

Good guys have selective vision, she wrote and underlined.

Parker pointed his marker at a young woman in the front row who squirmed with delight (and dread) that the great Parker Mangall had singled her out with his writing instrument.

"And yet," he continued without asking a question, "there is *that* moment when the literary mirror is held up before the protagonist's face, *that* moment when he becomes aware, or self-aware, of the way he appears to the rest of the world, and realizes his flaw is an unseen zit on the end of his nose, of which, until *that* moment, he has been blissfully ignorant."

Unconsciously, the young woman touched the end of her nose checking to see if she was the source of Parker Mangall's metaphor. Thankfully, no.

"The best authors write into reality the tragic flaws of beautiful characters and enable the reader to *empathize* with what the protagonist now knows." As his voice lowered, Mangall hefted the weight of his genius with his hands.

Write into reality tragic flaws of beautiful characters.

Hana placed her pen on the desk in front of her and folded her hands primly. It was then that she noticed Baxter, with his thinning, pre-middle-aged hair and round face, punctuated with a buttonish nose poking out from the center, like a macadamia nut beneath chocolatey brown eyes, staring at her. He blushed and looked away.

Chapter 1

After an appropriate amount of time, another glance revealed Hana's fingers, long and thin, tightened resting now on top of the desk. The sinews in her hands stood out against pale skin, which led to wiry-strong forearms, which led to… She picked up the pen and wrote again.

A story doesn't have to be real, but it has to have real emotion.

For the three previous Wednesday nights, Baxter had listened to Mangall's mid-week drone about protagonists and antagonists, the difference between analogy and metaphor, heck, the usual function of prepositional clauses, with bored disinterest. Frankly, Baxter was getting pretty dang tired of protagonists, prepositions and participles. He wanted to do some actual writing.

On a whim, Baxter raised his hand.

"Yes?" Mangall stopped his pontification and pointed dramatically at Baxter with his omnipotent-conch-shell-green marker. "Do you have a question or a comment?"

The rest of the class, consisting of grey-haired sixty-somethings, a handful of university students, and a few J.K. Rowling wannabees, turned toward Baxter. Interrupting Mangall was tantamount to abject public humiliation.

"Both," he said.

"Enlighten us, please."

At that moment a strange, fleeting vision entered Baxter Burnside's mind, one where he ripped the green whiteboard marker from Mangall's hand and stuck it up the professor's insight. Baxter cleared his mind and spoke. "Why are there no books where the bad guy is the good guy? Because I want…"

"There are plenty of books," Professor Mangall interrupted with a sneering smile, "where the antagonist goes through a re-birth, a transition from malevolent to benevolent, from…"

"Yeah, yeah, yeah, I hear what you're saying." Baxter volleyed the interruption to Professor Mangall prompting the class to collectively gasp and react like spectators sitting courtside for a particularly intense tennis match. "But what I'm talking about is: Why aren't there stories about really bad guys, who do really bad stuff, and get away with it. Like real life."

The professor chuckled condescendingly and crossed his arms. His voice, both in tone and volume, dropped precipitously. "I'm sure I can speak for most of the class, and perhaps the entire human race, when I say, people don't read books to be reminded of the random, thoughtless mayhem of life. We are outraged when an author destroys love, or hope, or, or, or…"

A young student, with green hair, a nose ring, and numerous tattoos obliterating much of the skin on her arms, filled in the blank space of the professor's list. "Happiness."

"Yes, yes," he turned the green marker on her and pointed appreciatively at her hopeful face. "Happiness. We don't want to be reminded that life, in almost every instance, is decidedly *un*happy and *un*fair."

"But what about a bad guy who is just born bad and really likes to destroy love, hope and happiness?' Baxter insisted.

"Do *you* want to write a book about that?" the professor's sarcasm echoed in the room.

Frozen like a deer in the headlights of an onrushing car, Baxter couldn't speak. Slowly he lowered his head, unable to see Mangall's look of vindication.

Chapter 1

Baxter's keys jangled loudly on the kitchen counter. He had not meant to drop them so indelicately, but he was frustrated with Mangall. The professor was obviously intelligent and able to communicate, but his arrogance burned Baxter. Nothing would have pleased Baxter more than to find a way to publicly humiliate the professor, but it was not going to happen. It was not in Baxter's amicable nature to draw attention to himself or humiliate others.

But he *wished* he could be like that.

As he thought about the myriad ways in which Parker Mangall could be metaphorically bloodied and smeared, Baxter rounded the bench and entered his kitchen. The room was small and woodsy as if a lumberjack had decorated it. The wallpaper was themed with rustic farm implements and tools. In various places, the paper had peeled like the wrinkled skin of an old person (his mother had skin like that), and it had yellowed along these scars. The motif was not entirely his fault (or choice). His parents, Betty and Burnie (his real name was Art, but everyone called him Burnie), had installed the cupboards themselves. They - meaning Betty - then decorated the shelving with knickknacks and cutesy serving spoons with saccharine sayings like, *Stir is a beautiful day,* which Baxter did not notice anymore. If it were up to Baxter, he would have redecorated everything, but his parents came over far too often. Betty, especially, would have been hurt if Baxter had disposed of the (her) decorations. Sometimes his mother asked him where the nice, Mickey Mouse cross-stitched towels had gone. Baxter didn't have the gumption to tell her he'd offloaded them at a garage sale.

Baxter opened one of the Burnside-Specialty cupboards and grabbed a box of cookies. After filling a glass with milk, he sat morosely at his small table, dunking cookies, and wondering how he was going to finish (more importantly – START!) his Creative Writing 102 assignment – The Novella.

For Baxter, writing a novella had never been a goal. Before Creative Writing 102, he would have spent more time gardening or walking or eating... anything but writing, or reading, for that fact. As he pondered the assignment, his mind wandered back to his Creative Writing 102 elbow buddy, Hana.

Their meeting had been accidental. On one of his afternoon walks, (a habit Baxter had begun when his mother told him he was starting to look a little portly) Baxter bent down to tie his shoe when an enormous, out-of-control dog careened into him knocking him into the bushes. Irritated, Baxter stood and prepared to launch his road-rage... until he saw the owner of the hound. The leash-holding goddess was stunning in her exercise gear, standing at least three inches taller than him, with short, mousy brown hair and three delightful little moles on her left cheek. On that day, Hana had been wearing sparklingly white tennis shoes and a mid-length summery dress. She was clutching the leash with a green plastic bag tied to it.

Baxter's words of outrage were checked quickly behind a fake smile, and he accepted her apology graciously.

"No, no, no," he said picking a piece of bush from his arm. "My fault. My fault. I shouldn't have been tying my shoe in the runaway dogs' lane."

Hana failed to understand the joke and held a hand over her heart. "Please. I'm sorry. Hund, my dog, he..."

The rest of her words were lost in what Baxter believed was love at first conversation. Her accent, her lilting voice – even the way she had to peer down at him – made

Chapter 1

Baxter feel slightly woozy. Those eyes, and the dots on her cheek, like tiny chocolate Kisses. Those lips...

He swallowed nervously. "Do you walk here much?" Baxter asked.

"Yes, in between my other duties."

Baxter quivered at the way she turned 'between' into '*betveen.*' He glanced down at her hands to surreptitiously check for a wedding ring. None. *Excellent.* "Where do you live?"

Eyes narrowing, Hana retreated a step from him. "I'm not sure..."

Baxter raised his hands. "No, I didn't mean... I didn't ask because I wanted to stalk you. It was just..."

He shouldn't have said the word 'stalk'. Hana raised her eyebrows, turned on her heel, and called Hund to her side so they could flee from the psychopath Hund had knocked over.

As good fortune would have it, a week later, they met on the same path. This time Hund was well-behaved, and she was carrying something in a plastic bag. Hana extended the gift and placed it in his hands.

"What is it?"

"A loaf of bread."

"What for?"

"Because I acted strangely last week. I can be... awkward." Her eyes were anxious, as if this kind of revelation was normally a deal breaker.

"No, no, I'll be the awkward one in this relationship."

Her hands twitched when he said 'relationship.'

"What I meant was, oh, damnit, I've done it again. There's no relationship," he motioned back and forth between the two of them. "I was just trying to be funny." He took a deep breath. "It's very nice that you felt like you had to apologize, but really, it's unnecessary."

While Hana grasped Hund's leash, Baxter stood with a cooling loaf of bread in his hands. Both humans tried to think of something – anything – to fill the clumsy, noiseless space between them. Suddenly, Baxter had a brainwave.

"What's your name?" he shouted his question almost in triumph.

Startled, Hana jumped. Hund barked once, then twice, warning Baxter that that kind of noise would not be tolerated.

"Hana," she responded nervously.

"My name is Baxter. Baxter Burnside."

"Nice to meet you." Neither was quite sure if it was proper to shake hands, so they didn't.

"I like your accent," Baxter said.

Blushing, Hana reached up with her non-leash-holding hand and touched her cheek. "I can't seem to get rid of it."

"Why would you want to? It's so… European."

She frowned. "I don't understand what you mean."

"You know, exotic, like someone from… I don't know… Canada."

"That's funny," she said.

"What accent is it? Norwegian? Polish?"

"Austrian."

"I was going to say that next."

He wasn't. In fact, Baxter had no idea how to identify accents. He was, though, quite pleased that he guessed the right continent.

"Where is your accent from?" Hana asked.

"I don't have an accent."

"Of course you do. To me, you have an accent. Have you always lived here in Vermont?" *Fermont.*

Chapter 1

He nodded, now staring at the bread in his hands, unsure whether to lower it, or hold it like a platter in front of him. "I've only been out of the States once, and that was to Niagara Falls. My parents thought it necessary for me to get some culture."

Hana smiled to be agreeable, but she was unsure of whether Niagara qualified as a deeply cultural, international experience. "We went on the Maid of the Mist and then…" his voice trailed off. Really, there was nothing particularly exciting about traveling to Canada. To Baxter, it just seemed like North Montpelier except for the gigantic waterfall running down the middle.

"Fascinating," she said distractedly as Hund arched his back to deposit last night's meal on the grass to their right.

"What kind of dog is that?" Baxter had never been around dogs. His mother didn't like the idea of an animal in the house.

Hana frowned as she put her hand in the green bag and plucked up the dog's excrement from the grass like the Easter Bunny's evil twin snagging chocolate eggs from a nest. "Hund is a greyhound."

"Oh."

"You've never seen a greyhound before?" She asked incredulously while tying the plastic green bag of feces with a bow. Baxter felt a wave of nausea roll across his stomach. The warm, squishy feeling of the…

"Baxter?"

Jolted back to the present, he was aware of the warm bag of squishy bread in his own hands. "Sorry, uh, no, I've never seen one in real life before, but I've heard of them. Something to do with buses?"

A Miserable Antagonist

Hund suddenly began tugging on the leash. "Yes," she said, "but... more... to do... with... dog... racing." As she was yanked back towards the path, her voice was jerky. "Would... you... like to... be pulled... along... with... me?"

Baxter Burnside felt a warm glow. It had been many years since a woman had requested his company on a walk. Not since Eris. He shivered. *That* relationship had been an abject failure marked by intense moments of mutual dislike, but he and Eris had stubbornly stayed together, right up until a month before their wedding date. When Baxter and Eris went for a walk to break off the engagement, Baxter felt a tremendous sense of relief, as well as a half dozen swats around the head and arms from his former fiancée. When he told his parents, his father's response was, 'Thank God we won't be dropping any money into *that*!'

"Yes, I would love to be pulled with you," Baxter responded as he attempted to catch up with her and Hund.

Hund drove them forward. Hana's long strides were able to keep up with the dog, but Baxter, unused to walking quickly, found himself breathless as he hurried behind her.

"So," he huffed, "what brought you to Vermont? The mountains?" Baxter forgot about the little mountain range which ran through Austria.

"No, no, I moved here for my husband."

Baxter's heart fell and his pace slowed. It wasn't as if he was preparing for marriage per se, but at least the possibility would have been a nice thing to ponder.

"Oh."

Hund stopped pulling and she faced Baxter without looking at him. "He died five years ago."

Baxter tried to frown, but it came out like a happy grimace. "I'm sorry."

Chapter 1

"He was not the kindest man in the world, but we were married for seventeen years."

Surprised, Baxter attempted to calculate her age: *Let's assume she was twenty-five when she got married, seventeen years of marriage, five years of widowhood, that would put her at forty-seven. That's only five years older than me!*

"I'm forty-five, if you're trying to add it up," she smiled.

He blushed. "Was it that obvious?"

"Your mouth works silently when you think hard."

"You saw that?"

"I did."

"You don't look that old," Baxter said lamely.

"Thank you. And how about you, Baxter Burnside. How old are you?"

"Forty-two."

She did not respond in kind because Baxter Burnside most certainly looked his age. Older, even. Neither the years nor his lifestyle had been kind to his appearance. The most appropriate adjectives to describe him were *fleshy* and *personality driven*. His doctor's descriptions were even less positive. *You've got some clogged arteries, Mr. Burnside. Perhaps it's time to lay off the doughnuts?* But he did, in fact, have a very nice personality. Many people had commented on his manners and complimentary nature.

"Interesting," she said instead.

"Why is that interesting?"

She turned away to follow the dog again. "We are almost the same age."

He chased after her. "So, your husband died, and you've decided to stay?"

"Yes. Montpelier is my home now."

"That's good." Baxter thought the way she pronounced *Montpelier* sounded like a ritzy kind of chocolate.

When Hund stopped again, Baxter put his hands on his hips and gulped oxygen. A Rorschach blot had appeared on his shirt in the shape of a heart over his heart. "What do you do for a living?"

"I am a florist."

"Huh," he grunted. "I wasn't expecting that."

"What were you expecting?"

"I don't know. A piano teacher, or something like that. You give off kind of a piano-teacherish aura."

"Is that good?"

"Very. Most piano teachers are wonderful."

"Do you play piano?"

Baxter pondered his musical ineptitude. His mother made him take piano lessons for two years when he was young, but his fingers were too short, and his sense of rhythm bordered on painful. But he did want to impress Hana. And the fact that he *did* take piano lessons gave some credence to a positive reply.

"I dabble," he responded, hoping that even if they did get married, she wouldn't be asking for a little ditty at their wedding.

"And you," she motioned with her leash hand, "what do you do?"

"I'm a banker." This *also* wasn't entirely true, yet it was close enough for plausibility. Baxter was a teller at a non-descript, cookie-cutter bank named Last National on the western edge of Montpelier. Though it had been established over one hundred years ago, the clientele had not changed much since its inception.

"I bet that's interesting."

"You'd be surprised. You probably know a thing or two about banking since you live in Austria."

Chapter 1

Hana blinked. "Switzerland is probably better known for its banking, but yes, Austria does have successful banks as well."

Baxter felt like an idiot. "Of course, Switzerland." Baxter attempted to outrun his stupidity. "I was reading a journal the other day…" When her eyes fogged over, he stopped talking. Somehow, the white lie wasn't getting any darker the longer he talked about it. "Say, what do you do for fun? Do you have any hobbies?"

Shyly, she batted her eyes over her shoulder. "It's crazy, really."

"What is it?"

"I… I'm taking a class at the University of Vermont in Burlington."

"Tell me."

Her eyes were magnetic – luminous – and echoes of dirndl-clad Austrian women yodeling in the mountains began to echo through Baxter's mind. "It's a creative writing class. You see, I've always had ideas, stories, you know, about faraway places and tragic people, love and anger... So, after my husband died, I had extra time and needed an outlet for it. There are stories I had started to write but never really thought I'd finish." Hana looked away as if embarrassed by the thought. "You must think me silly."

"Absolutely not. What's wrong with writing creatively?" Baxter said. "I think it's great, diversifying, finding out what you're good at. I've often wanted to do the same thing!" Baxter almost gasped at this much bigger lie. He wanted nothing to do with writing. *Reading* a novel was a stretch for him, but writing one? He might as well swim to the moon.

Her face lit up. "Maybe you'd like to join the class then?"

"Me? What? Er..." One hand remained on a hip while the other covered his sweaty chest. "I'm pretty busy during the day. You know, the bank job and all."

"It is okay! They are night classes!"

Aware that he'd made a colossal mistake, stepping directly in what Hana had recently picked up behind Hund, Baxter's mouth opened and shut like an air-breathing fish. "I don't know what to say..."

"I think you should say yes!"

"Well, I'll think about it. Where... um, it's been a long time since I've been to college. How do I register?"

"Everything is online, but if you'd like, I will give you my number and we can do it together." Her smile widened.

Now, trapped in an ever-tightening noose of his own stupidity, Baxter felt as if he had no option. "Okay, then."

Hana produced her phone. "What is your number? I'll call you and then you'll have mine." He gave it to her. After a brief pause, his phone rang. "There, now we are connected."

Despite his nervousness about agreeing to join a writing class, Baxter felt a thrill of the chase. He was a lovehound and she, a spotted love-rabbit. As he was about to respond, a very determined greyhound spotted a very frightened rabbit. The ensuing tug nearly dislocated Hana Stutz's shoulder. Crying out in pain and casting an *auf wiedersehen* behind her, (Baxter had visions of Maria von Trapp twirling about with a bunch of kids) she chased her dog across the green grass towards the small grove of trees where the rabbit desperately sought shelter.

It was not to be for the rabbit.

Escaping his owner's grasp, Hund easily outdistanced his prey and took captive the twitching, thumping rabbit in his mouth.

Chapter 1

Uncaring about the rabbit's painful demise, Baxter stared at his phone.

He had her number.

Chapter 2

Betty Burnside held the blue dishtowel in her left hand and grabbed a freshly washed plate from Baxter. She picked at something crusty with her fingernail and immediately returned it to him. Used to this kind of picking, he accepted the imperfect plate and dunked it back in the water. Scrubbing hard, Baxter removed the spot and handed it back to his mother, who, after a second inspection, nodded and dried the plate.

"Tell me again about this class you're taking."

Baxter was about to detail Creative Writing 102, but before he could speak, Hana stepped in next to him and took his spot at the sink. For the last six weeks, since they had been spending time together in the class, a genuine friendship had evolved. On this particular night, Burnie and Betty had invited themselves over to Baxter's house to both dine and meet Baxter's 'new romance,' as Betty had described her to Burnie.

It was the first time Hana had met them. His parents, or more appropriately, his mother, often queried about his 'love interests,' using finger quotes, insinuating that Baxter did *not*, in fact, have any real 'love interests.' When he told them about Hana, they were shocked. Since Eris Cromwell, the elder Burnsides truly believed that their precious son was destined for eternal bachelorhood.

This was the reason for Baxter's extreme nervousness about introducing them to Hana. Betty had a certain way about her – a cross between a Spanish Inquisitor and a Customs Agent. Her questions, although well intended, often set people aback. Questions like: *How long are you*

Chapter 2

expected to live? Are you finally divorced? And, Baxter's least personal favorite - *Have you always dreamed of being on welfare?*

"It's a creative writing class, Mrs. Burnside," Hana said as she towered over the diminutive woman who had ceased checking dishes for flaws and gaped up at the Austrian.

"Stop calling me that," Betty chided good-naturedly as she regained her composure. "My name is Betty. Call me Betty." Taking a step back, Betty handed the towel to Baxter who accepted it and began drying the dishes. "Creative writing. Well, that's fascinating. I can't ever remember Baxter being interested in literature."

"People take their time, Mom," Baxter said as he dried an antique, dimpled drinking glass and handed it to his mother for her to place in the cupboard. Betty was three inches shorter than her son, but much thinner. When she was younger, she had dark red hair, but now, at sixty-nine years of age, it was graying and habitually pulled back into the tightest of buns on the back of her head.

"I *know* that, Sweetheart, but the only books I ever saw you read were those comic books, what was it Burnie? The ones about the kids in high school, you know…"

"Archie and Friends," he grunted while staring at Baxter's twenty-nine-inch console television sitting on a small end table. "Archie."

"Oh, that's right."

"They're called graphic novels now," Baxter corrected.

"Kids' things if you ask me. Just pictures."

"That's what books are, Mom," Baxter said. "All books paint pictures."

"Well aren't you getting smarty-farty," she raised an eyebrow.

Hana interrupted. "That's what our professor, Mr. Mangall said. '*If the book doesn't paint a picture, it's simply loosely connected words destined for the wastebasket.*'"

Betty Burnside again scrutinized the tall, willow-tree-of-a-woman hoping that Hana would wilt under the pressure of her gaze. When Hana did not, she begrudgingly marked the 'can-stand-up-for-herself' box on Baxter's life-partner criteria sheet.

"Getting back to the creative writing class," Baxter continued, "we're learning the process for writing novellas – fiction."

Betty snorted. "You're going to write a novel."

Baxter jutted out his jaw. "It's a *novella*, a short novel. You don't think I can?"

"Color me skeptical."

Hana came to his defense. "Baxter has got some great ideas, Betty. He even challenged the professor on some common assumptions of novels."

Feeling justified, Baxter grinned. He finished the last dish and hung the towel over the handle of the oven door. "That's right, Mother."

"How did that go over?"

"Well… let's just say I have an idea."

"For a novel?" his mother questioned.

"A *novella*. I don't know, Mom. I suppose it's all quite ridiculous to you, but I enjoy it, and Hana has been very helpful. She's quite talented."

Betty's gaze bounced between the middle-aged adults who desperately sought her approval. "I'm sure she is, Baxter, but I'm worried your feelings will be hurt."

"I'm a grown man, Mother. I can handle it."

Her look said differently. "What is the process for writing this little novel?"

Chapter 2

Baxter didn't correct her again. She was doing it on purpose now. "It's all about the idea. To come up with something original. An author can write whatever they want. They can create or destroy or offend or do anything they want in the name of literature. It's wonderfully different than working in the bank."

"What's your *idea*?" his mother exaggerated the word.

"The bad guy wins."

"What?"

"The bad guy wins. You know – Lex Luthor or the Joker. They win."

"I don't know who those people are."

"Honestly, Mom, how did you survive the 20th century?"

His mother did not pick up the sarcasm. "By good, hard work. None of this fancy-schmancy online-computer crap. Why, your father and I worked our fingers to the bone so that…"

Sighing, Baxter backed away from the counter to interrupt her tired script. "…so that I could have the best upbringing available. I know. You've told me a million times."

Betty's face pinched. "You don't have to hurt my feelings."

"I didn't."

"Well, the way you're talking tonight is a good start for your novel – Sorry! *Novella!* Being the bad guy sounds like something you might be able to write about." Betty crossed her arms and tossed her head back.

Burnie shouted over the recliner. "Too far, Betty."

"You mind your own business."

Hana seemed alarmed.

"Well," his mother huffed with faux rejection, and searched the room, "it feels as if we've outstayed our welcome. Where is my handbag? Burnie, where is my bag?" Burnie did not respond.

For Baxter, this was the turning point in every visit he dreaded. Sometimes it happened early, sometimes late, but there was always that moment when both Baxter and Betty had had enough of each other. The progression from 'Hello, Baxter, it's good to see you,' with a hug and a lug of the basket of freshly baked goods, to 'Well, we've outstayed our welcome,' was as predictable as the ocean tides.

"Thanks for coming, Mom."

"Burnie, let's go." Betty extended her hand to Hana. "It was very nice to meet you, Hana. Burnie! Now!"

Grunting with effort, Burnie Burnside stood from his chair. Replicating the handshake with Hana, Burnie left the kitchen without speaking. As they trudged down the hallway to the exit, Betty began to quietly chastise Burnie about his general lack of speed. Burnie did not respond, nor did he accelerate.

When the door clicked shut and his parents left, Baxter leaned his back against it, ran a hand through his hair, and let out a whooshing breath. "Sorry about that."

"About what? They seem like lovely people."

"If your definition of lovely is stubborn and dismissive, then yes, my mother is it."

"Oh, don't be so hard on her," Hana responded. "It's obvious she cares about you."

Baxter harrumphed. "Cares about my income, my clean toilets, if I've been dusting, or my 'love life.'" He replicated his mother's air quotes.

"Those are good things to care about," Hana laughed.

"Well," Baxter said as he walked to the living room, "maybe *you* can adopt her as your own mother."

Chapter 2

Hana followed him. "Let's change the subject. Tell me more about your novella idea."

They settled into the empty living room. Baxter jerked the chain on an old lamp covered by a shade with tassels hanging from the lower rim. On the table connected to the middle of the stand, a half-finished coffee cup and small book of crosswords sat, still there from the morning. Hana curled a leg up underneath her and sat erectly in a threadbare sofa covered by a multi-colored afghan. Baxter plonked down on the chair his father had vacated. It was still warm. "The novella. Yes, well, it's nothing, really. I only spoke my mind because I was frustrated by Mangall. He's a lot of hot air, if you ask me."

"You're avoiding my question."

"Which one?"

She frowned.

"Okay. I think bad guys believe they're doing good in kind of a warped way. It's like…" his eyes rolled to the left as he sought the right words, "… like a virus. To the host, the virus is the bad guy. But really, the virus is just doing what it is made to do. From the virus' perspective, it's the good guy."

"That's very confusing."

He shrugged and searched the room hoping that one of his mother's knickknacks might help him explain what he meant. There was a cheerful ceramic bear grinning at him from the shelf above the television, and to the right, a photograph, delicately placed on a yellowed doily, of Baxter and his parents on a family vacation to a forgotten hamlet near the New Hampshire border. "If I have to write a novella, it might as well be something that no one else writes about."

"Especially in *our* small group," Hana smirked. "If you had to guess, what do you think they will write about?"

There were twenty-three students in Creative Writing 102; six in their small group. The purpose of the group was to share ideas, thoughts, writing tips, and create conversation. Their small group consisted of Curtis, a tall, early-retiree with an impressive head of salt-and-pepper hair; Lisa, an early twenty-something who couldn't figure out what to do with her life; Barbara, a highly-strung single mother with an incredibly perceptive BS detector; and Murray, a perpetual student and author-wannabe.

"Lisa, for sure, will write about something fanciful – unicorns, maybe."

Hana laughed. "And Barbara – something erotic, don't you think?"

"Murray will sketch an outline that no one will want to read. Academic, or something so pompous even Mangall will make fun of him."

"Curtis?" Her eyes shifted.

"No idea. Poetry?" Baxter studied Hana. Her eyes shifted when Curtis' name was spoken. "And you?"

"I haven't decided. Something about aliens or vampires." She noticed him staring and laughed loudly. "I'm kidding. I've got an idea about a young female musical prodigy who deals with unrequited love.

Baxter grimaced.

"Just because it's not your genre, doesn't mean it's not mine."

He held up his hands. "I know, I'm sorry. I didn't mean to reveal that expression."

"Yet, my idea will be much easier than yours. I cannot even begin to imagine how you are going to write it. Some people might hate even the thought of it."

Chapter 2

"I don't care what other people think," Baxter responded.

"You are lying, Mr. Burnside. I can tell. You *do* care because you are a very nice man." She tapped the sofa for the last three words. "You are the least bad person I know."

"I can be bad. I *can*," he stressed after she rolled her eyes. "And if I can't, I'll just have to figure it out."

"Do you have an outline yet? What about the opening paragraph? That's our assignment for next week."

Baxter felt his stomach lurch. As of yet, the first line of his novella had surpassed his talent; to write an entire first paragraph seemed overwhelming.

Unfortunately, his creative writing deficiency was about to manifest itself in a most blatant, obvious way.

Chapter 3

When students began to arrive at the Creative Writing 102 class, chairs had been arranged in six crude, amoeba-shaped blobs. By the time Baxter walked through the door, most of his small group was sitting uncomfortably across from each other, eyes darting, hands nervously dog-tagging the corners of their notebooks. Curtis, contrarily, wearing tan corduroy pants and a brown cardigan, was the epitome of calm. He sat serenely, arms folded, legs crossed. A bemused smile played across his lips as if he had been listening to something humorous.

While Curtis smirked, Lisa fidgeted nervously. Her hands worried in her lap, twisting and folding an origami elephant, before pausing to click her pen. Out and in. Out and in. The pen seemed symbolic of Lisa's indecision. Barbara was busy texting her babysitter about the complex needs of her children. It was then that Baxter realized Hana had not arrived.

"Hello, Baxter," Curtis welcomed.

"Hello, everyone."

Lisa, the young, Asian-American woman, with silky black hair framing an ovate face, punctuated by dimples near her smile, rocked in her chair and spoke rapidly. "Did you bring your opening paragraph? Your outline? Oh, I'm so nervous. I want you all to like it, but I'm sure you won't. Be gentle, please. But then again, be honest. I don't know. I don't know!" When she grabbed her hair, pen in hand, she accidentally drew a short, black line on her cheek. Furiously, she attempted to erase it, but it smeared instead. None of the others could quite bring themselves to tell her.

Chapter 3

"I brought mine," Baxter held up a crinkled piece of paper. At least a dozen ideas had been started on that piece of paper. Started and discarded. Started and discarded.

"Better hold onto that," Murray pointed at Baxter's crumpled paper. "It might go down in history as the beginning paragraph of a Pulitzer Prize in Literature."

"Why do you do that?" Barbara asked.

"What?" Murray's chin was resting on his forearms. He was the only one who had turned his chair around backwards.

"Why do you make fun of people? You know, contrary to your own belief, you might not be the next Steinbeck."

"Steinbeck," Murray sneered. "I've got some ideas Steinbeck *wished* he would have thought of." Murray's blue eyes squinted. Between them, a large zit had appeared during the last week, surfacing like a volcano from the ocean of flesh on his forehead. It looked as if he had encouraged the impending eruption multiple times.

"Sure you do."

"What are we supposed to be doing?" Baxter asked as he scanned the room of noisy students.

Lisa glanced towards the doorway. "Waiting. Professor Mangall had to step out for a second – he said it was an important phone call."

"Where is Hana?" Barbara asked Baxter.

"No idea."

"Are you two, like, a couple?" Lisa's voice squeaked at the end of her question.

"No."

"You spend a lot of time together."

"Yes, if a lot of time means one night of class per week." Baxter wondered how many other probing questions would be asked while Hana was absent.

"That's as much as I get with my boyfriend. He's always busy. His name is Jeffrey. Jeffrey plays golf and rides a motorcycle. Sometimes he goes fishing on weekends, and there is also the weekly poker game."

"It sounds like Jeffrey is avoiding you," Baxter said.

"No, he's just very busy."

The door at the front of the classroom opened and Parker Mangall stepped in like a magician from behind a curtain. He held up his phone. "Sorry about that, class. It was my publisher. They just need an edited draft for my *next* book." His smarmy voice caused Baxter's stomach to turn. Alternatively, a few in the class fawned over the great Parker Mangall, author of, *Be Better than Great: Be the Best!* Baxter Burnside did *not* fawn at the thought of Parker Mangall's publisher calling him. In fact, Baxter was highly suspicious that it was not his publisher at all. Publishers didn't normally call at 7:00 p.m., did they?

"I hope you all have the experience of working with editors even if they can be a pain in the backside." Baxter's lip curled with distaste at the professor's arrogance.

"Now, as you know, tonight is a night of beginnings. It is a first step into the majestic world of literary wonder. Until now, we've been training on the flatlands. But in the next moments, we're setting out for the cliffs of conjunctions, the crags of cadence, the peaks of pronouns; all these so you can, perhaps, with luck and practice, reach the heights I already have." He winked at the front row. Some of the girls giggled.

"Take out your ideas and begin to share them. Tread lightly, though. Be honest, but don't hurt each other." He paused. "That's my job."

Chapter 3

His laughter rang out hollowly amongst the anxious murmuring of the students.

At that moment, Hana burst through the back door, flustered and out of breath.

"Are you okay?" Baxter asked when she reached the circle.

"Yes… no… Hund… never mind." She sat down in a huff, opened her bag, and tossed her hair. "What did I miss?"

"The beginning of class," Murray said.

"We're just about to start sharing our ideas," Barbara answered. "Do you have yours?"

Hana held up her notebook. Chads dangled from the wire rings. It appeared as if a fistful of pages had been ripped out.

"Being the last one to arrive, perhaps you'd like to start?" Curtis encouraged.

"I think it's best if someone else does. I'm… not quite ready."

Murray tapped his chair. "I'll be happy to give you a template for excellence." He reached to his side for the fawn-colored satchel and extracted a spiral-ringed notebook, blue, with his name stenciled across the front. A pencil was stuck in the rings. He removed it, opened the book theatrically, cleared his throat, and took a deep breath. "I'll set the backdrop for you: a young man, suave," he pronounced it *suav-EH*, "in the prime of his life, removes himself from society and confronts his greatest fear."

"Death?" Barbara asked.

"Public speaking?" Lisa squeaked.

"Being mauled by a chicken?" Baxter responded.

A Miserable Antagonist

To each of these, Murray shook his head (with Baxter's he added *Ha ha, very funny*). "No, his greatest fear is his virginity."

"Virginity? That's his greatest fear?" Barbara was incredulous. "Good lord, there are some days I'd like to go back to my virginity and hug it, and tell it how much I missed it, and how I would never let it go."

"Please," Murray insisted, "this will be a serious book. I'll explore the desperate fear of every man, while my lead character, Desmondo Reyes, confronts the thought of being alone."

"There's a big difference between being alone and not having sex," Barbara said.

"Yes, yes, yes, I *know* that," Murray responded testily. "You'll just have to read it."

"Give us your first few lines, Murray," Curtis said conciliatorily.

Murray cleared his throat again. "Sex: The Final Frontier."

"Whoa, whoa, whoa," Barbara said. "Is that the title or the first line?"

"Both," Murray said. "Clever, don't you think?"

"If you're a Star Trek fan."

"You think you can do better? Go ahead. What's your book about? Frustrated motherhood?"

Hitting too close to home, Barbara blushed. "That's only a subplot."

"Mine's about a narwhal," Lisa interjected as she covered her face with her notebook. When she pulled it down, her black hair framed her face which had turned the unnatural shade of an almost-ripe strawberry.

Baxter and Hana shared a smirk. *Narwhal? Unicorn? Pretty close.*

Chapter 3

"What about you, Curtis?" Murray asked. "What's the idea for your novella?"

Curtis re-crossed his legs and put his hands behind his head. "I haven't thought of one yet."

Murray sneered. "Writer's block already?"

Shrugging, Curtis smiled. "It hasn't hit me." His eyes focussed on Hana. "Are you ready now, Hana?"

"This is very hard. I was hoping you would all take more time so that I could wait until next week."

"Oh, come on, Hana," Barbara insisted. "This is a safe place."

The inward monologue of every person in the group instantly disagreed with that assessment.

"It's... it's about a young female music prodigy living in Austria. Love and connections."

"What did you title it?" Curtis asked.

"The Weight of Her Tears."

"Oh, that's just wonderful," Lisa interjected. "I want to cry when I hear the title. Why can't I come up with good ideas like that?" She put her face in her hands and muttered, *Stupid narwhal.*

"No, no," Hana raised her hand, "a story about a narwhal sounds lovely." She paused. "Have you ever seen a narwhal?"

"I haven't, but I love unicorns. A narwhal was the closest I could get to a unicorn in real life."

"There's always the rhino," Baxter suggested.

"Baxter," Hana's voice warned. "Lisa, a story about a narwhal will be beautiful, I'm sure."

"What about you, Baxter," Murray said, "what's your novella about?"

Like a deer caught in headlights, Baxter froze. His true nightmare had arrived. The spotlight. Expectations.

Judgement. This ongoing dialogue had certainly *not* eased his fears about sharing his idea.

"It's about a bad guy."

"What kind of bad guy?" Murray said.

"One who does bad stuff."

"What kind of bad stuff?"

"Just let him talk, for Pete's sake!" Barbara exclaimed. Murray put his chin on his hands again but didn't stop grinning.

Baxter swallowed. "Illegal stuff. You know, speeding. Theft!" His eyes widened after he spoke the last word as if it was a profanity.

"That's the *bad* stuff? You're going to write about a shoplifter who drives too fast?"

"Lay off, Judgie McJudgerson," Barbara said. "This is a *creative* writing class. New ideas are welcome, kleptos, crybabies, and narwhals included." She nodded at Baxter. "Go ahead, Baxter. I'm intrigued."

"I haven't fully developed it, but there is this guy named," Baxter hadn't named him yet, "Packer Minshew, who is a rich, arrogant jerk, who always seems to have everything go right for him."

"Packer Minshew?" Barbara repeated softly and glanced toward the front where Mangall stood next to a pretty, young co-ed, his leg propped up on a chair. "Isn't that a little too close for coincidence?"

Baxter's reddened face spoke a thousand words. "The name doesn't matter, really, I can fix it later, but then there's this other guy named Herb Treadwell who robs Minshew's bank and... and gets away with it!"

The group was quiet until Murray deadpanned. "Wow. That's exciting."

"I want to write something different – where the good guy doesn't always win. Where the bad guy, misunderstood

Chapter 3

and underappreciated, tries to take life in his own hands and, and..." Baxter's face scrunched up, "Grabs life by the..."

"Balls?" Barbara finished.

"I was going to say 'horns,' but either way, appropriate."

"That's just Robin Hood redux," Murray pushed. "Robin Hood's not a bad guy."

"Are you sure?" Baxter responded. "From whose perspective? For the average Joe, the anti-Minshew, Robin Hood is a hero, but from the upper crust's perspective...? Robin is their worst nightmare."

"It's still Robin Hood," Murray said.

"So Herb Treadwell will be different. You can't help but hate him. Everyone in the book will detest him. He doesn't speak well. He's angry and belligerent. He... he... drives a crappy car."

"This keeps getting better and better," said Murray.

"I think it's a fine idea," Hana launched a rescue attempt. "It will just take some research."

"Research?" Baxter responded as the rest of the group turned their attention to her.

"The mere fact that you're writing a book about evil is quite courageous. Heroic, if you ask me, when you are such a nice guy." She nodded multiple times as if trying to convince herself and the others.

The others agreed. Lisa nodded wholeheartedly, while Curtis just smiled.

"But, but, I can be bad," Baxter stammered. "One time when I was in a busy parking lot, I was checking my phone, and someone was waiting for me to leave my parking spot, and they beeped their horn. I decided I would get out of the car and go back into the store."

"Did you really do that?" Lisa asked.

Sheepishly, Baxter lowered his head. "That's beside the point."

"Did you do it?" Barbara repeated.

"No. I felt bad, backed out, and apologized to the other driver." Murray snorted. "Look, I lied to you all, though. That's got to count for something!"

Hana reached out to touch his arm. "It's not a bad thing that you can't be a bad guy."

"And, by the way, not pulling out of a parking spot, is not bad – it's just selfish, or mean." Murray said.

"What's the difference?" Lisa asked.

Murray sat up straighter as if preparing to lecture to a class. "To be mean has to do with intent. Like, tripping someone on purpose. To be bad, well," he spread his arms, "*that* has to do with personality, or something internal. To be mean is how you act. To be bad is who you *are*."

"That's very insightful," Curtis said.

Murray beamed and patted himself on the back.

"So, what you're saying is, Baxter needs to find out what it's like to be bad, not just try to be mean," Hana said.

"Exactly."

"How will he do that?"

"HELLO!" Baxter interrupted. "I'm right here. You don't have to speak about me in first person." He stopped. "Sorry, I didn't mean to be…"

"Mean!" Lisa pointed at him.

"And it's *third* person, Baxter," Murray corrected.

He sighed. "What do I do now?"

"Read us the first lines of your idea," Curtis encouraged.

"I don't know if that's such a good idea…"

Chapter 3

"Come on, Baxter. Get it out of the way. Give birth to it. Force it out of your... mind." Murray's grin was malevolent.

"Okay," he said slowly. Opening his tightly wadded piece of paper, he glanced around the circle. Each face carried a different expression. Hana appeared nervous.

"*The Bad Guy*, by Baxter Burnside."

Groans. Throttled, but groans nonetheless.

"What?" he nearly shouted. "What's wrong with that?" Other groups stopped what they were doing to stare at Baxter. He raised one hand and apologized as they went back to their own idea developments.

"*The Bad Guy*? That's the title of your book?" Murray questioned. "You might as well make it. *Don't Read Me Because of the Boring Title.*"

"Would you chill out?" Lisa said. "Just let him read."

Baxter's hands shook nervously. "Chapter 1. Once upon a time, there was a bad guy named Herb Treadwell. People didn't like him at all."

When Baxter glanced up over his sheet of paper, the group's collective faces displayed mouths agape. Unsure of what to say, they waited for anyone else to say something first.

"Thank you, Baxter," Curtis said. "What a creative way to begin your first novella." He nodded ponderously as if he truly meant it.

"What you mean is, 'That sucks.'" Baxter lowered the sheet to his lap. "I knew I shouldn't have taken this stupid class. I'm not a writer. I just thought that this idea would resonate with people."

"It could," Hana insisted. "It really could. We will just have to work together as a team to help you develop the story. Won't we? Everyone?"

A Miserable Antagonist

All nodded except for Murray, who shook his head.

"How are you going to do that?"

"Perhaps," Curtis raised a finger and uncrossed his legs, "we, as a group, could do something entirely different than the other groups. What if we wrote Baxter's book together? We could research together, write together, edit together and then in the end, we could celebrate a collective work of art – the team novella."

"No way," Murray insisted. "*The Final Frontier* is *sooo* much better."

"Be that as it may," Curtis continued doggedly, "you can always write your *piece d' resistance* when you're finished with the class. As for me, I'm quite interested in the possibility of where Baxter might take us."

Hana studied the older gentleman in a new light. His response to Baxter's idea was an unexpected kindness she hadn't encountered in her former husband. "I'm in," she said.

"My narwhal idea was crap anyway. Yes for me." Lisa bobbed up and down in her chair.

All eyes turned to Barbara. "I'm tired of motherhood. Let's be bad!"

"Fine," Murray said exasperatedly, "I'll do it. But I don't want you all to be embarrassed when my chapters outshine all of yours."

Curtis clapped his hands once and smiled broadly. "Well, this is a fine turn of events. A true fellowship of the ring."

"Huh?" Lisa's face frowned.

"It's a reference to Tolkien. Lord of the Rings. The Fellowship... Hobbit, dwarf, wiz..." his voice trailed off.

Baxter was dumbfounded. "How is this going to work? Don't we all have to *individually* turn something in to Professor Mangall?"

Chapter 3

"We'll figure something out," Hana assured him.

The others waited expectantly for Baxter. After a slow second, he responded, "Okay, I guess."

"Great," Barbara clenched her fists excitedly.

Baxter Burnside felt something inside him start to settle, like a tuning fork at the strike of a perfect note. Whether it was hope, or happiness, or something far less positive – fear – he wasn't sure. Either way, times were a changin'.

Chapter 4

Baxter stood behind the bulletproof glass of his teller's station bouncing back and forth, left foot to right foot, boredom to excitement. Although his face did not reflect his inner turmoil, Baxter worried over the issue of 'badness' while he assisted customers.

Baxter had been working at Last National Bank for nineteen years, seven months and twelve days. He had taken seven sick days in total (required quarantine for COVID) and used his annual vacation time to diligently work on his garden. Until his chance encounter with Hana Stutz, Baxter had been quite comfortable cashing checks and opening accounts while imperceptibly allowing his life to flow past him. Sometimes he felt like an outsider in his own life – a character standing on a bridge, pointing at all the beautiful water gently burbling calmly underneath but unable to dip a toe in.

When the last customer thanked him, a lovely Mrs. Dalrymple, aged seventy-two, who as of yet had resisted online banking, Baxter glanced up and was shocked to see Hana and Curtis standing behind the yellow line waiting to be served.

They stood side by side. Baxter had never seen Curtis upright; he'd always been lounging in a chair on Wednesday nights, so the sight of him, at least a few inches taller than Hana, was disconcerting. Strangely, even though she was roughly twenty years younger than he, they looked like a well-matched couple. Baxter wasn't quite sure how he felt about this.

Chapter 4

"What are you two doing here?" he spoke through a smile without moving his lips.

"We would like to open a bank account," Hana said too loudly as she produced her ID and slid it through the slot in the window to him.

He didn't look at it. "What are you talking about?"

"We'd like to open a bank account," she repeated, her eyes widening, her head motioning towards a meeting room.

Baxter's supervisor, Lawrence Spago, a man of Italian descent, with a dense head of dark hair and a thick bushy moustache, was talking on his cell phone behind the rank of tellers. The conversation was heated as his elbow was pushed high up in the air. Larry's eyes narrowed as he caught Baxter glancing back at him. Instinctively, even as he argued with someone on the phone, it seemed as if Larry knew that something out of the ordinary was occurring. He took great pleasure in supervising (and correcting) his employees' activities.

"We would like to open a bank account," Curtis pressured for the third time.

Baxter sighed and took out the forms. "All right, *sir*. I'll need some identification, social security number…" he rattled off the list until Curtis interrupted him.

"It's a sensitive account."

"I don't know what you mean." Baxter turned to his right where his colleague, Bernadette Walters, chatted amiably with a woman and her small child. Normally in a conflict-of-interest case like this, Baxter should have given Hana and Curtis to her, but she was busy.

"Is there a place we can speak privately?"

"I'm a teller. When we open accounts…"

Hana's eyes widened.

"Fine," he shook his head. "Let me log out and we'll take the meeting room over there."

"Thank you, Mr. Burnside." She pointed at his name plaque and grinned.

Moments later, Baxter opened the small meeting room where he pulled back the chair behind a desk and placed his hands in front of him. He motioned for them to sit. As this was not normal procedure – tellers rarely left their bulletproof cubicles – Baxter felt (and looked) nervous.

Still playing the game, he turned towards the computer. "What are you guys doing here?" he whispered.

"We've had a few ideas," Hana said.

"Who is we? You two?"

"Yes, and the others. Except for Barbara. She hasn't responded to the email yet."

"Even Murray agreed, although he is being curmudgeonish about it."

Baxter turned in his swivel chair to 'check' their identifications. Curtis' face smiled up at him from his driver's licence. *Huh*, Baxter thought, *he's sixty-two years old. He's aged well.*

"What ideas are we talking about?"

Curtis casually crossed one long leg over the other. He was wearing khaki pants and a polo shirt. Baxter resented the fact that the older man carried himself so easily, as if life *was* but a dream.

"To write the story, Baxter, we," Curtis pointed to Hana, "felt the need for some experience in the *motivation* behind your despicable character role – Herb Treadwell, as it were. We're not sure if you, or any of us, know how to develop an antagonist like that – the 'bad guy'." Curtis used quote fingers which annoyed Baxter because of his mother's overuse of the gesture. "And if you/we don't know how to

Chapter 4

develop a character for lack of reference, how in the world will you/we be able to write about him?"

"*Write* about him?" Baxter said as his eyes shifted above their shoulders to where Larry Spago cruised like a shark behind the tellers with his hands on his hips, suitcoat pulled back to reveal a gray vest with a pocket chain dangling from the left pocket. "*Write* about him? I don't even know how to write, *period*."

"Then this will be good for you." Hana opened her purse which lent itself to the charade. Thankfully, Larry turned his eyes away from them. "As your writing group, we feel it might help to roleplay some scenarios, or better yet, act out a 'bad-guy' scene, so you can start the team off on the first chapter of the book."

"Roleplay scenarios?"

"Yes," Curtis nodded. "We're getting together this weekend to act out some situations where a book's bad guy might, you know, be engaged: murder, arson, grand theft larceny…"

"What the hell is that? Do you mean grand theft auto?" Baxter swallowed.

"It's just a 'for instance'. Of course, we're not going to actually *do* that one…"

"We could even do a bank robbery," Hana said.

"Shhh!" Baxter shushed loudly and angrily with a finger to his lips. "Are you guys crazy? Coming into the bank and saying those words? That's like buckling into a plane and mentioning to your armrest neighbor that you sell bombs for a living."

"I'm sorry," Hana apologized. "We didn't mean to upset you."

A Miserable Antagonist

Baxter shook his head. "Look, I appreciate the help, but I'll come up with my bad guy idea on my own. You guys can get on board after that."

Hana's face fell. "We're not sure we can wait that long."

Muttering under his breath, Baxter pushed the licenses back across the desk. "I'm beginning to realize that this whole writing thing might have been a mistake."

"Are you joking?" Hana leaned forward. "You have come alive since you first attended the class. You have started to stand up for yourself. You are becoming creative, you…"

"I'm not going to break any laws," Baxter said firmly.

"We are not asking you to break any laws," Hana said, "only *pretend* to break them. Come on. It might be fun. It *will* be fun." Her pleading eyes gripped Baxter, and it felt as if his soul was being squeezed out by the force of her beauty.

"I don't know."

"We're meeting at Curtis' house, Saturday afternoon about 4:00."

Baxter's mouth pinched and he glanced toward Curtis. "I don't have your address."

"I'll text it to you," Curtis said.

"Thank you." Hana spoke to Baxter but looked at Curtis who had tented his hands in front of his mouth.

"You won't regret this," Curtis promised.

"That's what people always say before they *most certainly* regret what is about to happen."

Hana and Curtis gathered their belongings and stood. To keep up pretenses, they both reached out to shake hands with Baxter. Their tallness made Baxter feel disadvantaged, and even more when Curtis outgripped him. Baxter hated that about larger people. Unfortunately, Hana pulled her hand away quickly.

Chapter 4

After they left, Baxter resumed his position at his teller's station. Unable to erase the previous conversation from his mind, Baxter jumped when Larry moved into the cubicle behind him.

"What was that all about?" Larry asked.

"They wanted to open an account."

"Why did you go into the meeting room?"

"Because they want to set up a joint account to buy a house. It seems they're quite in love." Oddly, Baxter felt a thrill at lying to his boss.

"Well done," Larry said and turned on his heel.

Maybe being a bad guy isn't so hard, Baxter thought as Jefry Moosen, a fifty-year-old undertaker, plunked a bowl of change in front of him to be counted by a machine. Momentarily, Baxter wondered why a funeral director would have so much change. Baxter attempted a smile at the grave Moosen, but the stern man's gaze felt like he was shoveling out Baxter's soul.

Wincing at the weight, Baxter hefted the bag of coins and deposited them into the counting machine. As it shook and sorted them, Baxter felt a similar shaking and wondered if he, too, was being sorted out.

Chapter 5

There were few comparable homes to Curtis Schachman's house, which sat on a ridge overlooking the capital city of Montpelier. The mansion, part of the inheritance from his grandmother, was from 'old money,' or that's what she used to tell him. How they came into their 'old money' was never fully revealed, only whispers regarding his Great Grandfather Toquay's foray into rumrunning during Prohibition. Needless to say, the neighbors couldn't keep up with the Schachman's and distanced themselves using tall hedges and needlessly large fences. Curtis had to use binoculars to glimpse the next house up the road.

The lane leading to the Schachman residence was as picturesque as a postcard. Dense trees arched over the road, their branches like leafy arms waving happily in the breeze. A white picket fence evoked visions of the great American dream as it lined both sides of the lane. Sunlight leaked through the tops of the trees and dappled the asphalt driveway.

Hana was the first to arrive. She showed up well earlier than the rest under the pretense of preparing for their activity. She wore a summery yellow dress and matching shoes. While waiting for the others to appear, Curtis and Hana arranged furniture in the front large living area into a circle. Cream-colored chaise lounges and matching antique chairs sat in front of a painted mantle portrait exhibiting the baleful stares of Grandmother Loretta and her husband, Raybehr, inheritors of the estate from the alleged rumrunners. From the looks of the portrait, Curtis certainly took after his grandfather.

Chapter 5

When class had dismissed the previous Wednesday night, Hana had approached Professor Mangall and questioned him about how they should be creating their stories. Mangall, in his very pompous way, told her that 'In order to elicit the greatest emotive resonance from the reader, the writer should, in every case, have a full knowledge of the proclivities of both protagonist and antagonist.' When she asked the professor what he meant by that in simple terms, Mangall stuck his nose up in the air and said, 'If you cannot *feel* the very thing your character *feels*,' he gestured with his hands in such a feeling way that Hana took a step back, 'then you cannot impress upon the reader why he or she should take you seriously.'

Thus, Hana and Curtis decided the team must manifest certain emotions to empathize with bad guys everywhere. To *feel* what a bad guy *feels*, they needed to get inside his head and run a few laps, upset a few apple carts, and maybe, while they were at it, lob in a few profanities. For her part, Hana couldn't imagine Curtis being vulgar, but then again, she had only known him for a few weeks. For all she knew, he could be Charles Manson's second cousin. But he didn't seem that way. What he did seem like was a perfectly content and handsome human being who enjoyed company.

And when she thought about Curtis, a warm feeling, like the moment fresh bread comes out of the oven and the butter begins to melt, arose from her heart. It had been a long time since she had felt that. Though Hana wanted to believe that she and her husband had been in love at one point, all signs pointed otherwise. The marriage had been one of convenience. They had met in Austria, high up in the Alps. Sunshine had been glistening on the snow and his eyelashes. He had been tall and handsome, chiseled, seemingly without physical blemish, but even then, he smelled of aftershave and anger. His worst moods were recognizable by the hue of his four-o'clock shadow. The darker the hair, the fouler the mood. He was not physically abusive, but his verbal tirades, and his constant nitpicking, had worn a hole in their marriage. Hana didn't want to call his early death a relief, but it was. Thus, it had taken five years for her to be open to a relationship again. Baxter was kind and gentle, and his personality seemed a nice transition to love, but Curtis was mysterious and beautiful. They were apples and oranges. At this point in her life, Hana was much more interested in citrus.

When Hana called Curtis earlier that week, they had met for coffee on Thursday morning to discuss how best to enact Mangall's dictum. The café was dimly lit and smelled of coffee beans, baking things, and early morning commuters with their hustling sense of importance and their inability to set down their phones to pay for their drinks. Hana and Curtis were more relaxed than the commuters, and they huddled in a side booth, enjoying their shared solitude while isolated by the wicker behind their heads.

Hana had spent a considerable amount of time selecting an outfit for their 'date.' This indecisive time raised questions of intent for her, questions of age differential, upbringing, and even wealth. But as Curtis sat across from her, hands engulfing a slowly cooling mug in front of him, her heart slowed. His eyes captured hers and his voice seemed like that of Clark Gable.

"We could pore over some serial killer cases on the internet," Curtis suggested.

"Yes, we could, but…" she let the word draw out, "it's very much like 'traveling' to another country by reading about it on Wikipedia. You might pick up some facts, but do you really understand the place?"

Chapter 5

"I get your point," Curtis responded. "What is your idea?"

"You'll think it's silly…" Hana said.

"How do you know what I'll think?" he asked. "You barely know me."

"Because if I was you, I'd think it was silly."

"What is it?" he asked.

"I think we should…"

"Yeah, that's stupid," he said before she finished. They both laughed. "Sorry. Go ahead." He motioned with his hands and his head tilted slightly to the side as if preparing to hear with one ear.

"I was thinking about actors and actresses when they're preparing for an evil part in a movie. They study the role. Get into the character. You know what I mean?"

"Mm hmm."

"I was thinking of having a roleplay party." Her pupils dilated, and she covered her mouth as if embarrassed by the idea.

"Explain."

"On Saturday, I want to invite everyone from our writing group to enact some of these crimes. Maybe we could do a roleplay where we draw a particular crime from a hat and write a short scene describing that person's motivations, feelings, etc…"

"A deeper 'for example' would help," he said.

"Okay. Let's say I drew from the basket of crimes …" she paused, "… arson. The 'actor' would have to act out how he or she is thinking and feeling as the crime is committed."

"Interesting."

"For someone like Baxter, he would have to delve into the part – act bad, be bad – so that he could write about it."

"What happens then?" Curtis asked.

"Each of us would write one hundred words describing what we saw. Not just our parts, or our roles, but what it felt like to see it from the outside. Creatively speaking, none of us will see the same thing in the exact same way. Hopefully, this will help us hone our writing skills."

"Can I make one amendment?" Curtis asked.

"Of course."

"Let's have it at my place. I've got plenty of space. Besides, I haven't really had much company lately, and it will do me good to have some noise in the place."

"All right. That would be lovely, thank you," said Hana.

"There is just one thing you should know, though. My house is... how shall I put this... rather large."

Rather large had been quite an understatement.

At first, Hana thought she had missed the lane, but her GPS insisted she go back one hundred yards to a black, wrought-iron gate, with the words **CALYPSO'S HILL** written above it. After turning the car around, she maneuvered it to the small black box outside her driver's window and pressed the button.

An accented voice, one she did not recognize, blared out, "Yes? How may I help you?"

"I'm sorry, but I'm looking for the Curtis Schachman residence. Can you tell me how to find it?"

The answer came in the form of a clicking sound and the gate swung slowly inwards. Stunned by the magnitude of the property, Hana drove her car slowly up the lane. Two

Chapter 5

hundred yards ahead she braked at a circle drive with a fountain in the middle. Streams of water spurted from the statuesque mouths of four horses and plummeted to the scintillating pool below. Surrounding the circular drive, two rings of yellow and red tulips swayed happily in the sunlight.

Built in 1911, the two-story house was immaculately maintained. The walls, painted a faint lemon-yellow, contrasted with white shutters, columns and doors. Yew shrubs dotted the sidewalk surrounding the house. A carefully manicured garden of mixed flowers and other shrubbery was positioned to the side of each wing of the mansion. When Hana stepped out of the car, she surveyed the grounds in wonderment. The sight reminded her of the opulent, aristocratic mansions in Vienna when she was growing up.

As she studied her surroundings, Hana was unaware that Curtis had come out onto the porch above her. Standing with his arms crossed, he smiled at her.

"Welcome to my humble abode."

"What is this place?" she asked as she approached him at the steps.

He followed her eyes. "It's been my home for many years. My grandmother left this to me in her will when she died. Quite thoughtful of her, don't you think?"

"How do you take care of it all?" She climbed the steps to meet him.

"I have some help."

"As in hired help?"

He shrugged.

"What do you do for a living to maintain a place like this?"

He touched her arm to guide her to the front door. "I'm retired, remember?"

"From what?"

Curtis touched the side of his nose. "Things."

After leading her inside, she marveled at the enormous chandelier sparkling in the front foyer at the base of a grand staircase. The white marble floor reflected the light from above. "Would you care for a tour?" he asked.

"Of course!"

They stepped to the left around the staircase, and he led her into a well-lit entertaining area which could have doubled as an indoor garden. Amazingly, in the middle of the room, sofas and comfortable reclining chairs were situated around a small fishpond with a trickling fountain. Behind the greenery, a floor to ceiling bookshelf contained hundreds of new and old books.

"This is incredible! If I lived here, I would never want to leave the house!"

He waggled his head. "That's part of my problem. I don't leave the house much – just on Wednesday nights. And, now when I meet you... all of you..." His voice fell off.

Hana plucked a book from the shelf. It was a first edition of *Great Expectations*. "I don't know if I should be touching this."

"Come on," he laughed. "Let me show you to our meeting room." They continued through the kitchen, which was a wide and spacious, well-lit room with stainless steel countertops and an island in the middle. There they encountered a husky man kneading bread. Curtis introduced his cook, Albrite, who nodded his head amusedly.

"You have your own cook?" she whispered as they left the room.

"Don't you?"

"Yes, of course. Me."

Chapter 5

Once they turned the corner to the room set aside for their afternoon activities, Hana fell in love with the space immediately. Everything seemed to be perfectly placed: the mahogany grand piano, the fireplace with an iron poker set in front, the luxurious chairs, drapes, and curtains. Even the portrait of Curtis' grandparents was proportional to the gravitas of the room.

"I feel like I've entered the house of a movie star."

"Hardly," he responded, but something in his voice seemed amused by the suggestion.

Curtis asked if she wanted something warm to drink, which she agreed to, and he went to the kitchen to retrieve it. While he was gone, Hana poked around the room searching for pictures which might add insight into the mysterious man, but there were few. Just his grandparents' large portrait above the fireplace and a few landscape photos.

"Are you looking for something?" Hana jumped when she heard his voice.

"I wasn't trying to be nosy, but there aren't many photographs."

"Just a bachelor."

"Did you ever have family?"

"I thought about it, but it never worked out for me. And you?"

Nodding, she turned fully towards him. "I was married for a long time. He died not that many years ago. No children."

"I'm sorry."

"You don't have to be. I'm content."

For the remainder of the afternoon, Curtis and Hana made plans for the group's time together. Just before 4:00, the doorbell rang.

"Should I get that?" Hana asked.

"No. Reyna will get it."

"She's your housekeeper?"

"No, just a homeless woman who enjoys answering my door." His eyes were mischievous above his coffee cup.

Moments later, a beautiful Hispanic woman passed without looking at them. She was dressed in a neat gray suit, and her hair was tied up behind her head. Reyna opened the door. Before she had a chance to greet the guests, an astonished Murray barged through her outstretched arm.

"Hey, everybody. Talk about a great place! Are you a Wall Street Trader or something?" Murray's eyes were stuck on the chandelier above him.

Curtis remained silent.

"Lisa's right behind me."

Seconds later, Lisa appeared in the doorway. Reyna greeted her silently with a nod, shut the door and returned to her post deeper in the house.

"Wow, Curtis, do you mind if I move in?" Lisa began to take pictures with her phone.

"Sure."

Hana welcomed the newest arrivals into the living room. "Please, make yourself at home. As soon as Baxter and Barbara arrive, we'll get started."

No sooner had Hana uttered the words when the doorbell rang again. Curtis held up a finger and retreated to the front door. "I'll get it this time, Reyna!" he called out.

Baxter was wearing a knit polo shirt and blue jeans. His thinning hair was slightly mussed as if he had awakened from a nap. "Are you the doorman?"

"Today, that's my role."

Baxter made his way ahead of Curtis to the living area where Lisa and Murray were finding places to sit.

"Hello, Baxter," Lisa welcomed gaily.

Chapter 5

Baxter greeted them in turn, first Lisa, then Murray. He smiled at Hana and followed Curtis into the kitchen where he was introduced to the Albrite, who nodded politely, and continued his business.

"Nice pad," Baxter said. "Almost as nice as mine." Albrite overheard the statement and smiled.

Curtis coughed into his hand and said, "I was blessed to have relatives with money. They left me the house and a sizeable estate."

"What a coincidence. My aunt and uncle are presently working on their wills to leave me the same thing," Baxter said, but his jealousy was apparent. Some guys had it all.

"What have you been doing today?" Curtis asked.

"A little of this and a little of that. Checked my investments. Counted my coin."

"Hope you made out like a bandit."

"The life of a banker, you know."

After the coffee had been served, the writers sat down in their respective chairs. It was an awkward, pre-conversation time that all gatherings encountered, when guests flicked from small talk to sipping drinks, checked out the surroundings, then their watches and phones, and hoped the discomfort would eventually subside. Soft mood music emanated from concealed speakers in the high ceiling. To fit his perception of the surroundings, Murray attempted to cross one leg over the other, but it was uncomfortable for him. Instead, he went back to being Murray, uncrossed them, and slouched in his chair. He did, however, begin to sip his coffee with his pinkie finger extended. Curtis and Hana sat side by side on the sofa. No one was quite ready to formulate the questions, forays into personal things, hidden things and just beneath the surface things. They were not yet

A Miserable Antagonist

far enough along in their relationships to wonder about families, motivations, and dreams.

The soft jazz melted into something more rhythmic, and Murray began to tap the arm of his chair. Baxter attempted not to stare at Curtis' lingering arm resting so close to Hana's. Thankfully, not long later, the doorbell chimed again. This time, when Curtis moved to stand, Hana grabbed him by the arm. 'Let Reyna get it.'

Curtis' face reddened and he sat down again. Baxter was disconcerted to see both Hana's physical touch and Curtis' embarrassment. *Why can't I be like Curtis?* Never having been a confident man, Baxter wondered what it would be like to have a mansion, servants, disposable income, Hush Puppy shoes and Polo shirts. Baxter wanted aristocratic looks and chinos, maybe an expensive gold watch dangling insolently around his wrist.

Instead, Baxter was a man with a small 1960's ranch-style house and turn-of-the-last-century clothing. He had just enough money to pay off his mortgage, and looks that aged like Blockbuster Video stocks. Hana's hand on Curtis' arm was a sure and certain reminder that Baxter would never be someone like Curtis. This particularly self-abusive thought continued to echo in his mind until Barbara stepped across the threshold and into the living room where her five classmates still sat awkwardly.

Murray's grin contrasted with Baxter's frown. Lisa clapped her hands daintily, then stood and approached Barbara to give her hug. The intimacy was unexpected. After the shock wore off, Barbara hugged her inelegantly with one arm while the other held her purse.

"Isn't this exciting!" Lisa said.

"That's one way to describe it," Barbara responded as she unlatched herself from Lisa's embrace. "Quite the place…"

Chapter 5

"It's a mansion!" Murray seconded.

"No kidding."

"May I take your bag and coat?" Reyna asked. Barbara awkwardly handed her accessories to the servant who then disappeared into a side room. Lisa escorted Barbara to an empty chair and took her seat.

Barbara scanned the room and noticed how the group had positioned themselves. Baxter sat alone in a wingchair to the left side of the fireplace; to his right, Curtis and Hana reclined on a divan separated only by the crack of two cushions. Murray and Lisa had positioned their chairs near each other on the right of the fireplace, in front of a handsome grand piano. Barbara sat down to their left on a plush, upholstered chair, arms cushioned but firm.

"As you know," Hana started nervously, "after our last class, we agreed in principle on Baxter's idea, but we," she motioned between Curtis and herself, "thought it might be good to spend some time together figuring out what this is. And, get to know each other, yes?" Curtis nodded and took this as his cue to speak. Baxter's expression darkened. He wasn't prepared for the more-than-platonic implication of '*we*'. Hana and *him* were supposed to be the *we*, not her and Curtis, and all of his…

"Taking into account Baxter's… personality, to connect him with the darker versions of life, we…"

"Whoa, whoa, whoa," Baxter interrupted. "I'm not the only virgin bad guy here. It's not like you guys are convicted felons."

Curtis said, "Of course not, Baxter." The other four tittered nervously.

"I think we all," Baxter circled the group with his hands, "have a certain deficit of badness, you know?"

A Miserable Antagonist

"What's the worst thing that you've ever done?" Lisa asked him.

Baxter's swallowed nervously. "Once, when I was younger I... I... broke a neighbor's window and blamed it on one of my friends." When finished with his confession, he studied their faces.

"No, you didn't," Murray said. "You're lying."

Baxter felt the blood rush to his face. "Okay! Okay! So I didn't do it! I lied. Is there anything wrong with that?"

"No, Baxter, of course not. You're a very nice person," Hana soothed.

"But I don't want to be a nice person! I want to be a bad guy!"

Murray snorted.

"Oh yeah? What kinds of stuff have you done, Murray?"

"*Lots* of things. Lots of *bad* things. When I was fourteen, my parents took me to the ocean for a vacation. They took me to Florida." He spoke the state's name as if it were the French Riviera.

"Ooh," Lisa cooed. "Florida."

"I know, right? One night, while we were walking on the beach, I saw an isolated house with the lights on. As we walked by, I noticed a young woman standing in the window. She was beautiful with long brown hair and slender legs. She had a small nose and wide eyes, thin lips and big..."

"Murray, too much information," Lisa warned.

"I was going to say, 'big ears'."

"Yeah, whatever," Lisa muttered.

"Anyway," he said slowly, "this girl's palms were placed against the glass. I wanted to leave my parents and run to that window to put my hands on the other side of hers. You know, to let her feel, that despite the barrier

Chapter 5

between her and the beautiful world, someone still noticed her. But there wasn't time."

The others subconsciously leaned forward.

"The next night, I snuck out of our apartment and wandered up the beach toward her house. She appeared in the window again, straining her eyes into the dark over the ocean." His voice lowered with secrecy. "I crept up the sand dune through the tall grasses. She didn't notice me. I approached, step by step, through the open gate, across the manicured lawn. For some reason, she still hadn't spotted me. Then it finally hit me."

"What was it?" Lisa asked.

"She was blind," Murray whispered.

"How could you tell?"

"As I neared the house, I looked into her eyes. They were milky, like they had scales on them. As I stood beneath her, so far below her, apart, a world of separation, I saw the door open behind her. It was a man, and he was holding…"

"What? What was it?" Lisa whispered.

"A knife."

Lisa's eyes went wide. "What did you do?"

"I tried yelling, but the surf was too loud. Then, I watched as the man with the knife approached her from behind."

"Oh, dear!"

"Slowly, he shuffled closer until he was standing directly behind her. Then the girl must have heard him, and she turned. There was only one thing I could do."

Lisa's fingers were curled up near her mouth. "What was it? What was it?"

"I jumped and SLAM! I pounded on the side of the house!" Murray clapped his hands and shouted at the top of his voice. The rest of the team nearly jumped out of their skins. Murray began to laugh at the top of his lungs. "I got you! I got you!"

"You little weasel!" Baxter shouted. "You could have just told us the truth!"

"Why?" Murray reasoned. "You didn't."

Baxter's eyes were fixed on Hana who seemed to be pulling her fingernails from the armrest cushions. "So the whole thing was a lie?"

"No, not all of it. I really did go to the beach with my parents, and there really was a girl standing at the window, but I didn't go and investigate."

"What DID you do?" Lisa cringed as she asked the question.

"I mooned her." Murray's guffaw of laughter echoed in the large room.

"Very mature, Murray," Baxter said.

"Yeah, whatever. At least it's badder than what you've tried to come up with. Breaking a window and blaming it on someone else..." he wiggled his fingers. "Oooooh, a regular Jeffrey Dahmer."

"Shut up, Murray," Baxter retorted.

For Barbara, this kind of interaction happened far too often in her house: adolescent spats, banging heads and cringe-worthy comments. As the resident mother of the group, she felt the need to change the subject. "Have you worked on your outline yet, Baxter? We need to get started on our group project."

"Of course," Baxter responded. What he meant was, *Of course not. I don't even know what an outline looks like. I'm in over my head. I'm so overwhelmed. I want to forget the whole thing.*

"And...?"

"First," Murray interjected before Baxter could begin. He spoke and touched his index finger, then consecutive fingers to illustrate his points. "We consider our characters.

Chapter 5

Then, work on the settings, a few metaphors, plot twists and such…"

Baxter's head swam. He still hadn't moved past, *Once there was a bad guy.*

"Then, we'll write the first paragraph and, once into the groove," he cracked his knuckles after touching all his fingers, "write the last paragraph. Easy." he smiled. "Then it's just fill in the big blank space in the middle."

While he spoke, Baxter noticed Curtis shaking his head.

"What is it?" Baxter asked.

"Interesting," Curtis said, "but you've missed the most important part of writing a book."

"Oh yeah? What did I miss?" Murray asked.

"You missed the point." Curtis leaned forward in his chair to move his focus from Murray to Baxter. "The point of writing a book is a critique of society, that you have something to say about life, about culture, about *you*," Curtis pointed at him. "You've chosen to write about this particular theme because it's important to you. Baxter, forget about writing for someone else. What do you want to say?"

"I could detail that in about ten words. I don't need a novel."

"What are those ten words?"

Baxter hadn't truly thought through 'what he wanted to say.' He had only joined the Creative Writing 102 class because he was interested in Hana. Now that Hana's attention had drifted from him to Curtis, the class seemed entirely pointless. It was déjà vu; he was great at nothing the rest of the world cared about. Nothing but being courteous, a good neighbor, a decent son, and a devoted employee.

"I'm tired of being afraid and I'm afraid of being alone."

Murray had been counting the words. "That's eleven."

Baxter shook his head. His unexpected honesty, and the profundity of his own statement, brought the group to silence. For Baxter, though he didn't know it yet, this open declaration of his life's truth was a flag-planting in his life. As a man who lived alone, ate alone, and worked alone in a small cubicle surrounded by similarly lonely people, Baxter Burnside was someone who desperately needed connection. Since the writing group had sprung up from the seeds of his discontent, something was going to change.

It had to.

Chapter 6

For they who gathered in the opulent space, surrounded by objects and symbols which most of them would never own, they began to realize the immense differences in their backgrounds and personalities. To be able to write together, to share together, and to understand the intricacies of narrative together, would necessitate vulnerability. Vulnerability was a precious commodity that none of them felt comfortable to share with the others. Not yet, at least.

Finally, Murray had had enough chitchat. "Well, are we going to do something, or should I finish picking my nose and go home?"

"Thank you for the gentle nudge, Murray," Curtis said and nodded at Hana.

Nervously, Hana pulled at a tendril of hair which hung in front of her ear and dangled along her neck. To Baxter, this tress seemed like a tender vine amongst the limbs of a rain forest. While she toyed with it, he watched her lips and eyes move. So soft. So…

"Right, Baxter?"

Startled from his reverie, he saw that Hana was looking expectantly at him.

"The most fun way would be to explore the emotions of the bad guy by roleplaying them."

"Uh, sure."

"How is this actually going to work?" Lisa asked, chewing diligently on the cuticle of her right thumb.

"Each of us we will write down a crime…"

"Then what?"

A Miserable Antagonist

"Then, we'll individually draw one from a hat and develop a scenario that we will depict – act out – what is on the piece of paper."

"Oh, great," Baxter moaned. "We did something like this at our staff Christmas party a few years ago, except everyone was three sheets to the wind. I still don't know how there wasn't a lawsuit."

Her face fell. "We don't have to do this, I guess…"

Baxter held out his hands. "No, no, that's not what I meant, it's just…" he looked around the circle, "we don't really know each other that well yet. How can we trust each other enough to roleplay if we don't know the *real* play?"

Others nodded slowly. Lisa looked like a Bobblehead during an earthquake.

"Let's get to know each other, then," Curtis responded. "We need a common question, but not something banal like, 'What's your favorite color?'"

"How about the name of your favorite YouTube channel?" Lisa suggested.

Murray was the only one who agreed. "I'll go first. My favorite channel is PewDiePie."

Everyone except Lisa seemed bewildered. She enthusiastically supported his choice. "Oh, yeah! I love him. So funny."

"What about you, Baxter?" Lisa urged.

"To be honest, I don't really watch YouTube."

"Well, what television channel do you watch?"

Baxter thought about the cathode television in his living room. It had been a recycled gift from his mother when they bought a forty-five-inch LED television for Burnie to watch his car races. Baxter's TV was more of a decorative accessory than a tool. As the group's eyes fastened on him, Baxter grew uncomfortable. To tell them the truth, that he really enjoyed documentaries, seemed

Chapter 6

geriatric; but to lie to them seemed to break the intent of the entire exercise. Or maybe, that *was* the point?

"I really dig ESPN." The fib slipped out with difficulty. Baxter Burnside emphatically did *not* like ESPN, nor did he enjoy sports in general. The thought of sweaty men (or women) fighting over a ball, or driving like crazy people around an oval track, seemed antithetical to the evolutionary process.

Everyone knew immediately that he was lying. They stared at him, waiting for him to own up to his falsehood. Murray broke the silence.

"What's your favorite sport?"

"Uh, baseball."

"Team?"

Frantically, Baxter tried to think of a team – any team – when suddenly he remembered one. "Yankees!" He shouted.

"You like the Yankees?" Murray's eyebrows raised. "Who's your favorite player?"

"Uh, I like them all."

"What about Big Papi?" Murray's eyes glinted malevolently.

"Who?"

"Big Papi – you know, David Ortiz."

Baxter's face turned red. "I thought you said Big Bopper. Didn't he play for the… another team?"

"No, Big Papi."

"I…" Like a swimmer desperately seeking a life ring, he scanned the circle for any kind of help. The women stared at him. Finally, his gaze landed on Curtis who closed his eyes and shook his head slightly.

"I… no, I don't like him…" Baxter's voice came out like a question. Fortunately, Curtis nodded.

"Oh, okay." Murray backed down.

"How about you, Hana? What's your favorite channel?" Baxter asked.

"The GC. Gardening Channel."

"Oh, that's nice."

"The question *was*, 'What's your favorite *YouTube* channel. Not old person channel." Murray insisted.

"Maybe I do not watch YouTube," Hana said.

"All right, let's do it this way," Curtis attempted to pacify the situation. "Everybody gets a piece of paper and writes a question they want the others to answer. How does that sound?" They all agreed, and the paper and pens were handed out. Baxter wanted to know where people were born, thinking this was a quick and easily answered question. Others took their time. When Hana finished writing, she blushed, and folder her paper to put into the basket. She smiled at Baxter. *What question did she write down?* Baxter hoped it was something she wanted to specifically know about him.

When all the questions were in, Curtis drew one, unfolded it and read it aloud. "What was your first kiss experience?"

Baxter sucked in his breath and felt the world sink beneath him. Which first kiss? The *very* first one, an awkward fumbling in junior high with an equally inexperienced young girl who, after finishing the wet, smushy thing, began laughing and ran down the hallway into the dark. Or, his recent, *last* first kiss?

"Baxter, please go first," Curtis insisted.

"Why do I have to start?"

"Because we're all here because of you. Show some leadership." Murray stretched his arms up and then crossed them behind his head.

Baxter sighed. "Her name was Eris."

Chapter 6

"Baxter, can you begin again and make a story out of it?" Barbara asked.

"Yeah, all right. Let me think." The group waited expectantly. "Once upon a time there was a guy named Baxter B…"

"Aaagh!" Murray said. "Don't do that! Be creative."

For one of the first times in his life, Baxter Burnside felt the adrenaline of competition course through him. Not since the Independence Day Hotdog Eating Competition had he felt the electric surge. His performance, a close defeat – 14 hotdogs to 12 – followed by a disgusting episode of projectile vomiting, had turned him off to competition in general. But sitting in this room, surrounded by people who wanted the same things as he, made Baxter want to rise to the occasion. Suddenly, Baxter wanted to lead the team. Suddenly, he wanted to be the one who would show them the Promised Land of literary genius. Suddenly, he wanted to impress not only Hana, but most assuredly Murray as well. He studied their faces, took a deep breath, and began to tell the story as it should have been, not necessarily as it had been.

"In retrospect, my first kiss with Eris was underwhelming, less a lip lock than a lip knock." Barbara nodded and encouraged him with, 'That's better.'

"As with most intimate things for me, it was unplanned and unanticipated. Eris was, if I can be so honest, well above my pay grade. Beautiful, intelligent, athletic. Everything I thought I wanted in a woman."

"Why was she with you then?" Murray asked.

"Murray!" Barbara hissed. "Shut up!"

"What?" He scowled and sank further into his chair threatening to tip it over as it balanced on its two back legs.

Baxter restarted. "That was the same question I asked myself every day until the day we broke up, two weeks before our wedding." Now, they were very much interested. "As far as beautiful days go, the day of our first kiss ranked in the top ten."

"Ooh, that's a good line," Lisa said.

Feeling warmed by her compliment, Baxter continued. "As I did most Saturdays, I went for a walk along the Winooski. It was a cool May day, fresh breeze, you know the kind. As I walked along the path, I took pictures of various birds, greenery, one of the local wrens was singing gloriously. You see, I really like birds. One time…"

"Perhaps stick to the subject, Baxter," Hana encouraged.

"Sorry," he apologized. "There I was, taking pictures on the path, when suddenly, at the last instant, I heard someone approaching. Unable to stop, this jogging woman, with earphones in, happened to be changing music at the very instant I had spotted a yellow bellied sapsucker. Our faces connected, her lips against mine. Surprised and embarrassed, when I stood up, I saw that I'd bloodied her lip with my teeth. One of my teeth was almost knocked out."

"That's not a first kiss," Murray smacked his forehead.

"You wanted a good story," Baxter responded.

"That was so good! You're a good storyteller!" Lisa encouraged.

"No, I'm not. I just… well, that was an important moment in my life."

"Bloodying a woman's lip?"

"Yes… no… Look, I'm awkward around people. I spend entire days opening bank accounts and helping old folks get rid of their checkbooks. There's always a glass wall between us. I see them. They see me. But we never get

Chapter 6

personal. It's transactional, and as long as the debits and credits match up, my life seems in balance.

AND, I'm not a person who watches a lot of TV, relationships are hard, and this," he circled the group with his hands, "is very, very, very uncomfortable. The only reason I joined the class was because of Hana."

All eyes turned towards her. She blushed uncontrollably and touched her heart.

"What I mean by that is…" he fumbled, "… we ran into each other on the walking path, nothing like me and Eris, no bloody lips and loose teeth, only a common interest in walking. And for some unknown reason, she invited me to the class."

Happy with the description, Hana nodded. "No lip knocking," she repeated.

"So, what happened with Eris? Did you guys get back together, or what?" Lisa asked.

Fumbling for the right words, Baxter pondered what occurred with Eris. Physically, she was exceptional – blonde hair, trim figure, straight teeth without a hint of tooth decay (a must for him). Whatever physical charms she had, Eris used (and abused) them to the best of her ability. Unfortunately, it was her emotional appearance she couldn't disguise. Eris was manipulative and moody. She enjoyed arguing, and her combative demeanor put more strain on him than he could possibly have understood while in the relationship. He had continued with her only because she made him look good.

"No… well… I… it's hard to say, really. The relationship kind of just reached its use-by date and we parted ways." In reality, it was much more painful than that: shouted insults, impossible expectations and a genuine sense of mutual dislike. Ultimately, when it was time for them to break off the relationship, they had both been worn to the bone attempting to live up to Eris' lofty ideals for self-adoration.

"That's not a great way to end the story, Baxter," Barbara said sadly.

"I guess not all stories are destined for ever-afters."

They broke for drinks and appetizers. While they munched and sipped, Baxter felt two divergent things: hope and unease. Hope for a new way of explaining life, and unease that he would have to be far more vulnerable with these people than perhaps he had been with anyone so far in his life.

More than Eris. Even more than his parents.

"Okay," Hana interrupted the snack time. "It's time for the main course." She said it lightheartedly, but there was anxiousness in her voice.

Hana issued more paper and waited impatiently for the group members to submit a crime for the roleplay. Where Barbara finished hers quickly, Murray thought carefully, chewing the nib of his pen, and putting his entire mental energy into imagining a crime that no one else would think of. Finally, his face lit up. He lifted his pen exultantly and wrote. Scrunching it up into a ball, Murray smirked as he dropped it in the wicker basket in which Hana had collected the other papers.

"A reminder about what you'll do: each person will draw one of the pieces of paper from the basket. Don't show it to anyone. You must first write a narrative, telling a story with that crime. Choose what words you would use to describe the motivation, the thought processes, and the emotion, before ultimately detailing how you would carry out

Chapter 6

the crime. Humor is acceptable but remember that we're trying to bring out our inner bad guys."

One by one, they reached into the basket and withdrew a crime. A few giggled. Lisa smacked her head and bemoaned the fact that *'There is no way I'll be able to do this.'* Baxter unfolded his slowly and he felt the blood drain from his face like a crimson waterfall.

Oh no.

Prostitution.

"Uh, I'm not doing this," Baxter said.

"Don't worry," Hana assured him. "No one will judge you. Just don't start it with 'Once upon a time.'"

His eyes widened. *This is definitely not a 'once upon a time' thing.*

Baxter's mind whirled furiously. While some scribbled a few notes, Barbara clicked her pen, and Lisa tapped hers against her leg. Curtis smiled enigmatically as he casually wrote a few lines. As Murray crumpled his sheet of paper and started over on a new one, Baxter could do nothing but stare at the word. Other than the actual, dictionary definition of the word, Baster knew absolutely nothing about prostitution.

"Okay," Hana said nervously. "Who wants to go first?" No one volunteered. Hana's eyes pleaded with Curtis, who cleared his throat and stood. "I guess I'll be the sacrificial lamb," he muttered under his breath. Murray finally set down his pen and looked up.

Without preamble, Curtis set his feet and began to speak. "There is something erotic about heat," he began slowly, his eyes smoldering. "The feel of an unquenchable flame. It starts in your guts…" He tapped his stomach.

Baxter frowned to hear the firmness of his abs. "…and moves through your heart, pounding, pulsating, throbbing to be released." Closing his eyes, he lifted his hands and his fingers twitched. "To feel the searing, charring, melting aphrodisiac – the smell of smoke and memory, of things which used to be, which are now left in ash. This is why I do what I do. **I am fire** and it burns inside of me, untamed, unstoppable… **Undone**."

When Curtis finished, his eyes opened slowly to see the group staring at him, mouths agape, faces slackened with astonishment. It had been such a long time since Curtis Schachman had commanded a stage, but he hadn't forgotten how to hold an audience.

"Holy crap," Murray ran his hands through his hair. "I'm not following that."

"That was amazing, Curtis," Barbara intoned. "Were you an actor?"

"I may have trod the boards, once or twice." He blew on his knuckles and buffed them on his shirt.

"Whatever you used to do, you haven't lost your touch."

"Thank you," he bowed. "Now, what crime was it?"

Hana raised her hand. "It could have been *any* crime. Crime of the heart? Jealous spouse walks in on the lover?"

He shook his head. "Interesting, but no."

"I thought it might have been arson," Barbara said. "Unquenchable flame, and all that."

"That's the one. Now, do you think we could all do something like that?"

"A categorical 'no' from me, Curtis," Murray responded. "It's hard enough to write something on demand, but perform it?" He swiped his hands in the air at Curtis. "No way."

Chapter 6

"You don't have to do it exactly like I did. Enjoy it." Hana stared at the paper in her trembling hands. Barbara had already wadded hers up into a ball and deposited it at her feet. "Would you like to go next, Barbara?"

"I don't know. I'm kind of with Murray on this one. It's like being the next band on stage after the Beatles."

"Just do *your* thing," Curtis insisted. "Every book is written differently, so is our description of them. Don't use words that I might use, or the words of your favorite author. You be the author – the storyteller inside you - that wants to come out."

Barbara swallowed deeply and stood nervously. "I am pretty sure there's no miniature Sister Grimm inside me wanting to come out," she said under her breath. Sighing deeply, she turned away from them to speak towards the back wall and began. "I don't know how it happened, really," she began. "It started out as… as a dare, you know, one of those things where the friend you thought you could trust, told you to ***trust*** her." Barbara mussed her hair and turned. "Suddenly, you're standing in a darkened room, surrounded by a wall of smoke and mirrors and all you see is your bare… soul. Do you know what I mean?"

Transformed by her own description, Barbara seemed embarrassed. "And now I sit here with all of you, heart pounding in my chest, hoping that I'm not the worst of us all. We're supposed to take twelve steps, but I can't even make the first. I know. I know. You see, my friend gave it to me at a party, and now after years in and out of… this," she motioned with her hands to the circle, "I still can't quite get away from it. It's my life, my momentum, my reason to get up in the morning. And now I don't know if I can afford to live without it."

Suddenly, Barbara stopped and covered her cheeks. "I... gosh... that's hard. It was probably more autobiographical than I wanted."

"I don't know what crime that was," Lisa said, "but you did a great job of describing it."

"She's an addict," Baxter said.

Barbara blushed incriminatingly. "I'm not an addict. I was writing, er, acting like one."

In college, Barbara had made the decision, that after leaving her parents' house, she would do everything in her power not to be the chaste, likeable, pert cheerleader from White River Junction. College became her time for experimentation, to turn over many different colored new leaves. When the opportunity arose at a party for her to try marijuana, she hesitated, but finally gave in. After a few years and a few failed classes, Barbara needed her entire willpower to quit the habit. It had been painful. Very painful.

"This has turned out to be a very interesting afternoon," Murray said.

"You should go next," Barbara said.

"I guess I could get it over with."

Murray pretended to tie a bandana around his head and then rolled up the sleeves of his shirt exposing his puny biceps. Screwing up his mouth, he suddenly transformed himself into another person with a gravelly, Hispanic accent.

"Me and Carlos, we never shoulda got caught, but the pigs, they was waitin' around the corner, drinkin' coffee and eatin' doughnuts. So me an Carlos, we crawl up to the building and we take out the cans and begin to spray. Carlos, man, he is an artiste. People would pay to see his work, and when he finished, I thinks to myself, 'Self, we should take a picture, right? That would be **loco**!" Murray raised his voice at the word 'loco' and began to laugh maniacally. "So we

Chapter 6

take a selfie but Carlos lost his grip on the wall an' he started to fall. Oh, 'mano, that was funny, an' when he hit the ground, I heard his shoulder pop, and he was screamin' but it was so loud the pigs dropped their doughnuts and grabbed us. It was so loco…"

Everyone was quiet. As Murray pretended to take off his bandana, he asked in his normal voice, "What did you think?"

"That was…" Hana started and then began nodding, waiting for someone else to fill in her missing adjective.

"Racist?" Lisa inserted.

Murray's face fell. "I thought we were supposed to be creative. I was just trying to be creative," he grumbled. Hurt, he sat down.

"You're right, Murray," Curtis responded to the group's awkward silence. "The brief was to describe the crime – in your case, graffiti – and you did a very clear job of portraying it. Whether or not it was racist is irrelevant. That's the way you told the story."

"Thank you, Curtis."

"I'll go next," Lisa said.

The team waited patiently while Lisa smiled and stamped her feet slightly before abruptly, and fiercely, turning on them. Pretending to pull a gun on them, she unleashed a profanity filled tirade about disrespect, turf wars, and something to do with her disdain for Miranda rights. As she finished the scenario, she shot all five of the onlookers and then, for dramatic effect, blew on the end of her smoking finger. Baxter lost count of how many times he jumped or flinched at her words, sounds and actions. Unable to move, he sat with his eyebrows arched, fixed above his startled eyes.

"And…?" Lisa asked.

"I... have no... words," Barbara said, "other than I did not see that coming."

Murray nodded. "I really liked it when you pretended to cock your hat to the side and tell Hana she should prepare to find a grave for both her and her dog."

"That was pretty good, wasn't it?" Lisa clapped her hands and sat down.

"Wait, what crime was it?" Barbara asked.

"Who cares," Murray said, "it was murder in the awesomest degree."

Lisa winked at him and double-tapped him with her finger pistol.

"Baxter, are you ready to go?" Hana asked hesitantly.

"Would you mind if I go last?" Baxter was sweating. He felt the pooling under his arms and at the base of his skull.

"Of course." Hana smoothed her skirt and stood. As she pulled herself to her tallest, Hana seemed the epitome of an ancient Roman goddess. With high cheekbones holding a triumvirate of moles, hair swept back from her face, and long, lean limbs, she was stunning.

"My parents were paupers." She shook her hands, unsure of what to do with them. "Whenever we went to the supermarket, they would lean down to tell me, 'Just take one more apple. The storekeeper will never notice. 'Go ahead, **Schatzi**,' my father whispered in my ear. I loved it when they called me that. Little sweetheart. I would have done anything to have them speak that word to me. I loved being **Schatzi**."

"And so I did anything they wanted to earn their love. Most days after school, I walked through the market, my hands sticky, quick as lightning. The market keepers, they smiled at me – I was beautiful to them, too. They would give

Chapter 6

me things, small trinkets from behind the counter. While their eyes were searching for small gifts, I stuffed many others into my pockets. They would pinch my cheeks, leaving scarlet fingerprints, searing guilt-marks, and let me go on my way. I would whistle down the aisles, 'Always slow,' my mother would say. 'They won't guess a thing.' I never learned to feel guilty. Now, I can't help it. I see something I like. I take it. I see a gem, a ring, a heart…" Hana's eyes and mouth melted them, "… a dream. It's no longer yours, but mine, because I am *Schatzi*."

When she finished, there was silence. Then she bowed. The others applauded. "Oh, that was so good, Hana," Lisa said as she clapped madly.

"Was that robbery?" he asked.

"Close enough," Hana said. "Shoplifting."

"Shoplifting dreams. That's wonderful!" Barbara smiled. "I think I've had that happen to me."

As they cooed over Hana, Baxter realized he had not heard much of what she had said. Although her intonation was wonderful, and the life she had given the story was marvelous, he had been more worried about how he was going to impress his co-authors. He had never been more nervous in his life. And, to portray a crime like prostitution was… incomprehensible.

"Baxter?" Hana interrupted his thoughts.

"Hmm? Yes?"

"It's your turn."

His face reddened. Shaking his head, he let his chin rest against his chest.

"It will be okay," Hana insisted.

Sighing, Baxter stood and reopened his piece of paper. Murray, knowing that he was the one who had written the word 'prostitution', grinned happily.

"You'll be fine," Curtis urged.

This from an Academy Award actor, Baxter thought. Baxter found he had no words to describe how he felt about this crime. With a dearth of 'bad guy' language, he couldn't describe the feelings and emotions of a prostitute. Added to it was the very real knowledge that five relatively complete strangers were waiting for him to act it out.

This little dream had turned into a nightmare. Could Hana steal this one?

"Come on," Murray said.

"I don't know what to say. I…"

"Be creative," Curtis urged with his hands.

"Okay…" Baxter sighed slowly. He cleared his throat. "I… uh… tested… positive."

They all waited. "It wasn't a venereal disease," his face turned a deep scarlet at the thought, "but… but…" Silence ensued.

Curtis wanted to help. "What did you test positive for?"

"I tested positive for… sexy."

Chapter 7

Betty Burnside's hip was cocked under her apron. She stood near the stove humming softly while a pot of beef stew simmered on the front burner. Betty's hair was coiffed into a perfectly shaped ball of aquamarine goodness. Beneath her bangs, thin, pencilled-in blue brows perched over lightly shadowed eyes.

At one point in her life, Betty could have been considered a beautiful woman. Perhaps even twenty-years ago, in her late forties. Men half her age might have found her attractive, if not tempting. She had the kind of relaxed confidence that men desired. Though short, her stature belied the power of her will, and in her heyday, men inquired of the opportunity to date her. Casually, she cast them all aside, and eventually settled on Arthur Burnside, who, without knowing it, was chosen for his solidness, not for his combativeness. Burnie had been average in every way; his shoulders were neither broad nor narrow; his hair was neither thick nor thin; his voice, neither low nor high, carried just far enough for Betty to hear him calling.

But now that she was in her 60's, Betty found that time, effort, and bitterness had etched lines in her forehead and cheeks and had also left a furrow at the base of her throat. She rarely seemed pleased with her own appearance or the appearance of others. She was especially critical of young women and their clothing styles, which she often called 'Just shy of whore-ish.'

As a delightful foil, Burnie was a hardworking husband and father, notoriously forgetful and decidedly content with life in retirement. Good-naturedly, he put up with his wife's foibles. Burnie loved her in his own way, or loved the way she could be. Now that life had moved on, now that his wife was generally miserable and his son was entering middle age, Burnie was much more content listening to the roar of car engines zoom past the cameras every weekend rather than his wife's stinging critique of most everything, like his son's resigned moaning about his passive existence.

"Can you turn that down, Burnie?" Betty said. "I'm trying to talk to Baxter."

"Sure thing, hon." Burnie notched the volume down one slot which made absolutely no difference. The mere fact that he acquiesced was enough for Betty.

"Now, tell me about this party thingie again. What *exactly* were you supposed to be doing there?"

He told her.

"I'm not sure I understand what this is all about. Is this because they don't think you can write about… what is it again?" She went back to her stirring.

"About being a bad guy. They say I can't understand it."

"I think you're lovely, Baxter."

He turned his back on her and walked to the table. "And therein lies the problem, Mother. Loveliness is not going to help me write about a bad guy."

"You're really going through with this…" she waved her spoon, "… this writing?"

"A novella," he inserted. "Why not? It's not like I have a thousand other things to do on the weekends."

"You could always come over here more."

Zoom, zoom went the cars around the track. Faster and faster. Burnie pointed at the television and began laughing.

Chapter 7

"As tempting as that is, I'm enjoying getting to know new people. Curtis is fascinating, even though…" he almost announced Hana's shift away from him which would have given Betty more fodder for her grandmotherless future, "…never mind. His acting skills are off the chart."

"He sounds like a pervert to me," Betty said as she carried the pot to the stove. "Actors tend to be perverts. Kind of like politicians. I'm sure there's a study about that somewhere."

"Can you be any more judgmental?"

"Don't be disrespectful." Betty inserted her hands into cushioned mitts and pulled open the oven door to check the store-bought rolls.

"Sorry," he apologized. "But they're really nice people."

"What about the woman *your* age. Hennie. She seemed nice."

"Hana. What about her?"

"Is she still eligible?"

"Technically, she is single, yes."

"Excellent." Betty leaned over the counter. "Burnie, you've got five minutes. Go wash your hands before we eat."

He waved behind his head.

"Have you gone out yet?"

"You mean like on a date, or just to one of our writing group sessions?"

"That's not a date. When you have homework, that's a job."

Baxter sighed. "Then no, I haven't asked her out on a date."

"What are you waiting for? Don't tell me you expect *her* to ask *you* out. Men need to do the asking. They have all the power."

A Miserable Antagonist

Baxter didn't believe his mother's words in the slightest. Though the world was peppered with chauvinists, his father was not one. Despite his mother's commentary regarding the dating structures of the '60's being implemented in the '20's, Baxter would have liked the scenario better where Hana asked him out. It would have taken all the guess work out of whether or not she was interested in him. Unfortunately, Baxter had a sneaking suspicion that Hana was slightly more interested in the 'pervert' than him.

Once Burnie finished washing his hands, he moved to the dining area where he pulled out his chair and sat down. Rubbing his hands together, he gazed up expectantly at his wife who towered over him with oven mitts, hot pan, and tongs. She placed two steaming hot rolls on his plate and then told him to 'have some salad, or you won't have a movement.' Like Oliver Twist, Baxter held out his plate to his mother who repeated the process.

In the background, race cars continued to zoom across the screen. Betty dropped her mitts on the counter and stomped over to the remote to frustratedly poke the green off/on button three times before making the sound and sight disappear.

Disappointed, but not dismayed that the television had been silenced, Burnie followed her with his eyes back to the table.

Betty went back to the stove and ladled three bowls of beef stew into shiny yellow bowls. She'd had them since the '70's – a wedding gift – and Baxter had been told multiple times that this crockery would be part of his inheritance.

Baxter received the stew from his mother with thanks. The stew steamed in front of him, and his mouth watered. Baxter reached for a hot roll, broke it open, and buttered it.

Chapter 7

Even if he didn't always enjoy his parents' company, he had to admit that his mother was a wonderful cook.

Finally, she sat down, and they began to eat.

Burnie slurped mouthfuls of stew. The first one caused him to suck air and wave a hand in front of his mouth to announce that the soup was HAAAWWT. As Betty chided her husband with 'Of course it's hot, dear, I just took it off the stove,' she turned to Baxter to continue the interrogation.

"This 'novel' of yours – sorry, 'novella'," she used her fingers for quotes, even though one hand held a baked good and the other a spoon, "is about a bad guy. What does the bad guy do?"

"I don't know yet."

"How can you not know yet?" She tapped the table. "Burnie! Burnie! Can you keep your slurping to a minimum?" Now that all the skin had been scalded from his tongue and palate, Burnie ignored her. He seemed to be lost in his lonely little numb world.

"Because we're just getting started."

"You don't really know how to write, do you, sweetheart?" His mother's saccharine voice irritated him. Baxter knew the sound of that tone. It meant, *You're not really qualified to be doing this*. He'd heard it when he wanted to play football, or the trombone, or even ride his bicycle across town to the swimming pool. He thought briefly about Hana's portrayal of the dream thief.

"No, Mother. That's why I'm taking the class."

He didn't mean for his irritation to be vocalized, but she kept pushing him.

"I'm sorry," she said as she wiped her mouth. "I'm just asking."

"I just want…" Baxter tried to find the right words. "I just want you to be…"

"Proud of you? I am. Very proud of you. You've got a nice job and…" Her voice faded.

"I was going to say, I just want you to be supportive. Whether or not I succeed in writing a novella is beside the point. It's the journey."

"We are supportive of you. Aren't we Burnie? Burnie?"

"Hmmm?"

"We support Baxter, don't we?"

"Sure we do! We bought him his first car, and we gave him a loan for a down payment on his house. Yes, of course. We support you, Bax." Slurp. Slurp.

"It sounds like you've contracted a small case of ingratitude," Betty mumbled under her breath.

Although Baxter was used to these little digs and manipulatory prods, he was never quite able to parry them. Sooner or later, Betty Burnside would break through his defenses and deliver the coup de gras.

"I'm sorry, Mom. It's just…" he leaned back in his chair but somehow slumped at the same time, "…I don't know what I was going to say. You're right, of course. You've always been very supportive."

"There, there," she reached out for his leg and patted it. "You eat your stew and enjoy your parents' company. You never know how long you'll have us."

Baxter bent over his stew and stewed.

Chapter 8

Larry Spago was the manager of Last National Bank, and he loved to study his features in the office mirror on the back of his door. It was a three-foot mirror, just large enough to reflect the image from hip to head, but truth be told the mirror wasn't big enough to capture his enormous ego. Some women found Larry very attractive, though. He had a full head of black lustrous hair which he parted in a straight edge right down the middle. Bushy eyebrows jutted out over beady, close-set eyes – the mark of intelligence, his grandmother told him in her accented English. Larry's perpetual three o'clock shadow, with wire brush moustache above his lip, accented, rather than covered, the large chin dimple which was cavernous enough to catch small bits of food.

To compliment this well-groomed facial hair was an omnipresent fluff of chest hair which stuck out over the 'V' in his unbuttoned shirts. This little tuft of hair looked like the top of a gnome's head poking over a fence, but Larry had been told by at least one woman (only one woman, really) that it was sexy. Sometimes Larry accentuated his chest nest by dangling a gold chain through it. 'Pure 24 karat gold,' he would tell people, even though it was really 24 karat *plated* gold.

When he was in his twenties, Larry modeled for a calendar shoot. He still had his copy of the calendar mounted on the office wall at the bank, right next to his college diploma – *Lawrence Domenico Spago - Community College of Vermont 1981 – Associate Degree, Business*. Larry was prouder of that calendar (his favorite month photo being May of

A Miserable Antagonist

1984 where he posed in front of a fake, seaside background in a way-too-tiny yellow Speedo) than almost anything else in his life, even his college diploma. Donatelli's Pizza wanted Italian-looking models for their low budget shoot. One night, the proprietor, Alberto Donatelli, spotted Larry during dinner, and he offered him the job right there on the spot. Preening like a peacock, Larry signed on the dotted line as he winked at the two ladies he dined with. So hot. So sexy.

After straightening the mirror, Larry tamed the tips of his moustache by licking his fingers and twisting, and then shot himself in the mirror with finger guns.

Larry pushed his office door open, pulled his sport coat tighter over his chest, and tilted his head back to survey his financial domain. As the bank manager, Larry's role was to supervise and, if necessary, rubberstamp any particularly tricky loan applications. No one could remember the last time Larry had used his rubber stamp.

Baxter knew Larry was coming even before he was coming. His cologne led the way. Nose twitching, Baxter counted out the last twenty-dollar bill for an older man named Hebron Grossman and then put his head down.

"Baxter."

"Yes, Mr. Spago?"

"As soon as you're finished, my office."

One of these days, Baxter hoped Larry Spago would put him out of his misery and let him go. Although the income was nice, Baxter grew more despondent about his prospects each day. There was no joy in tellering. There was no happiness in counting out money and giving it to someone else. There was no joy in asking Larry if he could use the bathroom knowing that Larry would be timing him while he was gone.

Baxter turned. "What are we going to talk about?"

"Important bank matters."

Chapter 8

"Fine, Mr. Spago. I'll be right there."

Baxter locked his till, logged off his computer, and followed Larry sullenly through the large space behind the teller's booths into Larry's office. Larry closed the door behind Baxter and motioned for him to sit in front of the desk.

Baxter detested Larry's office more than most any other place in the world. In Larry's sacred space – his 'domain', as he had labeled it – too many ridiculous things happened. It wasn't simply Larry's patronizing way, nor his true inability to think strategically (or even sensically). No, it was his incapacity to create an atmosphere of workplace happiness. Larry's office was a direct representation of why Baxter disliked Last National Bank. Everything in it was about Larry and his love affair with himself. Larry had affixed photos of previous girlfriends on each wall. It was as if these large photos, even bigger than his bowling trophies and slow-pitch softball awards, on display in an illuminated small glass case in the back corner, were the real trophies in his life. On the south wall was a photo of Spago and a waifish blond with 80's high hair, both clad in fluorescent matching outfits, skiing in Aspen. The north wall contained a particularly buxom brunette with Larry, in a green Speedo, snorkeling in the Mediterranean. A photo on the east wall captured a redhead with large eyes and a face full of freckles as they posed in their mountain climbing gear in front of the Andes. Above the Mediterranean ocean scene in the middle was the 1984 Italian pizza calendar. He did have a nice head of hair, Baxter had to give him that. Larry's safe was hidden behind the calendar. Baxter had seen it once when he opened the door without knocking. Larry had been very angry about that.

"How is your day going, Baxter?"

A Miserable Antagonist

"All right."

"Not great?"

"I'm a teller, Mr. Spago," Baxter responded as if the statement could answer all questions.

Larry pondered Baxter from his rocking throne chair on the opposite side of the desk. "How long have you been working here, Burnside?"

"About twenty years."

"That's a long time, isn't it?"

"You tell me, Mr. Spago."

Larry tented his hands in front of his chest and moved suddenly forward. The movement startled Baxter and he jumped. "What are your aspirations, Baxter?"

"I'm not sure what you mean, sir."

"What do you want to do with your life? Do you want to retire as a teller? Do you want to live in Montpelier all your life? Do you have a girlfriend? Boyfriend…?"

Baxter frowned. "Why do you want to know?"

"Because I'm interested! I want to get to know my employees. What makes them tick. What makes them tock. What makes them go boom!" His fake laughter reverberated through the office.

"Can I go back to my booth now?"

Shaking his head, Larry came out from behind his desk. "Baxter, would you like a raise?"

This was not what Baxter expected. "Uh, sure."

"In order to get a raise, one needs to display a sense of go-gettem-ness. Do you have that?"

"I think so."

"Show me."

"Sir?"

"I want you to go out there and take charge of the front area. I want you to organize the tellers' schedules. I want you to solve disputes. I want you to manage the team."

Chapter 8

"Isn't that what *you're* supposed to do?"

"Baxter..." Larry said his name slowly, "...this is a perfect opportunity for you to show me that you have managerial potential. I want to give you more money, I really do, but I just can't throw it away."

"So, you want me to go out there and do your job?"

"No," Larry frowned and smiled at the same time. "Of course not. I want you to do *your* job, but also show me how well you could do *mine*."

"Will I get the same pay as you?"

"Let's not be greedy here, Baxter. One thing at a time."

"Okay... What do you want me to do first?"

Larry walked behind Baxter and placed his hands on his shoulders. Baxter had never felt more uncomfortable in his life. As his boss massaged his neck, Baxter stared at Larry's pinup calendar.

"That's the kind of attitude we're looking for," Larry said as he leaned over and whispered behind Baxter's ear.

Baxter grimaced.

"As you probably know, Carmen has not been pulling her weight in the bank."

"Carmen Valdez?"

"Is that her last name? Huh."

"No, I have not noticed that Carmen has not been pulling her weight."

"Well, she hasn't." He squeezed one last time. "It's time for Carmen to go, and I need you to tell her that."

Baxter started forward out of his chair to escape his superior's hands. "No way. Not gonna happen."

"She's an anchor on our bottom line, Baxter. A real drag. The board of directors is on my case about this, and we have to do something. You and me, we," he rounded into

Baxter's sight, "who are managers and possible manager material, can't have people like that weighing us down."

"She's twenty-seven and has triplets."

"She does?" Larry was astounded.

"Yeah, two years ago, remember? We had a baby shower for the kids. Three girls."

"I don't remember that."

No kidding, Baxter thought.

"She's been away a lot and I keep having to hire extra help," Larry said.

"Her kids are sick. What do you want her to do?"

"I want her to be at work," Larry responded.

"Have you tried talking to her?"

"Yes." Baxter knew that this meant 'no.'

"What did she say?"

Larry blinked and shook his head. "It doesn't matter. What *does* matter, though, is that you show me your managerial potential. Go out there and break it gently to her."

"No."

For a moment, Larry looked angry, then perplexed. "If you do this, I'll give you a raise."

"How big?"

"Four percent."

Baxter rolled his eyes. "Not worth the aggravation."

"Six," Larry countered.

"Fourteen." Baxter wanted to cover his mouth. He was stepping out on a very large limb. He had just murdered his morals and was now bickering over the price of the funeral.

Larry's face turned red. "Eight point five. Final offer."

"Ten percent, Larry." It felt so good to be a bad guy.

"Done." Larry extended his hand. Larry had been suppressing Baxter's pay raises for at least six years. Ten

Chapter 8

percent wouldn't bring Baxter even close to where he should have been three years ago.

Suddenly, Baxter felt a deep sense of dread. Although he and Carmen were not friends, he could only imagine how she would take it. Three children, a husband, and a small house on the edge of the city. For heaven's sake, she took the bus to work every day.

Larry hurried Baxter to the office door and opened it. "Go get 'em, tiger."

Head lowered in shame, Baxter exited the office. Leaving behind the wood panelled walls, the glamorized pictures, the trophy photos and trophy life, Baxter wished he could rewind the last ten minutes, and instead of being at his cubicle for Larry to approach him, he would be in the bathroom uncaring if Larry was timing him or not.

As the office door snicked shut behind him, Baxter thought he could hear the soft humming of the 1984 Italian calendar model. *Que sera, sera.*

The other tellers turned to stare at him. Unwilling (and unready) to lift his eyes, he trudged back to his stool. Bernadette popped her head around the corner. Her brown hair, each curl like a small Slinky, seemed patterned after a young Shirley Temple. Bernadette was a happy-go-lucky woman in her late 30's with a lovely personality. When there was information she wanted, she would get closer and closer until she practically plucked it from Baxter's teeth.

"Did you just get fired?" She asked excitedly.

"Unfortunately, no."

"What was that all about then?" She motioned with her head to Larry's office.

"He wanted to give me a raise."

"Oh really? Then what are you so sad about."

"Because I feel like a prostitute."

Bernadette's fake eyelashes threw off their moorings and fluttered like flags in a stiff breeze. "Did he... touch you inappropriately?"

Baxter flinched. "What? No! No! That's not what I meant."

"What did you mean, then?"

"He'll give me a raise if I fire Carmen."

"You're serious! OMG!" Bernadette covered her heart and mouth with her hands. "I can't believe he would sink that low. Getting you to do his dirty work. That's horrible!"

"I know," Baxter's chin fell to his chest.

"What are you going to do?"

"No idea. I guess I'll probably have to tell her."

"Do you need some help?" Bernadette whispered.

"Absolutely not."

Bernadette leaned closer to him. "We could just pass a note down to the end of the line." She glanced over her shoulder to the last booth where Carmen was smiling at a customer.

"You mean like fold one up, send it past Dan, Steve, Camille, and Sheena to eventually end up in Carmen's hands?" he asked sarcastically.

Bernadette nodded.

"Don't you think that's kind of callous?" Baxter asked.

"Is it any more callous than getting one of your minions to do it?"

"I see your point, but no thank you," he said.

Bernadette was interrupted by a customer in front of Baxter. "I'll be right back," she giggled.

Sighing, Baxter moved into his cubicle and looked up. Murray and Lisa stared at him from the other side of the glass. "What are you guys doing here?" he whispered forcefully.

Chapter 8

"We wanted to see where you worked," Murray said.

"Hana and Curtis told you, didn't they?"

"Yup."

"I don't have a break for another half hour."

"That's all right," Lisa said. "I want to open an account."

"Come on, you guys. I can't have everyone opening an account just to check up on me."

Lisa smiled. "I really do need to open an account. I've got cash." She flashed a handful of bills at him. "One hundred and seventy-seven dollars."

Another sigh escaped his lips. Baxter placed a piece of paper onto a clipboard and passed it through the slot. "You'll have to fill this out and then come back with one form of I…" Suddenly, to his right, there was a loud noise. It sounded like a scream of rage. "…D." Carmen's face was a mask of rage, and she was pointing at him.

He leaned over to Bernadette's cubicle. "What did you do?"

"I sent a note."

"What? Why did you do that? I didn't… Oh, crap. Here she comes."

Carmen Valdez looked like a bull, but Baxter was not *holding* a red cape, he *was* the red cape. Carmen was a large woman with meaty arms and sledgehammer sized fists. She was wearing a long, navy-blue skirt and a cream top. At her throat was a pearl choker. Though she usually had a charming disposition and a bright smile, she left them at her teller's desk. Carmen charged through the empty space behind the booths, stopped just short of Baxter, and rattled a piece of paper in his face. "What is this?"

"Uh… I… I don't know. I didn't write it."

She unfolded it and showed him the words. Everyone in the bank watched.

The note read:

> Dear Carmen,
>
> You seem to have done okay here at work, but Larry asked me to fire you. Sorry about that.
>
> It would be helpful if you cleaned out your desk without making a scene.
>
> Love,
> Baxter Burnside

Flashing a look of abject horror at Bernadette, Baxter stammered. Not one identifiable word was produced.

"This better be a bad joke, Baxter."

"Look, Carmen, I'm just the messenger. Don't shoot the messenger."

Her face fell. "Don't you realize that this job holds my family together? Without the income, we will fall apart. My husband will leave me…"

"Baxter, how could you?" Lisa scolded.

"Stay out of this," he hissed.

Carmen waited, still clutching the pseudo-pink slip. "Why, Baxter? Why?"

"He… Larry… he said if I did this for him, I'd get a raise. I didn't think he'd actually take me up on it."

"How much is he going to give you?"

"Ten percent."

"Ten percent? A raise? You sold me up the river for ten percent?" She began to bawl louder. "What I wouldn't do for a ten percent raise. Oh, how am I going to tell Pablo

Chapter 8

this? And the children? We might have to move to…" she swallowed dramatically, "Buffalo."

The rest of the tellers gasped.

"I don't know what to tell you, Carmen. I'm just doing what he told me to do."

Carmen placed her hands on her hips. "You march back in there and tell that miserable, no good, greasy… *pendejo*… that he'd better get his ass out here, or I'm going to lawyer up!"

"Maybe it's best if you told him that?" Baxter suggested.

"Oh no, no, no," she waggled a finger in his face. "You and your greed, they got you into this. Now they'll have to get you out of it."

"She's right, Baxter," Murray said. "You probably shouldn't have done that." The line of tellers nodded along with the customers.

"Please, Carmen, I'm sorry. I won't do it again. Would it help if I gave you my raise?"

A sly smile formed on her face. "That would be a start. Now go!"

As she shouted the last word, he jumped like a startled rabbit from his chair. Just as he was about to hurry back to the office, the door opened, and Larry Spago came out.

"What's going on out here? Why is no work being done?"

Carmen approached Larry and stood by Baxter. "Explain this!" She handed the note to Larry.

Face flushed, eyes widened, Larry dropped his hands that still held the note. "Baxter, I'm so disappointed in you. Don't you know a practical joke like this is grounds for dismissal?"

"What! You told me to fire her!"

"That's preposterous! I would never do that to a fine, family-loving woman like Carmen Volpez, mother of twins and such a hard worker."

"My name is *Valdez*, and I have triplets."

"I apologize," Larry raised his hands in front of him. "I'm so distraught by this little gimmick here that I misspoke."

"You told me to fire her!" Baxter repeated.

"Keep your voice down," Larry said.

Baxter obeyed.

"Now, Carmen, how can I make this up to you? How can we be assured that this disgraceful kind of thing never happens again?"

"I want a ten percent raise."

"Done," Larry said without hesitation.

"Me too!" Sheena said.

"And me," Steve shouted. Teri, Camille and Dan all nodded enthusiastically.

"Sounds fine to me," Larry smiled magnanimously. "You've all been such faithful workers. You deserve a raise."

"What about me?" Baxter said.

"After this stunt you pulled?" Larry's eyelids lowered. "You're lucky to still have a job. Now get back to work."

Carmen thanked Larry and waited for him to return to the office. When the door had shut, she grabbed Baxter by the arm. "You owe me your ten percent also."

"I didn't get a raise like you guys did."

Her eyes flashed. "It's for my emotional trauma." Carmen whistled as she strolled back to her booth to serve her next customer.

When Baxter finally plonked down again in his seat, Murray and Lisa stared at him through the glass. "I don't suppose that's how you saw that playing out," Lisa said.

Chapter 8

Baxter dejectedly shoved the clipboard through the slot. "Just fill it out and get it back to me."

Chapter 9

"The protagonist is heroic, but only tragically so," Professor Mangall intoned. "To balance the powers of good and evil, our hero must be strong, yet fallible; stoic, yet emotionally available."

One of the younger students in the class raised her hand. "It's hard to imagine Hercules or Perseus being 'emotionally available.'"

Baxter found himself nodding enthusiastically to her heroism.

"Isn't emotional availability a contemporary construct?" another student asked.

Mangall nodded and placed an index finger to his lips before speaking. "Point taken. Yet imagine the mythic tale of Hercules or Perseus without emotion. What would you have left?"

The students remained silent, and he dropped his finger to pour forth his wisdom. "As writers, without emotion, we run the risk of the *Twilight* series, or worse yet, *Star Wars I, II, and III.*"

"Hey," a young woman disagreed, "I thought *Twilight* was quite well done."

"Which is *why*," Mangall stared her down, "YOU will never write a best-selling novel."

While the student reddened and put her head down in shame, the professor moved to the whiteboard and lifted the magic green marker and began to scrawl angrily. "Give me the greatest protagonists in literature." He stared around the room. "Anyone? How about I get you started. Edmond Dantes. Hester Prynne. Even Bilbo Baggins? Scrooge? You

Chapter 9

know you've made it when your character becomes synonymous in everyday language."

The class stared at him with blank looks.

"Have you never heard of Dantes?"

"Is that the main character in that *Inferno* movie with Tom Hanks?" a young man asked.

Mangall's face registered shock. "Please tell me you're not confusing a Dan Brown book with Alexandre Dumas."

The student's face scrunched up. He had no idea who Alexandre *Doo-MAH* was.

"Hester Prynne anyone?"

"Didn't he play for the Chicago Bears for a while?"

"Good God," Mangall responded and lowered his head to his chest. "Does anyone at all, have even a rudimentary knowledge of literary history that includes a genuine love of character development? Scrooge, anyone?"

"I used to love him in the Looney Tunes," Baxter couldn't hold himself back. Barbara jabbed him with her elbow while he smiled.

"Victor Hugo's Jean Valjean is worthy," a voice spoke from the back of the room.

Curtis.

"Scarlett O'Hara, or if you'd like, Winston Smith."

"Finally," Mangall exhaled and raised his arms in the air as if calling for an 'hallelujah', "someone has read something."

A young man raised his hand. "I thought we were here to write, Professor? What does reading have to do with writing?"

Mangall repeated the question under his breath. "Listen, people, and listen carefully. If you do not read, if you do not hear the thoughts of previous generations, and if you casually disregard anything that hasn't been made into a screenplay, you can't **POSSIBLY** understand what it means to help the world become emotionally available."

He snapped the lid back on the green marker. "Can anyone else tell me what reading has to do with writing?"

Once again, Curtis volunteered. "I suppose reading opens your mind to new avenues of expression instead of trapping yourself in the easiest patterns."

"Say more, great swami," Mangall encouraged with a smile.

"If we don't read Shakespeare or Homer, or if we disregard Virginia Woolf and Jane Austen, we've basically stunted our own minds. Certainly, we can't understand everything they say to us. They lived in a different time with different priorities. But emotions never change. Fear is fear. Happiness is happiness. Love is love."

"You're going to make me weep, Mr…"

"Schachman."

"Tonight, as we continue the writing process, I want you to keep these things in mind. I'm sure some of you have already formulated your ideas regarding your novellas. You'll want to impress me with your vocabulary and your intelligence. You think by distracting me with big words I'll disregard your actual story. Think again. I'm not that easy."

The class tittered.

"Tonight, what I want to see in your writing is a first paragraph and an outline for the opening chapters of your novella. These two things are the most important tools I can impart to you for your future as amateurs. Without a great opening paragraph and outline, you might as well be writing young adult novels."

"We'd make more money that way," one of the students said to laughter.

"Maybe," Mangall sneered, "but you'd be selling out."

Chapter 9

"You were speaking of the protagonist…" Hana called out.

"So I *was*." He turned to the whiteboard again and re-popped the lid off his 'Marker of Power'. "Develop the story around the *character* of your protagonist. Emphasize both his good traits *and* his flaws."

"Or her," Lisa said.

"Yes, yes," Mangall replied testily, "we can quibble over gender later." He wrote on the board. "Don't choose a distracting name, but one that carries weight. It's got to <u>*mean*</u> something." He underlined the word 'mean' on the board. "Too many novels are shipwrecked on the reef of names."

Baxter noticed a few classmates scratch out something in their books.

"Next, locate your novella's setting either in a place you know, or one you have completely made up. It's no good drawing a location out of a hat and thinking, 'Oh, yes, Oklahoma would be a great place to set the novella,' when, in fact, you couldn't even locate Oklahoma on a map."

More scratching out.

"Most importantly, you need to know both your audience and what your audience likes. As you write, think about them."

Baxter tried to think about his 'audience' as Mangall instructed, but the only person he could think of that would possibly read *The Bad Guy* was him – Baxter Burnside, frustrated bank teller, lonely and disenchanted with the life he was leading. Should he just write the book for himself then? If that was the case, it might be easier than he thought.

Suddenly, Baxter Burnside grew quite excited about the prospect of writing something that he, himself, would enjoy. Thinking about how writing could be the one place in the world where he could control everything, from actions to emotions, to conversations, he picked up his pen, opened his notebook and began to scrawl an idea. As Professor Mangall droned on about what they 'should' do as writers, Baxter was caught up in what he 'could' do.

Writing was about to become fun.

Scanning the room, he felt the anxiety level rise. Other amateur writers were concerned with their grades, or worse, with Mangall's mark of approval. Baxter, though, was finding himself on a tropical island of one – remote, untouched and extraordinarily beautiful, one without judgement or failure.

Baxter had his idea.

Ten minutes after Professor Mangall's diatribe, Baxter's team situated themselves in the hallway, chairs circled, bags and backpacks at their feet. Lisa nibbled her fingernails worriedly. Barbara tapped on her phone, her mouth working as furiously as she thumb-typed. Hana's and Curtis' chairs were turned ever-so-slightly towards each other, another subtle implication that something was going on between them.

"I've figured out what the novella is going to be about," Baxter announced.

"What is it, Baxter?" Hana asked.

He spread his arms. "Weren't you listening to Professor Mangled? We're writing for ourselves! Nobody else!"

"That's definitely not what he said, and you still haven't told us your idea," said Murray.

Baxter took out his yellow pad and flapped it in the air. "We can do whatever we want! We're gods of words!"

Barbara frowned. "Have you been drinking?"

"No. Of course not."

Chapter 9

"It's probably what happened at work the other day," Murray said.

"You didn't tell everyone, did you?"

"No," Lisa said.

"Yes," Murray said.

"Damnit, you guys."

"You tried your best to be the bad guy, Baxter, and it didn't turn out so good."

His face flushed at the memory. "That's beside the point. When Mangall was talking, I thought, 'Why not write our novella the exact opposite of how he told us.'"

"Clever, Baxter, but I'm not sure that's such a great idea," Curtis said, as he leaned forward slightly in his chair, hands clasped across his knees.

"We choose terrible names and use settings we've never been to before. We use language that only means something to us. Damn the reader!" His face was furiously alight.

"Baxter," Hana smiled tentatively, "are you sure?"

"Why not? Let's be honest: none of us are going to be best-selling authors, so we might as well have a little fun."

"Speak for yourself," Murray said.

"Give us an example of what you mean," said Barbara.

Baxter held the yellow pad aloft. "For the next ten minutes, think of the silliest name possible, a place you've never been, and doing something you know nothing about. Then, let's see what happens."

Their eyes swivelled around each other. Finally, Lisa giggled. "Okay – that sounds like fun!"

They began to collectively type, scribble or tap nervously. Glancing at Murray, Baxter noticed the glow from the computer illuminating the small smile on his face.

A Miserable Antagonist

Barbara chuckled as she wrote on a pad of paper. Curtis leaned back in his chair languidly scrawling his idea on the pages over his crossed thigh.

Unsure of how to begin, Baxter noticed Parker Mangall hovering over a group of young women. With a smug expression, he pointed out the deficiencies in their work. One of the women glanced up at him, pained eyes, eyebrows stitched together at the bridge of her nose by his critique. As he pondered the scene, Baxter knew what to write.

When the ten minutes were up, each team member read their opening paragraphs and their thought process which informed what they wrote. Although Murray believed his idea was fresh and humorous, the only laugh he elicited from the group was from Lisa who giggled about his setting – somewhere on Uranus.

The others, to varying degrees, read with enjoyment. The exercise had opened a valve of creativity in the group. It felt good to write for themselves, not for a grade. For them, evaluation had taken the primary position of importance in their lives: for Barbara, it was how her kids graded her cooking, or other domestic activities, or the way her ex texted her; for Hana, it was her abilities to put together flowers; for Lisa and Murray, it was simply the letter placed above their papers or exams at college; and for Curtis? Maybe it wasn't. Baxter, though, felt the heavy weight of external critique every day of his life, whether his parents or his peers.

Which was why, in that situation, when Baxter cleared his throat, he felt no trepidation. The others had given it a shot and survived, so why shouldn't he?

"Archimedes Chumpy was a bad guy with bad habits. It wasn't *just* that he chewed his fingernails and picked his nose. No, Archimedes was a stone-cold killer."

Chapter 9

"Archimedes Chumpy? Archimedes Chumpy?" Murray interrupted with a snort. "Out of all the names, you chose Archimedes Chumpy?"

"You must really like it because you spoke it like Ali Baba opening the cave," Barbara said.

"What?"

"Just be quiet, you two," Hana hushed. "Let Baxter finish."

"Do you want me to read the opening sentence again?"

"No," they all said in unison.

Baxter continued. "He lived in Boise, Idaho. In his house, he was surrounded by his trophies – pictures of his victims and a glass jar full of chewed fingernails." Baxter glanced up to see them cringe.

"Ugh, that's disgusting, Baxter," Lisa said, as she pulled her fingers from her mouth.

"Which part? The killing or the fingernails?"

"The fingernails, of course."

Baxter learned a very important thing at that moment. People were only interested in bad guys if they were disgusting people. A handsome bad guy was boring. A well-cultured assassin would cause people to flip the page. But a jar full of fingernails? Bring it on.

"When Archimedes got up and took his morning shower, the sound of his last kill still echoed in his ears."

"What did it sound like?" Murray asked.

Baxter smiled. "Meeeeeow, raahreoorh!"

Lisa's face disintegrated into disgust. "Wait. Archimedes Chumpy is a cat killer?"

"Yup. And a good one too. The Kitten Murderer."

"You're a sick man, Baxter Burnside," Murray said.

A Miserable Antagonist

Frustrated and perplexed, Baxter raised his hands. "Whoa, whoa, whoa. Let's pause here and separate the story from the writer. The task was to write about a strangely named person in a place that we've never been before doing something we know nothing about. You guys already knew I was going to write about being a bad guy!"

"You can't *totally* separate the story from the writer, especially when you *know* them," Lisa said. "Now every time I look at you, I'm going to think that you kill cats."

"This is ridiculous!" Baxter was flabbergasted.

"Why didn't you pick something nicer, like an arsonist or, or… a strangler, heck, a nursing home assassin?" asked Murray as he leaned over the back of his chair. "But a cat killer? Jeez, psycho."

"What about you guys? Your stories were just as bad as mine! Murray, a chicken named Elgar? Curtis, Zanzibar Ermine – a scuba diver with a death wish?"

"Uh, uh, Baxter," Lisa stated firmly. "You crossed the line. You need to unwrite that."

"How does one *unwrite* something? How do you *unhear* it? Or *unsee* it?" Gesticulating wildly, Baxter grew even more frustrated. "Who draws the lines for ideas, or books, or movies? Have you never seen a movie and thought, 'That was the world's worst piece of garbage?'"

Murray's head bobbed. "Yeah, I saw *Pretty Woman*. I wanted to scrub my eyeballs with bleach."

"There, finally, someone with some sense."

"But we know you, Baxter," Hana said. "We know what you're like. You could no more kill a cat in a book than you could in real life." She said this hopefully.

"I could. Yes, I could. I could kill a cat in a book, and I'll show you."

Chapter 9

"No, no, that's all right," Hana responded. "How about we stick with something more realistic. Some kind of theft?"

Exasperated, Baxter stood up. "What do I know about theft? Nothing! I work in a frickin' bank where they frown on that kind of activity. I haven't stolen a damn thing in my life, but I'm sure I could write about it."

The others shook their heads. "You *could*," Barbara said, "but you don't know what it feels like - heart thumping, pulse racing, scheming, absconding... ooh, that's a good word. I'm using that one." She scribbled the word on the paper in front of her.

"And *you* do?"

She shrugged but didn't look at him. "Not like steal-from-a-store kind of theft, but I've stolen things from people."

"Like when."

Barbara's face reddened. "I borrowed my neighbor's *Friends* series on DVD, and when she asked for it back, I told her I had already returned it."

"Psh..." Baxter said, "Everybody's done that."

"Have you?" Lisa asked him.

"Well, no... but I could! I could steal things!"

"There you have it," Curtis said.

"Have what?"

"We'll do what Barbara is proposing. We'll scheme, plot, and execute a theft."

Baxter's face darkened. "That's not what I meant. Not at all."

"Are you chicken?" Murray jabbed.

"Yes! Yes, I am! I don't want to get caught. I don't want to go to jail."

"But if you get away with it..."

A Miserable Antagonist

"I don't want to get away with it. I just want to write about killing cats."

"Stop! Saying! That!" Lisa covered her ears.

"That's a great idea, Curtis. What should Baxter steal? A car? A computer? A million bucks?" Murray rubbed his hands together.

"Not going to steal anything," Baxter insisted.

"Who is a person that you wouldn't mind stealing something from?" Curtis asked. "Think of this as your Robin Hood moment."

Without conscious thought, a few people flashed in front of his eyes. Carmen, yes, but not because he didn't like her, or that she could stand to lose money, but simply because the bank episode was still fresh in his mind.

Bank? Larry Spago?

Then, an idea formed in his mind.

Oh, wow…

Chapter 10

The Sunday pot roast smelled delicious, but Baxter Burnside was far too nervous to eat.

"Why are you so jumpy this afternoon?"

Baxter studied his mother as she busied herself in the kitchen. While wearing her traditional Sunday afternoon apron that read, **PROUD TO BE A SALAD DODGER**. Betty motioned to a drawer. "Can you hand me that meat fork?"

Baxter grabbed the fork from the drawer and handed it to her, handle first. She laid it on the counter then put on her oven mitts. Like a surgeon preparing for a triple bypass, she held her hands up in front of her and nodded to Baxter to open the oven door. Hot air exploded from it and superheated his face. Betty grabbed the baking pan and extracted the roast. Baxter closed the door and turned the oven off.

As Betty began to slice the roast, Baxter noticed that his father had fallen asleep while watching another car race. Even though the volume was far too loud, Burnie did not find a late morning nap particularly difficult. As Baxter approached him, heart pounding in his chest, he saw the item which he was about to steal.

His dad's television remote.

What made the moment even more tense was the fact that his father snorted when Baxter reached for it. Jerking his hand back, Baxter leaned over to see if he was still sleeping.

"Baxter, can you wake your father, please? It's time to eat."

A Miserable Antagonist

Startled, Baxter looked up at his mother who was not watching him. "Yes, Mom," he mumbled. Baxter quickly reached down, grabbed the remote, and stuffed it into the back pocket of his pressed khaki pants. Then, gently, he touched Burnie's shoulder.

"Dad. It's time to eat."

His father, who sometimes slept with his mouth open, snorted awake. "W… wha… who?"

"It's time to eat."

Burnie slowly recalled where he was and put the footrest down on his recliner. He grunted as he pulled himself up, and then searched for the television remote. As the TV blared the sounds of the race cars vrooming past the camera, Baxter realized his mistake.

"Where's the remote?" his dad asked.

"Did you set it down beside you?"

Flustered, Burnie turned in circles. "No, I thought it was right there, on the arm of my chair."

Baxter's face flushed. "Maybe you knocked it on the floor?"

Burnie checked around the chair.

"What are you looking for?" Betty asked.

"The remote!" Burnie shouted. "I can't find the remote."

"It looks like it's in Baxter's back pocket," she pointed with her oven-mitted hand.

Reaching behind him, Baxter touched the remote and his face reddened. "Oh, yeah, I must have picked it up and forgot…" His voice faded out.

"Just turn the TV off and put the remote on my chair."

Baxter looked at the thing in his hand. The remote was a symbol of who he was – an insignificant, inanimate object with many buttons, each offering a different

Chapter 10

manipulation. When someone pushed his buttons, he moved quicker, or slower, shut off, or turned on. They could predict his whole week of programming just by selecting the guide menu. He was a functional, useful human able to circumstantially change the things around him, but only at the whim and viewing pleasure of others. Both his parents, but especially his mother, knew *exactly* which buttons were useful and those that were inconsequential. She knew how to raise the volume, change the channel, and adjust his settings quite well.

Baxter shut the television off and dropped the remote on the arm of his father's chair.

After the meal, Baxter helped his mother do the dishes while his father moved back to the living room. Burnie turned on the television and positioned himself for his second, if not third, afternoon nap.

"He gets tired a lot," Betty said.

"Don't you?"

"No, not really. I sometimes get some pain in my hips, and shoulders and back, a little bit of eczema, ooh, and there's a nice sized bunion on my foot. But I don't get tired..."

Gazing down at his mother, Baxter saw the ravages of time on her body. He was surprised he hadn't noticed it before. Maybe he'd been far too interested in himself. He felt guilty about being a bad son.

"You're a good boy," Betty patted his arm and hung up the dish towel.

On the way home, Baxter thought about his mother's casual statement and suspected, unfortunately, that she might be right.

Chapter 11

To raise children was to invest heavily in the business of exhaustion. To do it as a single parent was to buy the whole company and borrow on one's reserves of strength, hope, patience and happiness. For the last two years, Barbara Hariman had reached the limits of her strength and savings, and it felt as if life was about to foreclose on her. When Stan left her on the front porch holding their then two-year-old son, Barbara could see the inevitable future as he peeled out of the driveway.

Life alone. Scrimping. Saving. Grieving. No life.

Almost impassively, she watched Stan roll away from them down the street. Selfishly, he had waited for Evelyn, who was twelve at the time, to leave for school so he wouldn't have to face her. It was the worst of his deceptions. Instead of acting like a grownup by taking responsibility for telling Evelyn that he had been cheating on all of them – first with Barbara (messing around with a colleague at work) and secondly with his children (cheating them of a stable transition from childhood to adolescence) – he whistled all the while he left them, twirling his car keys on his finger.

Barbara had done her best to retain a small sense of normalcy in the Hariman household, but she knew she couldn't keep it up much longer. Not unless there were some big changes.

Finally, one night, Evelyn, who had every right to be angry at both of her parents, sat her mother down at their undersized and scarred kitchen table laden with dirty dishes and scraps of discarded food and said…

"Mom, you need to take care of *yourself*."

Chapter 11

Barbara wasn't sure whether it was her daughter's thoughtfulness or the sentiment itself, but the cracks that had been showing broke open.

"Evelyn…"

The tears were symbolic of all the things which had become salty in her life. So many nights she lay in bed planning revenge against Stanley, or his floozy, or the teachers at school who didn't understand the magnitude of what *she* was going through, or her boss, whose deadlines were unreasonable in the current situation. Yet when the tears came, they seemed more of a baptism than tsunami.

As she blinked them away and held her arms out for Evelyn who, for the first time in ages, allowed herself to be hugged, Barbara felt a release.

"What do you think we should do?" Barbara asked her daughter after kissing the tear-moistened crown of her head.

"I think you should take that class you always wanted to."

"What?" Barbara pulled Evelyn back and gripped her shoulders lightly.

"I remember things. Before Dad left, you told him you wanted to take a creative writing class – you know, some time for yourself – and Dad said, 'Don't be ridiculous. That's a waste of time and money.'" Evelyn touched her mother's cheek. "You should do it."

So, she had. And every Wednesday night, Evelyn would babysit her four-year-old brother and nine-year-old sister.

Of course, the dream was much easier than the practicality. Wednesday nights weren't particularly easy for a single mother to leave the house: chores needed be done, baths taken, homework finished, and stories listened to. It was a forty-five-minute drive to the university, 90 minute class, and forty-five minutes back home. That was without talking to any of her new friends. What was supposed to be three hours had morphed into four or five. Even though it was a struggle, Evelyn held up her end of the bargain.

Which was why Barbara was so intent on making sure the class was worthwhile. Evelyn noticed how much her mother benefitted from interactions with other adults, but Evelyn also reaped the rewards of greater trust.

Barbara tapped her teeth with a pencil trying to put together the first paragraph of a novella she hadn't planned on, and a story she knew nothing about. It felt like going fishing, only not knowing which species she was fishing for, or where she was casting her line.

"Mom!" Barbara's middle daughter Kelsey shouted. "Ev is annoying me!"

"Keep up the good work, then," Barbara called out without looking up from her pad of paper.

"Mom!"

How do I start writing? What do I say? What do I want people to feel?

"Mommy." Her son Tommy sidled to the edge of her seat and pulled himself to her leg. Already, his thumb was buried deep in his mouth, and he was cradling his blanket under his chin. Sighing, she reached down and lifted him onto her lap. He nestled his head in her shoulder. She was trying to break him of the thumb-sucking habit, but sometimes it was easier to let him go than to suffer the consequences of weaning.

Evelyn sauntered into the kitchen and opened the refrigerator. Finding very little to her liking, she turned towards her mother. "What's for dinner?"

Her train of thought interrupted, Barbara frowned. "What?"

Chapter 11

"Dinner. Food. Fuel for body cells."

"Whatever you decide to make."

"But it's your turn. I made dinner last night," Evelyn pouted.

"You can probably see that I'm a little busy here," she motioned with her head at Tommy.

"You're always busy."

Barbara put down her pencil and sighed. "Okay, Ev, not too busy for you. What's up?"

Evelyn plopped down in her chair to slouch opposite her mother and brother. "Life isn't fair."

"What happened?"

"Nothing happened. It's just the way it is. We spend our weeks working, our weekends cleaning, and during it all we pretend that Dad isn't a jerk."

Smiling, she rocked Tommy. "What would you like to do?"

"I don't know. Something different. Like you – you're taking a class."

"You're taking lots of classes."

Evelyn planted her chin in her palm. "I *have* to take those classes. You take a class because you want to."

"You're right. That isn't fair."

Looking down at the pad, Evelyn smiled. "Looks like you've got writer's block."

"You can say that again."

"What are you supposed to be writing?"

Barbara glanced at the blank page. "Frankly, I'm not sure. I've told you about Baxter before, haven't I?" Evelyn nodded. "We decided to write this story about a bad guy who is good at being bad, but I can't for the life of me figure out why Baxter feels so strongly about writing this. We've seen enough bad guys in our lives."

"You can say *that* again."

Barbara reached out and touched Evelyn's cheek. "I want you to be happy."

"I'll be happy when you are, Mom."

"Let's be happy together." While still holding Tommy, Barbara pushed her writing equipment to the side. "I've decided something."

"What is it?" Evelyn asked.

"On my Wednesday nights, or whenever my class gets together, I'm going to hire a babysitter for your brother and sister. That way, you can have some time to just be your fantastic teenage self and not worry about them."

"We can't afford that."

"I can't afford to have you bored with life."

Evelyn hugged her mother again. "Thanks, Mom."

"Don't do drugs," she said with a laugh.

Murray Coleman glanced down at the growing mountain of discarded opening paragraphs written on lined, yellow sheets of paper. He was frustrated – frustrated by his inability to make headway on the assignment - and even more, his inability to impress his co-authors with his writing ability. From a purely literary perspective, they seemed so far beneath him, and yet, miraculously, they were picking this up faster than he was.

Murray glanced around his dorm room. Surrounding his books, assignments, and homework, were empty pizza boxes with their accompanying white plastic tents to keep the box from smushing the pizza. There were opened bags of chips and empty soda cans. It was a pigsty. Although he was used to the mess, sometimes he needed to get out and get away from it all. Shutting his computer, Murray grabbed

Chapter 11

his room key, put on his flannel shirt, and headed down to the common room to play some pool.

For the last three years, Murray had lived alone, which suited him well. The only roommate he ever had, which was during his first year, was insistent on bringing friends over until all hours of the night. Murray was somewhat jealous, but to a greater degree, he just wanted his own space. He didn't want someone complaining about his cleaning habits (or lack thereof); he didn't want anyone waking him up in the morning or in the afternoon. At this point in his life, he simply didn't want anyone else.

Until, that is, he found the Creative Writing 102 class.

Murray had seen a poster in the hallway with the seductive title: **WANT TO BE THE NEXT BEST-SELLING AUTHOR? CREATIVE WRITING 102 WITH _AUTHOR_ AND PROFESSOR PARKER MANGALL. SIGN UP NOW!!!**

To be honest, Murray knew next to nothing about Parker Mangall, and what Google spat out did not suggest that the Professor was on his way to becoming a best-selling author. His goofy title (*Be Better than Great: Be the Best!*) did nothing to convince Murray to take the class, but he did happen to see a pretty college girl yank off one of the tabs before he did. Fortunately, on the first night, Murray saw the young woman carrying a pink backpack which she hugged tightly to her chest.

Lisa.

As Murray stood over the green felt of the billiards table and studied the layout of the balls, he held the cue in front of his face. The common room was empty. Everyone on his floor, maybe even the entire dorm, had either gone home to their parents for the weekend, or were holed up in their rooms bingeing Netflix or playing video games. Murray did not particularly enjoy either of his parents' houses. He was also uninterested in watching movies. There were no new stories anymore. No new ideas. Even this 'idea' of Baxter's seemed trite. Murray was sure, despite agreeing to this little charade of writing a group novella, he could write something far better.

And yet, as he stared at the yellow **1** ball, Murray became circumspect about his actual literary talent. The ideas which he produced always seemed well-formed when deep in his own head, but after speaking them aloud to the others, he heard them through their ears. *The Final Frontier*? How stupid.

This psychological flagellation was a continuation of the things Murray had learned to believe about himself. He was not very good at anything. He was not very attractive. His ideas were infantile and unnecessary. To top it off, Murray was frightened of what others would think. Thus, the critique he gave to his classmates was in the form of sarcastic pinpricks to protect his own psyche. Now, though, as the group worked through Baxter's 'Herb Treadwell' idea and the 'amazing-awful-bad-guy-thing,' Murray found his creative mind curiously working harder trying to place his own puzzle piece into the space. And if he could do that, maybe he could fit himself into other spaces…

"What are you thinking about?"

Murray wheeled, surprised to see Lisa standing in the doorway.

"I saw you through the window as I was walking past."

"Spying on me?"

"No, you just look lonely."

He leaned back over the pool table and lined up a shot. "Just enjoying some peace."

Chapter 11

"Yeah, I know that feeling."

"Do you want to play?"

She hesitated in the doorway. "I was just..." Pointing behind her, her voice faltered when she saw his face. "Yeah, I'd like to play, but I'm not very good."

"You don't have to."

She approached the table. "Don't be a baby. If I say I'm going to do something, then I will. I'm playing, and it's not because I feel sorry for you."

"I wasn't..."

She ignored him. "Now, where do I find a stick-thing?"

"You mean a *cue?*"

She rolled her eyes. "Whatever."

Murray pointed to the pool cues in the corner. Because the dorm rec area tended to be less-than-well-looked-after, multiple cues were missing tips or were broken in half. Cracked chalk cubes were scattered across the room on windowsills and shelving. Lisa selected the least-worst of the cues and chalked the tip. As Murray re-racked the balls, Lisa took up a position at the other end of the table. "Are you going to break?" he asked.

She shrugged. "I'll give it a shot." He lifted the rack exposing fifteen precisely packed balls. Lisa knuckled two fingers and placed the cue on them. Sticking the tip of her tongue out between her lips, she aimed, drew back the cue and with one swift motion pushed forward. Unfortunately, she missed the center of the cue ball and it careened off to the side. Murray caught it before it could wreck his perfect rack.

"You see-sawed your arm when you shot."

"Really? Thank you for your guidance," she responded sarcastically.

His face reddened. "I'm just trying to help." He rolled the ball slowly back to her.

Lisa grabbed it and replaced it on the white dot. "Are you going to be super-sensitive about everything I say?"

"Would you like me to be?"

She smiled. "That's better." Murray studied her as she once again positioned her fingers, cue, and tongue. Lisa had a tiny nose and sharp cheekbones. Her black hair dangled over her face, and she tossed it back over her left shoulder. She wasn't beautiful, but cute, *like a caramel bunny*, he thought. Lisa clanked the break again, but this time, Murray was too slow to grab the cue and it broke the rack slightly. Only the yellow ball separated from the pack, but it was enough for Murray to feel the need to re-rack.

"Jeez, you really *are* bad at this."

"I told you so."

As Murray focused on the process of correcting her mistake - lining everything up perfectly tight, in order, numbers in place, colors appropriately positioned - he pondered the weirdness of his feelings for Lisa Kelly. She was different. Her clothes, t-shirt, and blue jeans were a few styles passé but not cool enough to be retro. She had luminous eyes and an expressive, nervous mouth which seemed to be in a perpetual tug of war whether to be startled or amused. Perhaps it was the best way to describe her: caught in the middle - in an androgenous fade, somewhere between male and female, power and passion, beauty and plainness.

"Are you almost done?"

He cleared his throat. "Hold your horses. I'm just practicing racking because the odds are I'm going to have to do it again after your third attempt."

"Shut up."

Chapter 11

This time, her aim stayed true, and the balls broke apart, not with power, but with something like curiosity, as if the balls saw something on the bumpers that made them want to get closer. Lisa raised her hands exultantly as if she'd just won the game.

"Nice job," he stated wryly. "You almost got one in."

"I aim to please."

The game progressed. Murray sank a few balls, scratched, and then handed the white ball to Lisa who stared at it in her hand. She stared at him without comprehension.

He pointed to the other end of the table. "Put it in the kitchen, anywhere you want, and sink a ball."

"The kitchen?"

"I didn't make up the term."

"That's stupid," she said as she placed the cue ball behind the dots and lined up her shot. Once again, she clacked it off the side.

"Go again. Replace it."

She shook her head. "No. I'm not going to get better by you feeling sorry for me."

"Whatever."

It wasn't until the second game that Lisa started to sink a few balls. Each time she did, she strutted and danced, rubbing it in. Murray laughed. He was aware of the mixed feelings: being attracted to her, yes, but somewhat platonically. For many years, his parents had pestered him about a romantic relationship because, as his mother would espouse, 'That's what young people need most in their lives.' Now as this newness unfolded before him, Murray was suddenly certain he just needed friends, first. The others in the creative writing group were fine, but Lisa was his own age, and they both went to UV.

It was good.

A Miserable Antagonist

"Do you have any brothers or sisters?" Murray asked.

"No, not that I know of."

"What does that mean?" Murray rubbed the end of his stick with blue chalk.

"My parents are divorced. My mom ran away when I was nine. My dad told me she struggled with fidelity."

"He told you that when you were nine?" Murray leaned over and shot. Missed.

"No, stupid. When I was older. But in his words, there was a good chance I had multiple half-brothers and/or sisters running around somewhere."

"How does that make you feel?"

"What, are you my shrink?"

"It's your turn. Shoot."

When she hit the cue ball, it caromed into three other balls leaving the orange **5** ball balancing precipitously on the edge of a pocket. "Aaaagh!" she groaned.

While Murray lined up his shot, she leaned against the wall. "Me and my dad, we just got along. It doesn't really make any difference if I have brothers or sisters. Why would I need them?"

"I always wanted a brother or sister," he revealed.

"Then you're a lonely child, too."

He shrugged and pocketed a striped ball leaving only the **9** left for his side. "You could put it that way. I don't really feel lonely. Sometimes I just like to be alone."

"Me too. But I also like people, especially the writing group. That's a pretty fun class, isn't it? Old people and us trying to write a novella together."

"Color me skeptical."

"What do you mean?"

Chapter 11

Murray placed the **9** near a corner pocket for his next shot and stood up. "That Curtis guy seems a little shady."

"Like a pedophile?"

"No, not like that, but like someone who's got something to hide and needs an outlet to relieve his guilt."

"That's weird."

"I'm just sayin'."

"What about Baxter? He's pretty different."

"Very."

Lisa deposited her teetering **5** ball into the pocket and lined up the **7**. "But it's not like a *bad* different. Like a *nice* different. Does that make sense?"

"No."

"I feel like he's caught between, like… like… well, do you remember when you shed your adolescence and became an adult?"

He rolled his eyes as she missed every ball with her next shot. "I'm not sure I've completely moulted," he responded.

"That's what Baxter's personality seems like to me," she insisted as she stood directly opposite him in his direct line of sight.

"Can you move out of the way? You're distracting me."

"Sorry," she moved three inches to the left and he shook his head. "Baxter seems like he's caught between the first part of his life and the one he really wants to live."

The statement caught Murray off guard. "That's good. You should write that in the book."

"You mean it?"

A Miserable Antagonist

"Yeah," he grunted as he struck the cue ball sending the black **8** into a pocket ending the game. "How about we go get some pizza?"

"Make it ice cream and you're on," she extended her hand for a shake.

He grabbed it feeling the smooth, warm skin of her hand. "Let's go."

Chapter 12

Hana called Baxter a few days later. After a long workday, punctuated by Larry Spago's continuous, annoying prodding that he, Baxter, even after the last fiasco, should begin to display more leadership abilities, Baxter was happy to go for a walk with her.

They planned to meet along the path overlooking the Winooski River. It was the best time of year in Baxter's opinion. Autumn colors were beginning to decorate the tips of the deciduous forests. The fiery display more than made up for the bleakness of winter when the cold north winds shredded Vermont's interior and left a shivering mess in its wake.

The Winooski snaked through the base of the foothills and wound through the shuddering trees. For some reason, Baxter always wondered where the river started and how it continued to flow even in the dry times. Where did the water come from? Why didn't it dry up? Why…?

His thoughts were interrupted by Hana, who had surreptitiously approached him from behind. "Baxter?"

He jumped. "Oh, hi. How are you?"

"Good. Good."

"Where is your dog?"

"I walked him this morning."

"What did you want to talk about?"

"Can we walk?"

"Yes."

Side by side they began to stroll along the natural path over molehills, under branches, and along the river. The water burbled beside them.

"Let me start by saying this, Baxter. I think you are a talented writer."

"I most certainly am not," he scoffed.

"Okay, maybe not talented, but creative. Is that better?"

"In a completely unrealistic way, yes."

"During the course of our class, it's been enjoyable getting to know the others. They have their oddities, but so do we all."

"What's yours?"

She laughed. "I'm prone to fear. I'm not a huge fan of crowds. I get… jumpy." She shook her hands out and looked embarrassed.

"What's wrong with that?"

"It makes going to class relatively difficult."

"Ah," Baxter nodded knowingly.

"I also don't know how to talk about my feelings." She swallowed and looked at him.

"Any specific feeling, or emotions in general?"

"Just a few specific ones. But feelings… for someone else. These are the hardest."

Baxter's heart began pounding. *Does she have feelings for me?* If someone like Hana was attracted to him, she of true kindness, altruism, and a healthy dose of beauty, maybe his life would turn out all right after all. His mother would stop razzing him, Larry Spago would have to give him his dues, and he might even move out of his house. Maybe to the hills – live near Curtis, rub it in a little.

"Tell me more," Baxter responded, swallowing heavily.

"You sound like my therapist."

"You have a therapist?"

"I have since my husband died. It helps."

Chapter 12

"And what does your therapist tell you about sharing your feelings for someone else?"

"She says I should take the leap."

"Okay…" he said slowly.

"Here goes." Hana stopped Baxter by grabbing his arm. "Baxter, since I met you, I… can't explain it… you impress me by your kindness and your willingness to try new things. When I see you, I… my heart skips a beat because I know we can talk about anything."

"You feel that too?"

Her face turned red. "Yes."

"I thought you didn't like me," he blew his cheeks out. "I find you so attractive, but you never really speak to me. You're always sitting beside Curtis, and he's handsome and debonair and sophisticated and, Jeez, he's like freaking Harrison Ford. But to find out that you…"

"Baxter…" she stopped him.

"Yeah?"

"I know that I can talk to you about anything, especially how…"

"You can say it," Baxter said, ready to be drawn in for their first kiss, which he'd imagined (and reimagined) at least fourteen times. But not on a walk, not like his first interaction with Eris. He shook his head not wanting the image of his former fiancée to invade his mind. His first kiss with Hana should not be while strolling along the trail, birds squawking around them, car horns and sirens echoing softly from the city below. Instead, they should be standing on the balcony of an expensive restaurant, maybe in New York, he in a suit, she in a sheer dress. He would be wearing thick-soled shoes and she, flats. They would be holding expensive glasses of champagne. When he professed his love, Hana would blush and touch the moles on her cheek. With great confidence, Baxter would take the drinks from her hand and set their flutes to the side. Delicately, Baxter would reach up to touch her face, where she would kiss his palm and tell him almost casually how much she adored him. In the background, Peaches and Herb would be singing *When he touches me, nothing else matters*. Hana would lean in, lips parted, eyes closed and…

"Especially how I'm falling in love with Curtis."

Peaches suddenly murdered Herb and the record screeched to a halt.

"What?"

"That's what I'm trying to tell you. Because I can talk to you about anything, I know you can look past your attraction to me. I don't want it to be awkward between us, but I have no one else to talk to."

Baxter leaned his head back, face tilted towards the sky. "Dammit! How can it not be awkward? I just vomited my feelings all over you about how I thought you wanted to be with me, and it turns out you liked Curtis all along."

The pit in Baxter's stomach grew larger. Instead of Hana seeming less attractive, Baxter found her even more desirable now that she was virtually unattainable. Not that she was attainable before his profession of adoration, but still…

"It won't be awkward for me, I promise." She reached out for his hand. He allowed her to touch him. "Can we talk about it? Please," she pleaded.

"Yeah, I suppose." He kicked at a stone and sent it clattering down the slope beside them.

"Thank you," she said and leaned in to kiss his cheek. No kiss had ever been so disappointing. They started to walk.

"I'm worried that he's too old for me."

Chapter 12

"You think?" he said morosely. "He's old enough to be your father. Or, or, at the very least, a crusty uncle."

"I know, but he doesn't seem old, you know."

"Unfortunately, I do."

She began to gesture expressively with her hands. "His mind is so agile, and he's so beautiful. The way he speaks, and have you seen how calm he is?"

"Do you want me to fall in love with him too?"

Hana laughed. "I went to his house the other night. We had dinner and then I…" She shook her head and smiled. "What should I do, Baxter?"

"About what?"

"About the relationship. Should I continue? The age thing could really be an issue."

Baxter wanted to tell her that age was *definitely* going to be an issue. In ten years, Curtis would be wearing adult diapers and they'd be living in a nursing home. Baxter imagined him with dentures and shivered. He would wear old person clothes and drive a scooter while Hana, only in her fifties, would be strolling next to him.

Unfortunately, Baxter could sense that Curtis was not one to let himself go. He seemed like a gentle, kind man with intelligence to match.

"You should go for it. What's the worst thing that can happen?"

"He could die while we're making love."

"Oh, for Pete's sake. You went there. Did you have to go there?"

"I was just trying to lighten the mood."

"Well, the mood certainly did change." Baxter kicked another pebble in the middle of the path. Another stone, another missed opportunity.

"So I should give it a shot."

A Miserable Antagonist

Baxter looked up at her. "If I were you, I'd give it a shot."

"Thank you, Baxter."

"Whatever."

Chapter 13

Curtis sat in his home library with a newspaper opened in front of him. He wore comfortable corduroys and house shoes, and his blue button-down shirt was tucked neatly into his pants. As he attempted to focus on the financial page, his mind strayed to Hana. Though they were almost a generation apart, there was something *older* about her; timeless, maybe, and her simpleness, in the best sense of the word, beguiled him. It allowed him to overcome his reservations about the age difference.

He'd only felt this way once before. It had been a brief fling, a dalliance between two stage actors who couldn't stop acting once they'd left the stage. She, a young starlet-wannabe, had seduced Curtis and made off with his best intentions. Hurt and embarrassed, Curtis felt the break-up was the terminus for his romantic life *and* acting career. Even though the producers of *Death of a Salesman* pleaded with him to return, Curtis couldn't drag himself from the pain and he aborted his modestly successful acting career to enter the business world.

So, it was strange that Curtis found himself wanting to get back into acting, even if it was not on stage. To teach some of these burgeoning artists a thing or two about composure, form, spacing, wording and translating it to literature, was both enlightening and enjoyable. Granted, Curtis had never really worked a day in his life – at least in the work-ish sense of the American Dream. No, Curtis had used his inheritance from his rum-running great-grandfather and turned it into a multi-million-dollar retirement. Everything in his house, from the decorations, the furniture and the fixtures to the garage and its… complexities were a result of a privileged and fortunate life.

The inheritance was more than modest. With it, Curtis found that he was extraordinarily gifted in working stock market trends and what they had left him was multiplied many times over. Still, he felt guilty about a few shady investment strategies. He ashamedly enjoyed the fruits of his grandfather's illicit labor, and now his own. Would he tell Hana about it? What would she think?

Setting the newspaper down, Curtis pondered Hana. What had captured him so utterly was her purity. There was no guile in the way she treated him or any of the others in the group. It was as if she was a holdover from the 1940's, a graceful Greta Garbo. With her face and figure, she was made for the silver screen, and yet here she was, caught in Montpelier in a creative writing group.

Curtis knew this was the way it was for every man and woman experimenting with romance. To invite the other into your home was to invite them into your history. Sometimes history was a beautiful thing, sometimes not. The accumulations of time and treasures were opportunities for conversation, but sometimes they were impediments and distractions from the words that needed to be spoken. Hana, thankfully, had accepted his residence in stride, and after meeting the staff, had wandered the rooms in awe, and settled into the chair across from where he was now sitting. She had one leg curled up underneath her, sipping at a hot chocolate, and talking about life.

The past was past, it had been said, but why, as he studied her, did it feel as if the past had opened the trapdoor and stuck its ugly head up at him in the present?

Chapter 13

Opening his yellow pad, Baxter felt that it was time to write. Summoning whatever creativity he might have buried within him, he took a deep breath and put pencil to paper.

The Bad Guy

By

Baxter Burnside

Chapter 1

Herb Treadwell was...

Baxter chomped on his plastic pen. It was already pitted with toothmarks. He tried to recall what Mangall had said during the very first class he attended. Every protagonist needed a character flaw...

... an extraordinarily average guy. If Herb was a superhero, others would have dubbed him Captain Nice, or Mr. Invisible. When Herb left the house every morning, he never closed the door behind him without first checking and rechecking that he had his keys, his wallet, and a certain watch that didn't keep time. It simply reminded him of...

Baxter quickly felt that this exercise would be one of catharsis, maybe even self-diagnosis. The very averageness of the novella would reflect an intrinsic part of his own character. And this was a flaw. Most certainly, this was *his* flaw.

> ... the desperate circumstances in which he found himself a widower. If not for that watch, that extraordinarily average Timex, Herb, too, would have been dead.

For what seemed a short time, but what was actually well into the dark hours past midnight, Baxter continued to write. From the onset of the idea, that Herb Treadwell was the averagest guy ever born, imbued with gifts to love women and to thieve (a cross between James Bond and Butch Cassidy), the story did not just seep from Baxter's fingers – it exploded. Once the dam had been broken, Baxter found a rhythm of imagination he'd never experienced before. Although his prose was unrefined, repetitive, and often full of grammatical errors, it seemed thoroughly irrelevant because Baxter was writing for an audience of one.

Himself.

With very infrequent breaks, Baxter pushed on, letter after letter, word after word, sentence, page and chapter. When the sun rose, Baxter felt weak. He had expended every ounce of energy held captive within him and had dumped it onto those yellow handwritten pages.

He finished chapter four ending with…

> In the abstract hour of night, 2:38 in the morning, Herb Treadwell finished his plans for the greatest robbery of all time. What made him

Chapter 13

most uneasy was the thought, 'How could robbing a bank be so easy?'

Of course, the real-life Baxter Burnside knew that robbing banks was almost impossible, but his alter ego, Herb Treadwell could do whatever the heck he wanted, and twice on Sundays. He wasn't going to get caught, that was for sure. He was going to spend the money on himself. Nobody could do a darn thing about it. Because in Baxter's book, the bad guy was going to finish first.

Yawning broadly, Baxter flipped the yellow pad closed and inserted his pen into its correct spot in the desk drawer. Behind him, his bed was still made. Its comfort was appealing, but Baxter had to get to work. For brief seconds, Baxter's body attempted a mutiny over his mind to call in sick, but Baxter had never done that. Not once. Not in the almost-twenty years he had worked at the bank.

After showering and shaving, Baxter crawled into his work clothes - brown slacks, white shirt and blue tie, and then tied the laces on his leather shoes. They were fifteen years old. Certainly, he could have used new ones, afforded them even, shoes with better insoles with true grip on the bottom, but going to the shoe store seemed overwhelming. He liked these shoes, anyway. He knew them, and they knew him.

It was 8:24 by the time Baxter walked through the side door of Last National Bank. Squeaking in just under check-in time, he hung his jacket on the coat tree in the staff room and made his way to his teller's desk where Bernadette was already preparing her computer and till.

"Good morning, Baxter. A little sleepy sleep-in today?"

A Miserable Antagonist

Baxter spun his chair out of the way and logged in. "I actually didn't go to sleep last night."

Bernadette raised an eyebrow and spoke with a fake French accent. "A little amorous company last night?"

"No," he said slowly. "I've been doing some writing."

"Really?"

"Yes," Baxter punched in his computer password. "I've been taking a creative writing class. I'm writing a novella. That's a short novel."

"What's it about?"

"Being asked to fire one of your colleagues," he responded without looking at her.

"I hope you're not still sore about that. I *honestly* thought I was trying to help."

He stopped to look at her. "Your best foot forward was to write a 'You're-fired-but-don't-be-angry' note thus putting me in danger of justified dismissal?"

"Like I said, I'm sorry."

Baxter didn't respond.

"Look, Baxter, I'll make it up to you somehow."

"How? Are you going to petition Mr. Spago to give me the same raise that everyone else got?"

Bernadette's cheeks flushed. "No, but…"

"But what?"

"We could make out sometime."

Incredulous, Baxter shook his head. "And making out with you will somehow replace the self-respect I lost for telling you about what Mr. Spago wanted me to do."

"I just thought that… well, it doesn't seem like you ever have any… female company and…" she touched her cheek, "I'm a female and I could supply the company."

"Oh, for Pete's sake," Baxter mumbled. "Do I come across as completely desperate?"

Chapter 13

"Kind of." Bernadette turned back to her own station as Chad-the-security-guard unlocked the front door and assumed his position of staring-into-nothingness for the rest of the day. Chad was a meaty kind of fellow, with muttony fists, connected to pot-roast forearms, leading to a ham-ish neck that flowed out over his collar. If there was anyone in the bank who had a worse job than Baxter, it was Chad.

"Great," Baxter responded.

"I didn't mean that in a bad way," Bernadette continued. "I just mean that your… desperateness is kind of cute… like a puppy that doesn't get the attention it needs, so it waggles its tail really fast, and sticks its tongue out…"

"Stop. Just stop. You're not making it better."

"I'm trying to make amends," she pouted.

"All right, Bernadette, you know what you can do? The novella that I'm writing is about robbing a…" he lowered his voice, "… a safe."

"In a bank?"

"Shhhh," he quieted her with his hands. "It has nothing to do with reality, only dreams of revenge."

"Against Spago."

He didn't say anything.

"Wow! That's so cool! What can I do?"

A patron approached Baxter's window. He lowered his voice so the person couldn't hear him. "Keep your eyes open for someone who seems *shady*, you know what I mean?"

"Shady. Got it. Then what?"

"Good morning, sir," Baxter greeted a frequent customer, a wild-haired man with wide glasses and four rings on each hand named Matteo Neil. Matteo was an El Salvadorean immigrant who had escaped with just his Guess jeans and a red handkerchief stuffed with food. He dropped a bag full of coins in the stainless-steel dish to be counted. "I'll have that for you in just a little bit." Baxter took the bag and dumped it in the counting machine. Bernadette followed.

"Then what?" She rubbed her hands together.

"Then you can take a few notes about their appearance – describe them as best you can. Then imagine them in a scenario where they might…" he looked around, "do some damage."

"Aye aye, Cap'n." She saluted him.

"Please don't ever do that again," Baxter said as he ripped off the receipt at the change counter and walked back to his cubicle.

Around lunchtime, as Baxter yawned into the back of his hand for the 79th time, Bernadette leaned over from behind her cubicle. "Stop doing that! You're making *me* yawn."

"I can't help it. I told you, I didn't sleep last night."

"Me either. I was so excited to…" she stopped talking and pointed indiscreetly. "OMG. There's the character for your novel!"

Baxter glanced around for a downtrodden man, or an out of place security guard – maybe a jumpy Matt Damon, but there was no one of that description at the end of her point. "Where?"

"Right *there!* The woman by the watercooler."

There was only one woman sitting by the watercooler and she might have vied for the crown of Most Beautiful Woman in Montpelier. Wearing a knee length skirt, black tights, high heels and a white blouse, the woman appeared as if she'd stepped off a catwalk.

"She looks like *either* a bank robber *or* a movie star," Bernadette said.

Chapter 13

When the woman turned towards them, Baxter gasped.

"Do you know her?"

"Excuse me," Baxter said hurriedly and stood from his chair. "I need to go to the bathroom."

"Baxter!" Bernadette called out. "Who is it?"

As quietly and quickly as possible, Baxter hurried to the bathroom where he stared at his reflection in the mirror above a marble sink. He grimaced as he placed a hand in a globule of pink soap drying on the edge. While scrubbing the soap from his hands, Baxter gazed into his reflected eyes, red from lack of sleep, which stared back at him in bewilderment.

Eris?

Baxter calculated how long he would have to wait in the bathroom before she left. He assumed it would be at least twenty minutes depending on whether she was there for a loan application or a deposit. He hoped a deposit.

After ten minutes of scrutinizing his reflection there was a knock at the door. "Baxter," Steve's voice was muffled on the outside. "Are you all right?"

"I'm just going to the bathroom."

"Are you sick?"

"No. I'll be out in a little bit."

"Are you dropping a deuce?"

"Shut up, Steve. I've just got some stomach issues."

"Diarrhea?"

"Go away!"

After a pause, Steve knocked on the door again. "I just want you to know there's a woman out here who wants to see you."

"You take her."

A Miserable Antagonist

"Believe me, bro, I'd like to, but she looked at me as if I was a booger on the underside of a desk."

With one last look in the mirror, Baxter sighed. "One minute." Splashing some water on his face, Baxter felt better but dreaded the thought of talking to his ex-fiancée.

"Put your big boy pants on, Baxter," he murmured to himself and opened the door.

When he returned to his cubicle, Eris was standing on the other side of his partition. She hadn't changed. Actually, she might have looked even better than when they broke up. If her personality wouldn't have been Wicked-Witch-of-the-East-ish, he would have melted at the sight of her. She was roughly the same height as he, but trim around the waist. Her flowing brown hair was unstyled, which made her even more attractive. Light makeup accentuated her cheeks and green eyes. All the other men in the bank were staring, even some of the women.

"What can I do for you, ma'am?"

"Baxter, is that any way to talk to your old flame?"

Baxter squirmed in his chair. "I'm sorry, ma'am. It's a conflict of interest to serve people we know."

"Stop, Baxter. It's me, Eris. Let me in."

He shook his head.

"I'm not here for a loan or a deposit, but I need to talk to you about something."

"My phone works," he said as he averted his eyes. He could feel her drawing him in again.

"You've blocked me."

"For good reason."

Bernadette followed the conversation with the intensity of a tennis fan at Wimbledon. "I'll take over. You can meet with her."

Chapter 13

"No," he insisted. "If this woman wants to meet with me about something personal, she'll have to wait until after hours."

The door to Larry Spago's office opened, and he approached Baxter's cubby with a greasy smile. He had been watching the monitor in his office and had seen Eris pull up in front of Baxter.

"Hello, Miss. Can I be of assistance?"

"Your employee will not speak with me."

"Is that so? What seems to be the problem, Mr. Burnside?"

Larry had never called him 'Mr. Burnside' before, and Baxter was certain he did not like it at all. "The customer wants to have a personal conversation, but I have chosen the appropriate professional response which is to speak with her after hours."

Larry looked at his watch. "We don't want to upset our customers, Mr. Burnside. If you're so worried about keeping tabs on your time, take your lunch break now, then resume the position when you're done with your conversation." He smoothed his moustache as if it had adjusted while he spoke.

"Thank you so much," Eris winked at Larry. His smile broadened.

Bernadette leaned closer to Baxter and spoke out of the side of her mouth. "Gag me."

Sighing deeply, Baxter logged out of his computer and pushed his stool back, nearly ramming it into Larry Spago. Larry told him to 'Watch it!' and walked backwards to his office never taking his eyes off Eris.

Baxter led the way to the conference room while the rest of the bank watched them.

A Miserable Antagonist

Eris followed Baxter into the room and shut the door behind them. Taking a seat on the opposite side of the table, he motioned impatiently with his hand for her to sit.

"What do you want?"

"I want to talk, Baxter."

"You do realize how inappropriate this is, don't you?"

"Your boss didn't seem to mind," she smiled lasciviously.

"He has a weakness for beautiful, difficult women."

"Aw, you still think I'm beautiful?" She touched her hair.

"Back to the topic at hand…"

Without pretext or context, Eris dropped a bomb. "I think we should get back together."

Unable to control his surprise, he shouted, "What? ARE YOU FRICKING KIDDING ME?"

Eris glanced behind her at the bank foyer where every single head was still turned toward them. An older gentleman, Dan Tulio, who was propped up by his walker in front of Steve's cubicle, frowned and shook a finger at Baxter.

"Will you keep your voice down and act like an adult. Jeez, Baxter. I just told you that I care about you, and you just about popped a testicle."

"You… you don't care about me." He almost choked on his amazement. "You only have feelings for yourself."

"That's not true…"

"It is! Remember when we were together, and we'd go out, and you'd make me sit with my back to everyone else so they could all stare at you? And… and… you'd fall asleep every time I was driving. Remember the time when it was your turn to take out the trash and you got so angry about it, you threw my shoes away?"

Chapter 13

"I was different then."

Baxter leaned back in the groaning chair and linked his hands behind his head. "So was I. No way, Eris. No way."

"Please, Baxter, I have nowhere else to go." Her pleading eyes were always the most difficult thing for him. Large circles of desperate, needy manipulation.

"Don't do this to me," he whispered. "It was hard enough the first time."

Sensing his hesitancy, how she had sliced his sympathetic artery, she circled like a shark smelling blood. "Everything will be different. I promise."

Baxter knew her promises were worthless. Still, they did have some good memories, although he struggled to think of them at that crucial moment.

"What exactly do you want?"

"I want to move in with you."

Simultaneously, his heart raced and fell. "What happened?"

"Nothing," she lied. "I…"

"What?"

"I miss you, that's all." She was hesitant to explain that her last boyfriend, the owner of a Montpelier car dealership, with slicked-back hair and a gold tooth, had kicked her out of his life after she wrecked one of his Cadillacs during a shopping spree (with his money).

"Why do I get the feeling that you're not telling me the entire truth?"

She leaned forward over the table exposing a shadowed, diving neckline. "Because our ending was so difficult the last time. But it's a new day, Baxter. The two of us. The Duo. Brad and Angelina. Ross and Rachel. Sonny and Cher."

"Didn't all those couples break up?" Baxter asked.

"But *we're* getting back together, don't you see? We'll find *real* happiness."

"I don't know," he hesitated.

"Baxter," she said softly, "I'll make it worth your while."

"Eris, I don't..." he swayed.

"Then that's a yes?"

His mind was an unwavering no, but his body desperately wanted someone to share time with, even if it was Eris. He was lonely. After Hana's rejection for the much older Curtis, and Bernadette's strange proposal, Baxter felt like Eris might be his last chance to slay bachelorhood.

"Okay," he said quietly.

"Great!" Eris said and walked around the table. Knowing full well an entire audience was watching, she pressed in close to Baxter's body, leaned down and began to kiss him deeply on the lips. As she pulled away, she playfully bit at his lip. Then, with a seductive smile, she turned to walk from the room.

"I'll see you tonight, roomie."

Speechless, Baxter felt his lip to see if it was bleeding. It was.

As Eris cat-walked past the Last National patrons, in front of the other tellers and towards the suddenly-alert Chad, who had sucked in his gut and puffed out his chest, she lifted a hand to them. While she did this, Baxter Burnside remained in the small conference room, head now resting on the desk in front of him.

He had no idea what just happened or why, only that his life was about to become infinitely more complicated.

Chapter 14

Despite Professor Mangall's best efforts to impart his wisdom, one group in the class decided to sweep his little nuggets into the literary dustbin and build their own, anti-establishment narrative. When Mangall began reading the musings of Baxter Burnside and his compatriots, he felt his ego begin to tear. Not only had Burnside and Co. ignored every shred of Mangall's advice regarding what makes a perfectly good novella, they had done exactly the opposite.

Mangall knew there was always a smart alec or two in every class, and their efforts were generally erased with a pointed criticism or sharp rebuke. But never before had students gone to such great lengths to dismiss him like Baxter Burnside and his friends had. Mangall was a published author, for cripes' sakes.

Unfortunately, as he continued to read Burnside's version, Mangall grew uncomfortably aware that it was not bad. To be lip-bitingly honest, it was quite good.

In fact, the simplicity of the writing, and the strange storyline, albeit childish and ridiculous, made it annoyingly apparent that Burnside had at the very least a smidgeon of talent.

Mangall sat in his office reading the rest of the rubbish his class had produced and was thankful that they had done exactly as he had instructed. They had turned in run-of-the-mill, dime-a-dozen, starter novellas, easily replicable and easily graded. Though they had completed the assigned task, Mangall felt uncomfortably aware that he was doing the class no favors by supressing their creativity. Now, the literary mirror, the one exposing his own protagonizing flaw, threatened to crack under the weight of his gaze. Sighing, he turned away from his sense of guilt and transferred his flaw to Burnside.

Here was a story about Herb Treadwell, a complete nobody, engaging Parker Mangall in a life of undramatic intrigue. Baxter Burnside's style was loose and lacked vocabulary, but the way he strung poignant 'what-if's' together and hopes for the common man, it could really come to something.

Mangall took off his glasses, rubbed the bridge of his nose, and stared through the rain-spotted office window. It was early evening, just after dinner. The remnants of his Reuben sandwich remained on a small white plate beside his computer keyboard. The odor of sauerkraut and caraway seeds still lingered in the room. Picking up the last piece of his sandwich, he swallowed it in one gulp, licked his fingers, and ran his tongue along his teeth to retrieve any seeds or bread before class. As he wiped his hands on his pants, he spotted through the streaked window, an extraordinarily attractive woman, and his teeth cleaning ground to a halt.

Her hair seemed to follow her, to race to catch up with her for fear of being left behind. The woman's tanned face, glowing from outdoor activities, and her strong firm legs were eye-catching. Shockingly, the man walking beside her was Baxter Burnside. They seemed engaged in lively conversation, although Burnside, trailing slightly, seemed to be pleading with her to do something. She did not miss a step.

How in the world did a putz like Burnside end up walking side by side with a drop dead, gorgeous woman like that?

Some guys had all the luck.

Parker Mangall did not have all the luck. Most nights he walked home to his quaint, two-story house six blocks

Chapter 14

from campus wondering why he did not have a spouse, or even a girlfriend. He was a talented, published author, a university professor, with an income well above the mean household. His home was quaintly furnished, clean, though dark, and tastefully decorated with curiosities – things that brought back memories. An old steamer trunk. A small cask. Various steins he'd collected on vacations across Pennsylvania – by himself. But there were no pictures, no frames with laughing faces beside roaring waters; no alpine adventures; nothing to suggest he'd lived a life outside the university.

Nothing to suggest he'd lived a life at all.

Though he had been cursed with bad eyes resulting in his need to wear thick glasses or contacts, and a somewhat doughy complexion, in his own mind, Parker believed he was attractive. At the same time, though, he was ignorant of his own personality flaws. That he could distance himself from women simply by opening his egocentric mouth was lost on him. In this, Parker failed to understand that even if he was the most intelligent person in room, he was also the least-liked.

As Beauty and the Baxter ascended the front steps of the university, Mangall knew that in a few moments they (or at least Burnside) would open the door and enter the classroom. Tonight, Parker would be returning their first drafts. Usually, this was one of his favorite moments as he, a *real* author, would rip out the keel of most of the students' dreams, shipwrecking them on their own ineptitude. Because writing was *utterly* subjective, professors like Parker Mangall used their position of authority to destroy any who might threaten their own naval supremacy on the seas of book-writing.

A Miserable Antagonist

But to see Burnside – Parker spit the name out in his mind – succeed in both writing and love, was wholly frustrating for Mangall.

Following close behind the couple was the annoying young man wearing a t-shirt and holey jeans. Parker sifted through the papers and located the one he thought belonged to the boy – Murray. Ah, yes. *The boy who couldn't.* He'd seen his type before: lots of hot air and marshmallows, but nothing else. Mangall dropped the paper back on the stack and noticed the next people, the oddly matched couple – the silver-haired gentleman and the tall, German-accented woman. Completing the misfitted group was the young Asian girl and the perpetually tardy mother. They were the group collaborating on Burnside's novella. If the first twelve (incredibly short) chapters were any indication of the final product, Parker Mangall was about to be miraculously impressed.

As they filed into the classroom, Mangall displayed the first PowerPoint slide, a photo of Stephen King with the slide title – *How to Write Like His Royal Highness* – as a backdrop. He stood at the front, arms crossed, waiting for the class to file in and take their seats.

In the back row, the six writers of Burnside's small group sat next to each other. The beautiful woman who had been walking with Burnside sat beside him near the end of the row. As the din increased, the woman checked her reflection in a compact mirror. Touching her lips with gloss, she smacked them a few times. Parker Mangall was mesmerized.

"Quiet down, everyone. Let's get started." Gradually, the murmurs ceased. When they did, Parker was captured by the beautiful woman's eyes, and he fumbled for words. "Now… uh… I've been… er…" He breathed deeply once and started again. "I assume the noise is about the grading of

Chapter 14

your papers." Excited murmurs. "I've had a chance to read through them. Though some have struggled, one in particular has captured my attention."

Each student desperately hoped that Professor Mangall would call out his or her name. They would proceed to the front of the class, under the watchful eyes of Stephen King and Professor Mangall, and receive their accolades, perhaps a laurel wreath or golden medallion. "I'm going to read the first lines of a paper and then this student can claim his or her work and give us some insight into their literary process." Parker was veritably certain that Baxter Burnside would not be able to give a cohesive outline of how he wrote what he did. Or he hoped he wouldn't.

"Here we go…"

"Herb Treadwell was an extraordinarily average guy. If Herb was a superhero, he would be dubbed Captain Nice, or Mr. Invisible. When Herb left the house every morning, he never closed the door behind him without first checking and rechecking that he had his keys, his wallet and a certain watch that didn't keep time."

Every eye searched the room, especially those in Baxter's small group. Lisa put her hands over her mouth and smiled delightedly while Hana patted his shoulder. Parker paused and waited for Baxter to claim his work. Although Baxter's face reddened, he did not respond. The class rumbled with anticipation as they jealously searched for the author.

Finally, when the suspense had sufficiently heightened, Mangall shook the small sheaf of papers out to Baxter. "Mr. Burnside, don't you want to claim your work?"

Eris appeared shocked, unbelieving.

"Uh… no, that's all right," Baxter mumbled.

"What?" Mangall responded incredulously. "I just praised your work, and you won't *stoop* so low as to accept my praise?" The others laughed nervously as Mangall stalked up the stairs towards Baxter and paused, three steps below his table.

"No," said Baxter right after Eris jabbed him with her elbow. The rest of the group wondered what he was up to. "It's not that. It's just…"

"Spit it out," Mangall bullied. "You don't think it's very good?"

"It's not that either."

"Then what is it?"

"I didn't write it for you or your praise." The class gasped and looked at the red-faced professor who seemed on the verge of apoplexy. "What I mean is, I wrote it for me and for us…" he motioned to his friends. "It's bonded us, I think."

"He's right," Lisa said. "It's a group project and we think we've got a great idea."

"That's what I said," Mangall responded testily.

"I'm sorry about that, Professor. I meant no disrespect but, I mean, that guy up there," Baxter waved a finger at Stephen King, "he is probably a good writer and all, but if you were to interview him, he might say he writes because he loves telling stories, not because he needs people to like them. The success part, that's just a by-product of liking what he does."

"You don't know who that is?" Mangall jabbed his finger towards the face which bore a slight resemblance to Mangall's.

"Does it matter?"

"OF COURSE IT MATTERS! To make it in the literary world is to chisel one's name into the pantheon of world changers. To sell millions of books, to have stories

Chapter 14

made into movies, to… to… be *known*," his voice lowered, "is the greatest of all accomplishments."

Baxter closed his eyes and sighed. This kind of confrontation was exactly what Baxter did not want. Having various people in his life - his mother, Larry Spago, Eris – continually gaslight him had a cumulative effect. Now that Professor Mangall had joined the queue of browbeaters, Baxter resorted to what he knew as his 'turtle syndrome.' To pull his head in and protect his heart and brains. That was what he did best.

"I'm sorry, Professor Mangall. Of course you are right."

At his side, Eris crossed her arms and harrumphed. Baxter knew what that meant. He'd get a tongue-lashing when he got home, but Baxter was done with the spotlight. Glancing around the room, he could sense how badly the rest of the class felt for him. A few were shaking their heads.

Strangely, though, Hana rose from Baxter's other side. Without Baxter realizing, Hana had placed her hands on the table in front of her, palms down, forceful and stabilizing. At that moment, Professor Mangall symbolized everything she had detested about her husband. The way he spoke. The way he stood. The way he resisted listening. His pomposity. When Mangall attempted to publicly humiliate Baxter in front of the class, she couldn't help but shield one of her newest friends, the one who had spoken honestly to her in spite of his own needs. Baxter's selflessness, innocence, and goodness had to be protected.

"Excuse me, Professor, but the greatest of all accomplishments is not to be *known*, but to *know* people. In that, our group has already succeeded."

All eyes turned to Hana. Like the sun rising above the eastern hills, Gandalf with his glowing staff and horse, her face radiated goodness. Baxter's mouth dropped to his chest. Eris' frown deepened from a ravine to the Grand Canyon. Professor Mangall's flabbergasted face attempted to catch up with her words and the depth of what she had spoken. "Yes, but… well… to know… as opposed…"

Mangall's spluttering was satisfying for Baxter; yet at the same time, he felt sorry for the professor. Nobody should have to feel the public shame of a dressing down, even one as publicly critical as Parker Mangall.

Suddenly, he felt a tug on his left arm. "Do something!" Eris hissed. "Be a man. Be brave. Do this. Accept his praise instead of relying on…" she waved her hand toward Hana who had retaken her seat and was leaning into Curtis.

Lowering his head, Baxter stood slowly and moved out from behind the long table and along the aisle towards Mangall. Standing one step above the professor, Baxter cast a look over his shoulder where Hana and Eris sat on opposite sides of his empty chair. Where Eris scowled and moved him along with a sweeping gesture, Hana's hands covered her mouth. A tear had formed in the corner of Hana's eye, but she was smiling behind those delicate hands. Curtis' arm was resting on the back of Hana's chair.

It felt like an interminable walk to the base of the amphitheater-like room. Each step with Mangall to the front, each footfall downwards, was a descent into the unknown. For Baxter Burnside, perhaps this moment, more than any other in his life, was a journey of courage. To confront those in authority, and to place himself in a position of vulnerability, had been previously unthinkable. With the support of five others, Baxter felt a stirring of hope as he stopped near Mangall's podium.

"Thank you, Mr. Burnside," said Mangall, bowing sarcastically and offering his green marker to Baxter. "Now,

Chapter 14

if you would please enlighten us on your path of 'knowing others' through writing."

Nervously, Baxter felt his pulse pound. He clutched Mangall's marker in his hand. It felt foreign, hard, like a squire wielding a sword for the first time. He shifted from foot to foot until he glanced up and saw his entire team smiling at him. Lisa gave him two thumbs up.

"Herb Treadwell is third person autobiographical," his voice was a question to Mangall. He breathed a sigh of relief when Mangall did not correct him. "I learned that from you." Mangall crossed his arms and nodded towards the class, his ego stroked. "When we started to write, we - us," he pointed toward his teammates, "we wanted to write something from our own perspectives and styles but held together by theme and direction. It might not be a novel concept," he chuckled nervously at his pun but stopped when Mangall did not laugh, "but we're writing it for us. If you like it, Mr. Mangall, that's great, but if you don't… it doesn't really matter." Baxter cleared his throat nervously and scratched his nose as he waited for Mangall to respond.

From his right, a surprising question arose, not from the professor, but from one of the other students in the class. She had dark hair, enormous brown eyes, and wore baggy sweatpants and a bulky matching sweatshirt with the UV logo, an angry looking mountain lion leaping through a large letter V, fangs and claws extended. "What is your novella really about?"

Baxter turned towards her and breathed a sigh of relief. "It's about an average guy named Herb Treadwell who is tired of the fake niceness of others and sickened by what seems most important to them. Like, money and power and looks." Baxter's eyes unconsciously flicked towards Eris, but he quickly looked away knowing that if they lingered, he'd be in trouble.

"He's a bad guy, but a misunderstood bad guy. The problem is, as I was beginning to write, I didn't know much about being bad, you know what I mean? It's not that I don't know what it is – I do, I can define it. I know it when I see it. But to describe it in writing, it felt strange, like I was hurting someone. So, we've been doing some roleplay to understand evil and how to write about it. Curtis is really good at it." Baxter pointed at him.

"Roleplay?"

"Maybe we could try it during class some time?" Baxter glanced at Mangall who shook his head. "Basically, we put crimes into a hat and then draw one out. We take ten minutes to *feel* the *emotion* of the crime, and then we act it out and write down our thoughts. Each one of us attempts to describe what we saw and then we compare perspectives, critique the writing, and figure out where our story might go."

Various students were taking notes. One group buzzed excitedly about replicating Baxter's idea.

"Thank for that exciting little diversion, but there isn't time for this tonight, Mr. Burnside. We've got a full PowerPoint presentation about Stephen King and his methodology for writing best-selling novels." Mangall shooed Baxter back to his seat. The class groaned in disappointment.

"Can we try it just once?" the young woman asked. "Maybe Curtis could show us how it's done, and then when we break into our own small groups, we might be able to write about the emotions of our own stories better."

Chapter 14

Feeling as if his class had been hijacked, Mangall wanted to say no. Because their faces were so expectant, Magnall felt himself backed into a corner.

"Oh, fine," he said frustratedly.

Smiling, Baxter nodded enthusiastically. "Curtis, would you feel comfortable doing a little improv?"

A grin played across Curtis' face. "Sure, Baxter."

Minutes later, after the class tittered excitedly and put crimes into an unused coffee cup, Curtis pulled one out, wrote a few notes, and stood in front of them. After mussing his silver hair and untucking his collared shirt, Curtis turned towards the class. He stuck one hand into his pants pocket.

"An accepted dare never seems to end well, does it? I remember the moment, the *exact* second, when my brain told my head to nod while my soul screamed – 'Do not do this!' And yet in that nod, I knew I'd find belonging, you know what I'm saying?" Incredibly, Curtis had transformed himself into a seventeen-year-old punk. "It didn't hit me until the jail door slammed shut, because of that nod, that simple gesture, I had agreed not just to stealing a car – my neighbor's car, a crappy little Mazda – but also to a life of anger and despair." He chuckled. "A stupid little Mazda…"

When his voice diminished, he paused dramatically. Then, he tucked in his shirt and reset his hair. The class erupted into applause. Hana stood, her ovation emphatic. The group whistled lustily and shouted.

Finally, after the cheering had finished, Parker Mangall resumed his place at the front. As he clutched his favorite green marker, the veins popped out from the tops of his hands. "That's very nice, Curtis, but Professor Gibson's Theater 101 class is on the other side of campus. This is a creative *writing* class."

A despairing silence settled over the amateur writers. Despite Mangall's harsh words, Curtis smiled appreciatively. To command an audience and to be appreciated for the artistry was something he had missed.

Mangall continued his diatribe. "It is one thing to scribble a hundred words of script and deliver it well. The audience can *see* what you're doing and saying. It is an entirely different thing to put together a coherent, cohesive plot and deliver it in a way that astounds the readers and *draws* them into the narrative well-beyond the visual. The reader must be made to believe the make-believe by becoming the cinematographer in *here*." He tapped the marker to his temple.

"After I finish my King presentation and return your first drafts, I want each of you to think clearly and honestly about what I've said. How do we use language to impel people to think, believe, or behave differently? That is the artistry and craft and impetus of the great writer which transcends the actor..."

Mangall spotted Eris in the back row. He could tell she was captivated.

Maybe the night wasn't lost after all.

Chapter 15

When the group reconvened after the tiresome Stephen King presentation, each person carried their first drafts back to the circled chairs. Interestingly, though the outline of the story belonged to Baxter, the writers had extended the narrative using their own thoughts, words, and emotions. For the women to write from a man's perspective proved difficult. For Murray, thinking of anyone else's perspective was a terrible task. The only one who hadn't struggled was Curtis, but his writing was also the shortest.

They each read through Parker Mangall's comments noting he had been hard on them, but not been unfair. On the bottom of Baxter's draft, Mangall had scrawled in all caps:

DON'T GET LAZY. FINISH THIS!

Eris leaned into Baxter's shoulder and pointed at the paper. "You got a B+. Why didn't you get an A?"

Frustrated that she hadn't listened to a word he had said, Baxter ripped off the handwritten grade at the top of the first page and popped it in his mouth.

"What are you doing?"

"I'm eating the grade. I don't care about it."

Eris wrinkled her nose in disgust. "You can be one strange human."

He shrugged.

"I got a C-," Murray moaned. "I've never had a C- before."

Lisa smiled and snapped her gum. "C+. This is awesome!"

A Miserable Antagonist

Curtis did not look at his draft but instead gazed at Hana's. The two of them, with their heads together, seemed content to read through each other's words. Their connection was not about the story, but *their* story. Baxter found himself envious because he was stuck with Eris. After she had seen his grade, she retrieved her phone from her bag and began to play Candy Crush.

While they continued to scan their drafts, Professor Mangall's shadow emerged between Eris and Baxter. "Now, do you have any questions?" He didn't wait very long before addressing Eris alone. "And who are you? I'm not sure I've seen you in the class before."

"Eris. Eris Chapman."

"It's nice to have you as a visitor. Are you here with someone?"

"Him." She pointed at Baxter who took no notice of either of them.

Mangall pulled up a chair and sat down next her. Flirting seemed as natural to Mangall as it was to Eris.

Ignoring them, Baxter said to the rest of the group, "Maybe we should talk about how it's all going to fit together and, most importantly, how it's going to end."

"There's got to be more romance," Lisa insisted. "Herb Treadwell definitely needs more kissing."

"Oh, please," Murray grumbled. "What the world doesn't need is another predictable love story."

"Says the student who got a C- instead of a C+," she retorted proudly.

"Come on you guys," Baxter said. "Our grades don't matter."

"Says you," Barbara pointed at him and then her paper. "It's your story, so you don't have to worry about the grade, but we're *all* paying for the class. We want a return on our investment."

Chapter 15

"Barbara," Baxter said, "this is *our* story, not *mine*. We're doing this together. I only had an original idea, but you guys have some really good stuff. I can't believe you didn't get better grades."

"It's Mangall," Murray whispered. "He's got it out for us."

"I'm sure that's not true," Hana said. "Professors are supposed to be objective."

"*Supposed* to be objective," Murray stressed. "Unfortunately, objectivity falls by the wayside when one is distracted." He motioned with his head to where Parker Mangall was now enthralled with Eris. His chin was on a closed fist, rapt by whatever she was saying. Eris, practiced in the art of flirting, curled a lock of hair around her finger. She batted her eyes coquettishly as if transformed by every response oozing from Mangall's mouth.

"Jeez, Baxter," Murray smirked. "I don't know how you pulled her out of the hat, but she is *waaaaay* out of your league."

Baxter rubbed the center of his forehead with his fingers. "Back to the story. Here's what we've got so far." As a team, they laid down the outline, but there were still too many opinions, and the plot holes were becoming plot craters. Whether it was Lisa's romance, Murray's sudden insertion of a robot, or even Hana's desire to add more descriptive, emotional language, the team was soon embroiled in a disagreement about the book's direction.

"Listen," Curtis finally interrupted. "This isn't necessarily a philosophical struggle. We all have an idea of who Herb Treadwell is. This is a literary identity crisis. But we also must understand the symbolism of the watch. Ultimately, we need to decide who Herb Treadwell really is, why time is standing still, and what will start the watch again."

Silence ensued. Then, Barbara asked Curtis, point blank, what he thought the last chapter should look like.

Smiling like a Sphynx, Curtis tented his fingers in front of his mouth. "When the reader finishes the last page, they must decide if Herb Treadwell has accomplished his task of being a worthy protagonist. If Herb has not, if the reader is not convinced, then we will have failed."

"But..." Murray started. Curtis silenced him with a finger.

"If we truly believe that Herb can carry out this crime, then we must describe Herb's ultimate reasoning, emotion, and the action. Until now, we've only been play-acting the emotions of breaking the law. We need to go deeper."

Baxter felt his heart drop. *Uh oh.*

"When you tried to take your father's remote control, what did you feel, Baxter?"

"Confused."

"As you would. You haven't done this kind of thing before."

Baxter's face felt hot. "But it was my dad, and I really didn't want to take anything from him."

"Very noble," said Murray sarcastically. "But that doesn't help the thematic development of the story."

"What have *you* done, Murray? If you're such a big talker, why don't you do something illegal or unethical?" Baxter didn't mean to be short-tempered, but Eris' fake, flirty laughter behind him was infuriating.

"I could," Murray folded his arms confidently. "I'll pick one."

"Pick one what?" Baxter said.

"Pick a petty crime and I'll do it."

Chapter 16

Baxter began to read. Incredibly, it had been years since he'd finished any novel, but by reading again, he found a systematic model for plotlines. The protagonist, in whatever fallible way, engages in an unknown display of courage. To carry the day, the protagonist (usually after falling in love, being spurned by love, or being oblivious to it) delves deeply into his or her reserves of awesomeness to find a way to win.

Because Baxter had never carried the day, nor had he fallen in love, or delved deeply into hidden reserves of awesomeness, he couldn't come to grips with how an *antagonist* could be transformed or reformed. Now that they were grabbing the antagonist by the horns, Baxter felt that he had to shape his outward appearance to change his inward.

Thus, part of his secret plan.

On the day his secret plan began to percolate, Bernadette was the first to notice that Baxter was more distracted than normal. While he worked in his typical, friendly, Baxter-ish way, his legs jumped.

"What is that?"

"What?"

"That banging on my cubicle."

He looked down at his leg which finally forced it to stop. "I'm excited."

Surprised, Bernadette leaned closer to him behind their barriers. "That's interesting. Is it the striking young blossom who's brought the light back in your eyes?"

"What? No! That's not it at all."

"Then what is it?"

A Miserable Antagonist

Baxter checked to see if anyone was watching. Steve and Carmen worked with customers. Larry leaned against his office door pondering the piece of something he'd recently excavated from his teeth.

"Can you keep a secret?"

"No."

"If I tell you something, can you please try not to tell anyone else?"

"I'll try."

"I'm going to be a bad guy."

Bernadette scrunched up her face. "What?"

"A transformation – evolution – from Boring Baxter to Bad Baxter."

"Still... lost."

"Remember how we're writing this novella, and we have to identify with the characters – emotions and stuff?"

"You're getting in touch with your inner bad guy?" Bernadette asked.

"That's the thing. I don't *have* an inner bad guy. Not yet. But I'm going to make one."

"How are you going to do that?"

Once again, he looked around and leaned in even closer to her. "I'm going to change my look, get a tattoo, grow a beard, maybe lift some weights, and talk like I've been in prison."

Bernadette burst out in laughter which caused the other tellers to stare at them. "I can only imagine what kind of tattoo you're going to get. Let me guess, a skull?"

His face flushed. He was so predictable that she guessed it on the first try. "What's wrong with that?"

"Nothing. But it was going to be a henna tattoo, wasn't it?" Her laughter continued. "And, and, and you were going to get it put on your back, right? Where no one could

Chapter 16

see it." Bernadette shook her head, leaned back, and motioned for the next customer to step up.

Annoyed, Baxter continued to talk to her while she served the patron. "You think you know so much about me. I was going to put it on my neck." He stabbed at the back of his neck.

Bernadette glanced at him out of the corner of her eye and smirked.

"So what if it was henna – there's no use ruining my skin for a stupid class."

Thanking the customer, Bernadette returned to him. "People ruin their skin all the time, Baxie. How many regretful drunk people show up with a tattoo on their inner arm or ankle with the name of someone they met the month before? Or they get inked with a popular symbol from a movie only to be ridiculed later when they actually grow up."

"Do you have a tattoo?" he asked.

"I do. It's a flower."

"Where is it?" he asked.

"Wouldn't you like to know…" Bernadette winked at him suggestively which made Baxter recoil.

"Oh, God, don't do that."

"You bad boy," Bernadette giggled as she brought her expression back to neutral to wave to the next customer.

While Baxter served his line of debtors and creditors, a stream of thoughts coursed through his mind. *Why shouldn't I get a skull tattoo on my neck? Why couldn't I lift weights? Why can't I grow a beard and dye my hair black?*

Because Baxter Burnside couldn't *imagine* himself doing any of those things… permanently. It wasn't that he *wasn't* a bad guy, it was that his imagination was stunted by stereotypes. For Baxter, rebellion lay in the length of his hair and the size of his tattooed pectoral muscles. When he thought about a tattoo, his mind went to henna, so that when he was done, it would fade away. When he thought about a beard, it was nicely trimmed. When he thought about lifting weights, a few bench presses might do him some good. But all these changes were temporary.

The reality for people like Baxter Burnside was that they must ultimately realize simply changing one's exterior was pointless without an internal revolution. No matter his skin, his hair, muscle tone or demeanor, Baxter could not truly understand the mind of the bad guy without becoming one.

The point of the exercise, at least in Baxter's own mind, was to think and behave so differently that Herb Treadwell took on flesh and became real. His flesh. His real. To encounter this 'different,' he had to make some permanent choices.

Baxter nodded at Timothy Detmerus, a large, middle-aged man with green hair, shaved on one side of his head. He had multiple tattoos on his arms and legs and carried a small cat. It used to be that animals were not allowed in public places, but the rules had relaxed, and it wasn't rare to find animal-people bringing their furry children to his teller's station. But the sight of the cat reminded Baxter of his bad-guy, murderous villain – a cold blooded killer. Cat killer. For a moment, Baxter tried to imagine what killing Mr. Detmerus' cat might be like, and he shivered. Baxter felt an unnecessary pang of guilt so great that he wanted to apologize to the man's cat before he'd even murdered it.

"What can I do for you today?" Baxter asked.

"I'd like to cash my paycheck," Timothy responded happily and buried his plump face in the cat's scruff. He handed the envelope to him.

"How would you like that?"

Chapter 16

"Can I get ten twenties, five tens and forty dollars of quarters? And the rest can go into my checking account."

Baxter began to count the money out.

"Mr. Fuzzpocket and I are going to the casino. Time to do something crazy."

Shocked, Baxter paused what he was doing and glanced up at the cat-sniffing man. Mr. Detmerus couldn't be much older than Baxter, but he was so different – not just the tattoos and green hair, or the mangy looking animal he carried – Mr. Detmerus actually seemed happy. He was taking his hard-earned cash to the casino. He imagined Timothy sitting in front of blinking, clanging machines, dropping quarter after quarter into the slots, hoping that his luck would change. Mr. Fuzzpocket would be wrapped behind his neck like a purring scarf, licking its paws, and watching out for someone like Herb Treadwell.

"Can I ask you a personal question?" Baxter said.

"Sure."

"Why did you decide to get tattoos?"

Mr. Detmerus studied Baxter over the freakishly fuzzy cat. "I think they represent who I am."

Baxter noticed that the tattoos were of cats chasing butterflies; a rainbow; the lunar cycle. Even if he was an Egyptologist, Baxter was unsure he could have deciphered what Timothy was trying to represent.

"Yes, but why a tattoo? What I mean is, why do you need other people to know... um... who you are in such a permanent way? Why not just have a conversation with them and say, 'Hi, I like cats, rainbows, and moons."

Detmerus frowned. "You wouldn't understand."

"What do you mean?"

"Do you want me to be honest?"

"It always hurts when people say that," Baxter responded as he peered from his peripheral vision at Bernadette who did not seem to be paying attention. "Go ahead. I think I can take it."

Leaning over, Detmerus placed Mr. Fuzzpocket on the small counter in front of him. The cat proceeded to purr loudly and push its head and neck into his chest. "You're a young-ish, white male, cute in a completely platonic way. Nothing about you stands out, and I think you like it like that. Hair nicely combed, clothes, dated – could almost be considered 'retro,' I suppose, but my guess is, style is not your primary concern." Baxter glanced down at his clothes and unconsciously touched his brown, striped tie. "Your hands are smooth and manicured, no facial hair. You must have worked hard to be so average."

"I guess you weren't lying about being honest."

He kept going. "I'd say you're desperate for people to like you, but you'd have no idea what to do with that if it happened."

"Does your alter-ego read crystal balls?"

Detmerus shook his head. The smile was derisive – haughty. "When you figure out your own life, then come back and judge mine."

"I wasn't... I mean... I was just asking..." His stuttering alerted Bernadette whose eyebrows pinched, perplexed at her colleague's discomfort.

Timothy retrieved his money and cat and whirled away from him with a flourish. As he tromped away, his green hair flopped restlessly over his right shoulder. Chad the security guard tried not to stare, but when Timothy pulled the door open, Chad couldn't quite refrain from following him with his head.

"What was that all about?" Bernadette asked.

Chapter 16

"I just asked him why he got tattoos, and he kind of went off."

"Here's a little word of advice, Baxie. Don't ever ask someone about their appearance unless you're into them."

"What? What does that mean? I talk with you about *your* appearance."

Bernadette touched her heart. "Oh, that's so sweet, Baxter. I had no idea you were into me."

"No! NO! That's not what I meant. How am I supposed to know…?" Bernadette ignored his protestations with a bemused smile.

Frustratedly, Baxter reflected on Timothy's words. He was right. Baxter was average. Retro, without meaning to be. He had soft hands and no facial hair. There was that one time Baxter had attempted to grow a beard. For three weeks his attempted jaw-hair-cultivation ended up in sparse patches of facial forest near his cheek bone, under his chin, and along his neck. It was so itchy that he gave up the experiment and shaved it. His mother didn't like it either, and she told him so.

As he watched Bernadette work next to him, he was irritated that she had read him so quickly and accurately. And his implication of 'into-her-ness' was exasperating. She had riled him just like everyone else. If there was any one thing bad guys weren't, it was predictable. Baxter definitely needed to be less predictable.

At noon, Baxter walked with Bernadette and Sheena to a local restaurant, Johnny Bing Bings, for a fast-food lunch. Sheena was an incredibly shy African American woman in her thirties who had short, curly brown hair, and an ovate face with round eyes and large lashes hidden behind thick glasses. Sheena had brought a book to lunch. While Baxter and Bernadette chatted, Sheena lost herself in the torturous lives of erotic fictional, fantasy characters with longbows and broadswords wearing little more than lingerie. Sheena ate slowly, chewing her food with something akin to disinterest, while the characters in her book eviscerated and tangled tongues with equal enthusiasm.

"The main character," Bernadette spoke as she brought her fried pickle and mushroom burger to her mouth and took a big bite. She spoke with her mouth full but held three fingers in front of her lips. "Herb Treadwell, he wears a broken watch because...?"

"Yes, because," he slurped his soda, "Herb Treadwell feels it necessary to be reminded of the moment when his life went down the crapper because of the good guy. Or girl, in this case."

"What's her name?"

"I don't know yet." Baxter unknowingly dropped a splatter of mustard onto his pants. Bernadette followed the trajectory to his khakis but said nothing, even when Baxter ignored it.

"What do you mean you don't know yet? Your book sounds really confusing."

"It is. It's supposed to be confusing because life is like that. Down is up, passion is boring, and life is death."

She wrinkled up her face in annoyance.

"Put it this way, Bernadette," he touched Sheena's arm, "Sheena, you can agree with me, too, you're a booksy kind of girl." Sheena glanced up from her tale of scantily clad heroes in loincloths and their buxom partners in rabbit-furred harnesses. She left her finger on the line. "In all those books you read, the good guy goes through a predictable journey, rides the same emotional rollercoaster, and ends up the hero, while the bad guy is administered the coup de

Chapter 16

gras," Baxter pronounced it *coop de grass*, the 'p' projecting a piece of pickle onto his lip which he licked back into his mouth, "in the most smack-your-head, oh, I-should-have-seen-the-death-kick-coming-to-my-head-in-slow-motion kind of way."

Sheena's bespectacled eyes roamed from Baxter's to Bernadette's. Sighing, she placed the book in her lap, a bestseller entitled *Desperate Dragonslayer Desires: A Destiny Cavehome Adventure*. "What are you suggesting, Baxter?" Her voice, deep and raspy, was entirely consistent with her cultivated look.

"That the bad guy gets to make hay!" He shook a French-fry exultantly into the air. "That the guy who is always hated, always rejected, always dismissed for everything, finally has his moment where he comes out on top."

"That goes against everything that a reader wants." Sheena said. "What you're suggesting is literary anarchy."

"So be it," he responded with a furious light in his eyes and popped the fry in his mouth. "I don't care about the reader. I don't care about entertaining people."

"Then why the heck are you trying to write a novel?" Bernadette interjected.

"Because it feels like it might save my life," he said quietly.

"Wait, are you dying?" Bernadette asked.

"No. Well, not in the traditional heart-stopped-brain-dead sort of way. But I'm dying from a serious case of the Routine, you know what I mean?"

"Not really."

"Jeez, you must have heard what Mr. Detmerus said. I'm nearing middle age; I'm a teller at a bank; I go home at night to an empty house. If I'm really adventurous, I'll walk down by the river and stop at the café to have a bite to eat. It's the same, day after day – nice Baxter and his neat little life – and all the while I want to be someone different. Someone who breaks the rules so I can *feel* something."

Bernadette and Sheena looked at each other but said nothing.

"Writing this story allows me some small feeling of control. As a writer, I can do anything I want. Worlds can be born, pigs can fly, bad guys can win. Anything. Have you ever thought about that?" He scrunched up the burger wrapper in his hands.

"No," they both responded at the same time.

"Well maybe you should take the class, too."

"I've got too much of a social life," said Bernadette.

"Me too." Sheena added, her hands subconsciously stroking the closed book on her lap.

Baxter tossed the wrapper towards the wastebasket. When he missed, he shook his head and retrieved it, and placed it in the basket. "The problem is, that when I try to write Herb Treadwell's story, to move beyond a clever opening and a decent idea, I can't figure out how to manipulate him. I can make him kill cats or elephants or camels – whatever. I get such a serious case of the Guilts after I write it, that I erase it, and by golly if I don't apologize to the imaginary animals I've slain."

"Yes, that is weird," said Sheena.

"So that's where I'm at. I'm going to try to change, do some bad guy things, so I can get on with my novella."

"Let me get this straight," Bernadette began picking up her trash and putting it on the brown plastic tray. "You want to get a tattoo and commit a crime so you can write better."

"YES! That's exactly it."

Chapter 16

Sheena looked around to see if anyone was listening to the conversation. "I think you need a holiday, Baxter," she whispered. "Or maybe a decent psychologist."

Baxter's laughter sounded as if he was choking. "No, Sheena, I don't need a holiday. I need to change my life."

Chapter 17

Hund strained against the leash clutched in Hana's hand. She chided the dog as he stopped to urinate for what seemed the seventy-first time on a nondescript tree where someone else's dog had peed many times before.

"Isn't this fun?" she asked Curtis.

"Of course. It's a beautiful fall day. I'm with you…"

"Yes, that is nice." Hund finished his business and went snuffling ahead, the humans followed dutifully.

"What would you like to talk about today?"

"You."

"What would you like to know?" he asked.

"Tell me about your acting. Was it a career or a hobby?"

Curtis gazed thoughtfully across the autumn tree leaves as they filtered the early afternoon light. "It started as a dare. One of my friends in high school dared me to try out for the school play – *The Crucible*."

"I don't know that one."

He shook his head ruefully.

"What was the dare?"

"There was this girl…"

Hana laughed. "Ah! There always is."

"Her name was Helen. She was a dreadful actress, but she looked nice."

"Tell me what happened."

A butterfly emerged from the foliage and danced on the currents. It paused, dropped suddenly when distracted by an inviting leaf, and flexed its wings open and shut.

Chapter 17

"On opening night, I was as nervous as a teen with a fake ID. Before the play, I alternated between nausea and restless panic, afraid that I'd forget all my lines. When the curtain parted for the opening scene, I looked out into the light and realized I couldn't see anyone. When I spoke, I was simply telling the story to the light. Then, as the play unfolded, I *became* Samuel Parris, and the power to become someone else was intoxicating. Strangely, it was only after the final curtain dropped and the audience applauded wildly that I remembered there were people out there." The butterfly floated up again and out of sight. "Maybe it's a metaphor for life, I don't know."

Hana studied his profile. He had a beautiful nose and long eyelashes. His gray hair emphasized his beauty rather than made him look old. "Have you ever been in a movie?"

Curtis' face expressed scorn. "I wouldn't sink that low."

"What do you mean?"

"Cinema isn't acting – it's… how do I put this… it's like faking an orgasm." Hana burst out laughing. "No, really," he continued. "Screen 'actors' spend a week practicing for a scene, memorize a few lines, and practice portraying their emotions for a closeup camera shot - knowing full well that if they make a mistake, the blooper reel will be as popular as the film. They can have as many shots as they need. It's all fake. There's no interaction with the audience, no connection."

"Why is it so popular then?"

"Because the camera lies. Modern people like being lied to. Movies makes the audience feel as if it is important to the actors. They're close up and placed inside the story. With theater acting, on the other hand, you must do the whole thing yourself. The set is static, and you must help the audience feel and participate in the story, not just watch it…"

Curtis' description was so vivid, and so passionate, that Hana felt herself blushing.

"Stage acting is wonderful and frightening. Like skydiving without a backup chute."

"Do you think I could be a good actress?" Hana giggled as she touched the side of her hair.

"With that face, my dear," Curtis mimicked Jimmy Stewart, "you could do anything. Anything at all."

They walked along a little further in companionable silence. Hana slipped her hand into Curtis'. It had never been like this with her husband. Jim didn't like to be touched, especially in public. They never took walks together. Hund had been her companion and protector far more than he. Hund had been steady and reliable. Jim, after their first years of romance, became withdrawn and spent long hours at work. When they couldn't have children, Hana felt ashamed, perhaps even blamed, and Jim drew back even further. By the time of his death, they barely spent any time together.

But now that she was with Curtis, someone who had both the inclination and time to be with her, she felt safe and comfortable. As Hund paused again to their right, she pulled his arm in close to her.

"What did you do before acting?"

She felt him stiffen slightly. "Oh, this and that."

Hana pulled away from him slightly, but she still held onto his hand. "That is an evasive answer I was not expecting," she laughed.

"Why do you ask?"

"Because I am interested. I want to know everything about you."

Chapter 17

Curtis felt a surge of fear. He wasn't ready. "If you're talking about my career, I... worked in investments."

"That sounds fascinating. You must have been very good at it judging by the size of your house."

He cleared his throat uncomfortably. "Yes, I suppose."

"Tell me about it. I am interested."

"It's very technical. I don't think you'd be quite as fascinated as you believe."

"Try me," she insisted.

Curtis Schachman had been very good at what he did. It was called Algorithmic Trading. With his initial money from his grandparents, Curtis started a company that developed software which worked through computers rather than humans. Computers could make trades infinitely faster and with far greater accuracy. Entering the parameters for when stocks should be bought and sold, the program would purchase or sell in this range quickly and with surgical precision. This kind of trading was something the rich did, not the average investor, giving the elites opportunities into vast amounts of wealth that others did not have.

But it was also a place of low morals. Although intensely regulated, Algorithmic Trading could be used to destroy people, businesses or, worst case scenario, entire economies. These 'flash crashes' happen quickly, wiping billions, even trillions of dollars almost instantaneously.

Curtis had instigated one of these flash crashes and ruined the lives of people all over the planet.

Two trillion dollars' worth.

In that algorithmic trade, Curtis pocketed 387 million dollars.

Though his finances were confidential, rumors had spread that Algonaut Enterprises had been responsible for the flash crash. In the aftermath, Curtis had received an envelope, which turned out to be a suicide note, from the owner of another Algo company who had lost almost half a billion dollars in less than three minutes.

Within weeks of receiving the note, Curtis, laden with a mountain of guilt, sold Algonaut Enterprises for 1.5 billion dollars and retired to his mansion in Montpelier, never again to purchase another stock.

"I don't know what to tell you, Hana. Just Wall Street stuff."

"Come on," she prodded him. "Tell me."

Curtis' jaw hardened. "It's time to go home."

Lisa knew that Murray was not the bring-home-to-your-parents type. If the statistics from their brief relationship held true, Murray would say something unapologetically offensive in the first twenty minutes which would set into motion a maelstrom of apologies and backtracking. Because Lisa's parents were disproportionately sensitive, having them meet Murray would be like setting an industrial fan inside a room of runway models. Thus, when Lisa and Murray went to the movies together, Lisa said nothing to her parents. It was better that way.

While she prepared for the movie, Lisa reflected on the way in which their relationship had grown. In the beginning, Lisa was jumpy and anxious about sharing thoughts and ideas. Both Lisa and Murray appreciated Professor Mangall's attempts to stir something literary inside them, but it wasn't until Baxter stumbled upon the idea that she truly felt part of the group. Lisa had very much enjoyed the roleplay night, and now that they were going to scheme a

Chapter 17

crime, she was happily anticipating the upcoming Wednesday night.

To fill the time before their mid-week creative writing class, they hung out, texted each other and discussed ideas. They'd settled into an easy, sibling relationship. On this night, after the movie, they would go to Dairy Queen, and load up on ice cream to discuss the film. On Saturday, they had watched an Indie film about homicidal, transphobic zombies. Murray believed he understood the director's intent – that all of humanity was dead, but alive, and bent on destroying anyone who was different. Lisa was equally certain that the movie was just plain stupid.

Lisa checked herself in the mirror once, then twice, turning sideways and around. She wore faded, high-waisted blue jeans and a tight black top. Pulling her hair up into a ponytail, she snapped the rubber band into place and blew a kiss at her reflection.

Her phone rang. "Hi, Baxter."

"Hello, Lisa. This is Baxter."

"I know. I just said your name."

"Sorry."

"What's up?"

"Are you still coming on Wednesday night? To Curtis' house?"

"Of course. I wouldn't miss it."

"I've got a few ideas I wouldn't mind running past you if that's all right."

"Well… I'm on my way to a movie…"

"That's okay. I'm sorry to bother you."

"No," she insisted, "it's fine. We can talk on the way."

"If you're okay with that…"

"Sure." Lisa grabbed her keys and made her way to the car. "What's on your mind?"

She heard him sigh into the phone. Lisa heard someone's voice in the background. Probably his gorgeous girlfriend. Baxter must have covered the phone because his reply was muffled and softened. Then, he was back. "I've been thinking about how to connect with bad guys and… well, I've got an idea…"

When Lisa arrived at the theater, she was bouncing with excitement. Baxter's idea was insane, stupid, really – like a movie with homicidal, transphobic zombies. All the same, it sounded exciting and worth exploring.

Murray was standing by the ticket counter impatiently checking his watch and tapping his foot. "You're late."

"I was talking to Baxter."

"About what?" They showed their tickets to the attendant who passed them through.

"Some research."

"I can only imagine what that is." Murray opened the door for her as they walked into the theater. It took a few moments for their eyes to adjust. They followed the glowing orange lights at their feet to find their spots in the stadium seating. Murray liked to sit in the back row to observe everything. Not just the movie, but people, too.

When they sat, Lisa leaned into him. "He wants us to go on an excursion."

"An excursion?"

"Yes. To the prison."

"What?"

An older couple turned around to stare at them.

"What?" he repeated softer.

"Baxter thinks that if we can get into the psyche of authentic criminals, we can write about them better."

"For what reason?"

Chapter 17

Other theater-goers twisted around to growl at them as the movie was about to start. "I think it's a great idea. Have you ever been to the prison before?"

"No, of course not."

"Anybody *could* become a criminal. Even me." The opening ads reflected a flickering red and blue light on Lisa's face which was only inches away from Murray's.

Murray's upper lip curled. "You wouldn't break the law if it slapped you in the face."

"I don't even know what that means."

As the movie started, he moved his head even closer to hers. His lips were only inches from her ear. "Let's say the government bans all young people from using their cell phones in public, citing the hazards of distracted walking as a rationale."

"That's ridiculous. They would never do that."

"You asked me what I meant – I'm giving you a for-instance. It's not going to happen, obviously."

"Oh."

"So they ban you and me and every other young person from even looking at their phones or you get fined."

"That's ageist!"

A middle-aged gentleman put a finger to his lips as he turned to them.

"Lisa," he hissed, "focus. If this were to happen, what would you do? Would you follow the law, or would you disregard it at risk of a fine?"

"I would…" Lisa knew that she'd follow the law even if she didn't like it. But she didn't want Murray to know that. "I would break the law! Damn the fines!"

"SHHHHH!" The old couple had had enough.

"Oh shh, yourself," Murray responded. "I know you're just saying that you would break the law, but you wouldn't. You'd hate it, but you'd stop looking at your phone."

The older couple, grumbling about the inconsiderate youths, arose from their seats, cast an angry look at them, and moved down the aisle.

"So what does that prove?" she asked.

"I agree with Baxter. It *proves* that we don't have tendencies for criminality, which is why we have a great need to interview a prisoner to figure it out."

"I'm so happy that you're up for this," she said happily.

In front of them, the opening credits of the movie began to roll down the screen. Neither was aware that their arms and hands were getting closer together, just within touching distance. Who would have known that being bad would draw people together?

Chapter 18

"You don't have to be so sensitive," Eris said, needling Baxter into a fight. "All I said was, 'Why don't you and your little friends give up this silly charade and take a real class.' What's wrong with that?"

"You don't know the first thing about taking classes." Baxter was annoyed that Eris had overheard part of his conversation, but it was inevitable. Now that she had moved in, and now that she had taken over redecoration and redistribution of his furniture, there was no place he could go for privacy. Already, his living room had an *Eris-y* feel to it: photos of her were positioned in places of greatest visibility; sitting just outside the bedroom door were her pink fuzzy slippers; a yoga mat was permanently fixed in the middle of the living room. Baxter believed this was so that he couldn't recline his chair. Every time he sat down to watch a movie, she perched herself on the floor in front of him and the TV, and began to distract him with poses. Down dog, Warrior, Luck Dragon – he didn't know their names only that their purpose was to impede whatever it was that he wanted to do. Once, he made the mistake of telling her to move, and she spent the next twenty minutes lecturing him on the importance of flexibility.

The bed now contained twelve immense, fluffy pillows, one in the shape of a pug's face. The bathroom had taken on the decidedly sweet smell of lavender and lemon, both of which made Baxter's lip curl. And the kitchen. The kitchen! His mother would be furious. The maternal knickknacks had been rearranged in such a manner that now his mother's cutesy tchotchkes were replaced with ribbons and sandalwood incense sticks. Baxter's house had been transformed into Bed Bath & Beyond. He didn't like it one bit, but he couldn't do anything about it.

"I know about taking classes. I went to college, too, Baxter."

"You took a modeling class, and it wasn't at college. It was in a photographer's studio." Baxter began to cut up vegetables for dinner.

"As if you know anything about college classes," she responded defensively.

The knife bit through a carrot with a loud thunk. "I'm a banker, Eris. Banks generally tend to hire college graduates."

She mimicked his voice. "Banks generally tend to hire college graduates." She sniffed. "You're a teller, Baxter. Have you even paid off your college loans yet?" Eris moved into position where she leaned against the sink, her assets pushed forward giving him full view of what she, and he, most valued about her.

Baxter wanted to remind her that he was the one paying the bills. This would have brought the next round of pouting and excuses that she just couldn't quite find the job of her dreams. Instead, he fixed his eyes on her body. He couldn't help it. She had curves where other women had crumpets.

Eris smirked. "Now, what are we having for dinner?"

"Chicken and vegetables."

"We had chicken last night."

"Would you like to cook?"

"Don't try to pigeonhole me into your sexist, misogynist ideas."

"I wasn't," he insisted. "I simply find it strange that the person who is not helping make dinner is the one complaining about it."

Chapter 18

"I'm not complaining. I just think we should have a well-rounded diet."

"You're complaining." Baxter put the tray of diced vegetables into the oven.

"And you're in a foul mood."

Turning to the sink, Baxter began to fill it to wash the dishes. Eris stepped with him and posed on the opposite side of the oven. "You were always good at that," he said.

She twisted her hair with her finger. "At what?"

"Manipulating me. Using your body as a distraction."

"I don't do that."

"Puh-lease."

"When have I ever done that?" she asked.

"How many examples do you want?"

"Just one." Eris arched her back and stretched her hands above her head. Her hope was to distract him from thinking of that *one time* she had manipulated him.

He watched her hands, then her arms, her slender neck and firm... He shook his head and closed his eyes. "Okay. Okay. Three months before our wedding, you sprung it on me, and I quote, 'I just want you to know that you'll be taking *my* last name on the marriage certificate.'" Eris smiled at the recollection but tried to hide it. "Yeah, you know what I'm talking about. I told you that there was no way in Blue Hades I was taking your last name."

"What's wrong with my last name?" She twisted to the side and gracefully bent over.

"Nothing. There's nothing wrong with your last name, but I'm not going to change mine to Cromwell. Baxter Cromwell. That's horrible."

She frowned. "You didn't want to change your name to mine because you thought it sounded horrible? I'm hurt." She wasn't.

"You're not hurt. I'm just wiser than I used to be. Remember, I almost gave in because you decided it was imperative, at that moment, to sunbathe."

"So?"

"It was October."

It was close. She almost got him to give in.

Knowing that the argument was mid-stream and Eris was caught on her back foot with her feathers ruffled, she positioned herself next to Baxter while he continued to wash the dishes he had dirtied to prepare dinner. "Why should I have to take your name? Is it because I'm a woman?"

He set the dish back in the water. "I never asked you to take my name. I never asked anything of you. But you were so adamant that I take your name, I knew it was the first brick in the wall you were going to build around me. You would take every opportunity to control me."

Eris' lower lip quivered. "I never realized you hated me so much."

"Ugh," Baxter groaned. "Please, stop. If you're going to live here, we're going to have different ways of conversing. No more arguing, or fighting, just for the heck of it."

"Am I really so terrible."

Yes, he thought. "No," he said with a sigh. "It's simply inconvenient timing for you to be here. I was just beginning to get my life back in order, you know? And then suddenly you show up. You still haven't told me what happened."

More pouting. "I'm an inconvenience." By the look in his eyes, Eris knew she guilted him into a corner. "I'm sorry," she said as she turned away from him.

"Eris…"

"I'll go out and find something to do tonight. You just enjoy your time here. Do some writing. Think about criminals while poor Eris has to be by herself."

Chapter 18

Baxter knew he'd been checkmated. Reaching his hands out to her, she allowed herself to be enveloped by his arms. As she laid her head on his shoulder, she smiled with malevolent glee.

Chapter 19

"Do we know anyone in prison?" Baxter asked.

Betty was so shocked, she almost dropped her mug of decaffeinated coffee. Baxter had shown up at their house, delightedly (and unexpectedly) for dinner. It was Tuesday night, generally not a time when Baxter would traditionally visit, but he felt it might be good to get out of the house for a while. Eris had accompanied him for the free meal, not the company. While Betty and Baxter sat in the small lounge area, Eris perched herself on a cushioned armchair across the room from Burnie who was (predictably) watching a car race. Instead of conversing, Eris played a video game on her phone.

"What kind of question is that?"

"I'm just curious if there are any felonish fruits dangling from our family tree." Baxter sipped his chocolate milk and waited for an answer.

"Does this have to do with your class? The bad-guy thing? Please tell me you're not planning to get into any trouble."

The question was indelibly Betty-nuanced. No, he was not *planning* on getting into trouble, but one never knew. And even if he was, he would not be *telling* her. "No, Mom. I mean, yes, it has to do with the class, but no, no trouble."

Betty's eyebrows knitted, and she crossed her arms primly. "That's not exactly a convincing response, is it, sweetheart?"

"It's a simple question, though, isn't it?"

"Yes, I suppose. But I'm not aware of any." She called out through the house. "Burnie, do we know any prisoners?"

Chapter 19

"WHAT?"

"Turn that TV down and come out here when I talk to you!" Betty shook her head as she waited for Burnie to make a grumbling appearance in the arch which separated the kitchen and the living room.

"I couldn't hear what you asked." Burnie's eyes were stuck partway open. Deep bags clung to his lower eyelids. Age spots marked his cheeks and temples. He looked tired, threadbare, like a shoe with all the tread worn down.

"Do we know anybody in prison?"

"No," he responded tersely and turned back to the TV. Two steps later, he stopped and faced them. "Except for your nephew, Jack. That sounds like a convict's name, doesn't it? Jack. What did he do again? I can't remember. He was a piece of work, that one."

"Thank you, dear. I'd forgotten about him. You can go back to your little car race now."

He bowed slightly and scooped one arm in front of his waist and the other behind his back. "Thank you, your highness."

"Oh, pooh," she waved at him but smiled. "Old fuddy-duddy."

"Jack's in prison?" Baxter asked.

"Yes, not too long ago. Drunk driving, or something ridiculously stupid. Why, Brenda was furious. When she called me, I think it was six months ago, she told me the full details, not that I can remember them all. It seems like I'm forgetting all sorts of things. You know, Baxter, when your mind starts to go…" she tapped her temple. "So anyway, Brenda called and…"

Baxter let his mother fill in the unnecessary details while he started his checklist of questions for Jack. She loved to talk. Betty loved rumors. She loved to pass them on.

Thus, the need to fill in the blanks with her own biased commentary, like gene splicing to finish the genetic code of a Tyrannosaurus rex. Baxter remembered little about his cousin Jack. He was ten or twelve years older, strong – oafish, really – with few brain cells. During family gatherings, Jack ignored Baxter or picked on him with his friends. Baxter wasn't surprised that Jack had ended up in prison. Some people just seemed destined for it.

"Where is he, you know, imprisoned?"

His mother stopped her ongoing narrative and lifted her coffee. It had grown cold, but it seemed not to bother her. "Chittendon."

"Where is that?"

"Burlington, I think." Burlington was where the University of Vermont was located, forty-five minutes from Montpelier. Because they drove that distance every week for classes, it would be easy to find the prison.

"That's wonderful," said Baxter.

"Wonderful? Why, that's a terrible thing to say, Baxter."

"No, what I meant was that we, er, I could go visit him to see how he's doing."

Betty's eyes narrowed. "What do you want to visit him about?"

Baxter held up his hands. "Nothing. Nothing, really. I think it would be good for us, I mean, me, to, you know, see the inside of a prison, and while I'm there, I could visit Jack. Catch up on old times."

"That's funny. You never really seemed to like Jack."

"Maybe I'm turning over a new leaf."

Betty held her coffee cup in front of her face as a warning. "Just don't get comfortable. A prison is no place for my Baxter."

Chapter 19

When Baxter arrived at the University of Vermont to collect Lisa and Murray, he was already frustrated. The steady rain dampened his spirits, but not as much as the fact that Eris rode along stating she wanted to keep tabs on him. This made the forty-five-minute drive an endless earful of all her travails. Baxter had forgotten how negative she was, and the longer she stayed with him, the quicker that memory returned. It was a tragic thing Eris was so beautiful.

Pulling up to the curb, Baxter honked the horn. Murray and Lisa appeared seconds later huddled under a shared umbrella as they raced to the car. Murray opened the door for Lisa, and she scooched across the back seat to sit behind Baxter. Murray shook out the umbrella and laid it at his feet before slamming the door.

"Make sure you don't get the seat wet," Eris said into her visor-mirror. "I don't want it to smell wet in here."

Murray frowned at her, leaned forward and punched Baxter's shoulders as they pulled into traffic. "I thought we could only have three people go into the prison, Baxter."

"I'm not going in," Eris answered haughtily as she checked her eyebrows and applied one last layer of lip gloss. "I'm making sure Baxter is a good boy." She smacked her lips.

Murray snuck a glance at Lisa who rolled her eyes.

"You're going to stay in the car at the prison?" Lisa asked.

"I might wait in the holding area. I'm interested... to a point."

Baxter ground his teeth and drove. Turning left on Highway 7, Baxter drove in silence. Lisa pointed to her right at an informational sign which read, *WORLD'S LARGEST FILING CABINET*. "Should we stop?"

"I think that would be very interesting," Eris agreed.

"As tempting as that sounds," said Murray, "I think we've got a much more important mission. Right, Baxter? How much longer is it?"

"Two minutes."

Exactly two minutes later, they stopped outside the Chittendon Regional Corrections Facility. It was a red brick building that appeared more like a library than a penitentiary. Baxter killed the engine and reached for his umbrella, but Eris was quicker and grabbed it before he could. Opening her passenger door, she popped the umbrella and raced to the front door in the rain. She turned and motioned with her irritated hand for Baxter to *Hurry up!*

"She's a piece of work," Lisa said. "It's so surprising that you broke off the engagement."

Baxter sighed. "Just another part of my existence that sucks the life out of me."

"Why don't you just dump her again?" Lisa asked.

Murray opened his door but didn't get out before saying, "Have you seen her backside?"

Lisa smacked him.

Murray and Lisa huddled under their umbrella and ran to the building while Baxter got soaked rounding the front of the car. He stepped into a puddle which added to his irritation. When he reached the others, Eris brushed at the water in his hair. He swatted at her hand.

"You're all wet."

"No kidding."

The reception area was neat and tidy. A stern-faced, uniformed officer, a woman in her late forties with a strong jaw and a hint of sideburns, glanced up from her computer. Behind bulletproof glass, she motioned them forward.

Chapter 19

Eris handed the wet umbrella to Baxter and took a seat.

"We're here to see Jack Ladham," Baxter said to the officer.

"Have you filled out the correct forms?" The woman had a large gap between her front teeth.

"Yes." Baxter reached into his satchel and produced the correct forms and identifications and pushed them through the slot. It felt strange to be on the other side of the barrier.

The officer studied them. Lisa smiled which seemed the wrong thing to do. People don't smile in prisons.

"It says you are related to the prisoner."

"Yes," Baxter responded. Lisa and Murray appeared surprised. "He's my cousin."

"Did you read through the rules?"

Baxter swallowed. "I scanned them."

"No touching. No contraband. Keep your hands on top of the table at all times. Keep your feet on the floor. At no time will you attempt to give anything or receive anything from the inmate. This includes contraband of any kind. The inmate will sit on one side of the table, and you on the other. Any disruptive behavior by you or the inmate will result in your immediate removal from the premises, and all attempts for repeat visits will be denied. Do you understand what I'm saying to you?"

"Contraband?" Murray asked. "Is that like a shiv?"

She regarded him dolefully. "You've been watching too much television, sir. But if you attempt to pass anything sharp to Mr. Ladham, you will find yourself in big trouble."

"Duly noted," Murray said, holding up his hands.

"Now, through security. We'll bring Mr. Ladham to you."

A Miserable Antagonist

After fifteen minutes, Murray, Lisa, and Baxter sat nervously in uncomfortable plastic chairs on the same side of a scarred, wooden table, Jack still had not arrived.

"I'm so nervous," Lisa murmured.

"Me, too," Baxter agreed.

"But he's your cousin," Murray scrunched up his face. "Why would you be worried about seeing him?"

"We're in prison, Murray. When we were growing up, our parents didn't tell us we had to keep our feet on the floor and hands on the table or we'd be prosecuted."

"Yeah, but he's still your cousin."

Baxter swallowed. "You'll see."

"What are we going to talk about?" Lisa asked. "Should we be taking notes?"

Handing them a copy of his notes, they scanned them. Lisa put hers under the table until Murray chastized her about keeping her hands on top or 'she'd get her butt kicked out of prison.' She quickly put them back on top.

"When he comes in, put the questions away. He might get suspicious," Baxter said.

"We'll have to remember what he says, though." Murray said. "Baxter, you should take the lead."

"As if I'm going to let you two scare him off."

Moments later, a steel door screeched opened and a beefy man with decaying blue tattoos on his arms was led to the table. Baxter, Murray, and Lisa stared up at him, conscious that their stares might annoy him, but it was the first time any of them had come face to face with a convicted felon. The guard reminded them to keep their hands and feet to themselves and then parked himself against the wall.

Jack pulled out his chair. It creaked under his weight as he sat down. "Baxter."

"J... J... Jack," he stuttered.

Chapter 19

"Long time no see." Jack leaned in over the table. "To what do I owe this unexpected pleasure." His eyes roamed over Murray and Lisa, but remained on Lisa. Unconsciously, she leaned closer to Murray.

"We were in the area and thought we'd stop and visit."

For a moment, Jack did not respond. Then, he slowly leaned back in his chair and rubbed his beard. "Who is 'we'?"

"These are two of my friends, Murray and Lisa." They lifted their hands simultaneously uttering an awkward 'hi,' attempting not to look nervous.

"And why would Murray and Lisa want to meet with me, along with my long lost cuz."

The three looked at each other. Murray motioned for Baxter to continue.

"Truth is, Jack, I'm taking a creative writing class at the University of Vermont, and… uh… we thought you might be able to help us."

"Intriguing," Jack responded. "How can I be of service?"

"We're writing a book…"

"A novella," Murray interrupted. "That's a shortened version of…"

"I know what a novella is, moron. I'm an inmate. Not an idiot."

Murray's face reddened.

"What's the *novella* about?"

Baxter cleared his throat. "It's about a bad guy who does some bad stuff."

"Sounds fascinating," Jack chortled. "How did you come up with such an incredible idea."

It was Baxter's turn to blush. "We thought maybe you could help us out with some details. Such as what it's like to… be arrested. You know, handcuffs and police cars and courts and all that…"

Jack raised an eyebrow. "Ask away."

"What did you do?" Lisa asked. "I mean, what are you serving time for?"

"I robbed a liquor store and stabbed the clerk. Just a little scratch, but they gave me six years for it."

"Huh," Baxter frowned.

"What is it?"

"My mom said you were arrested for drunk driving. That's what your mom told her."

Jack's jaw twitched. "That's about right."

"What do you mean?"

"Mom has always been embarrassed of me. I suppose she thinks drunk driving sounds better than robbery and assault with a deadly weapon."

"Why did you do it?"

"What difference does it make?" Jack glanced up at the yawning guard along the wall.

"It doesn't, I suppose, but… how did you decide to do it?"

Jack rubbed his jaw again. For the first time, Baxter noticed a scar running along his face from his left eyebrow to the lower part of his cheekbone. "Sometimes people just need to get robbed."

"That doesn't make any sense," Murray started.

"Not for you, a college pissant with his little girlfriend. You probably never even cheated on a test before. Been served a slice of the good life on a silver tray."

"She's not my girlfriend," Murray said.

Jack looked at Lisa. "So she's single…"

Chapter 19

Lisa shivered, but hardened her voice. "Keep your eyes to yourself, mister."

Jack laughed and leaned further back in his chair. "I needed the money, and I felt like a drink. The two intersected nicely. So, I took my car down to Regal Liquor, whipped open the door, threatened the clerk with a large Bowie knife, and found her willing to allow me to choose from the vast assortment of enjoyable alcoholic products." He spread his hands. "Is that enough description for you writers?"

"And the arrest?" Baxter pushed.

"You can't go anywhere without being recorded. I'd barely finished off the first bottle of whiskey when the cops showed up at my apartment."

"What happened then?" Lisa asked.

"The cops were real calm about it. They made me lie down on the ground. They handcuffed me and stuffed me in the back of the car."

"Did they read you your rights?"

He sneered. "You watch too many movies."

"What about prison? What's it like here?" Baxter asked.

Jack shrugged. "About like out there," he pointed towards a barred window. "Three meals a day, some exercise, lots of screen time."

That didn't seem right. "So it's not difficult?"

"Of course it's difficult, Cuz. I can't do whatever I want. No drinking. No sex. No freedom. I'll be fifty-nine when I get out of here. And nobody is going to hire a fifty-nine-year-old convict."

"I'm sorry."

"Do the other guys try and…" Murray started, but then snapped his mouth shut when Lisa smacked him hard in the arm which made the guard snap to attention.

"Try and what?"

He rubbed his arm. "Like, make the moves on you."

"Murray!" Lisa scolded.

Jack coughed into his hand and looked away from them. "Are you interested?"

"No!"

Baxter reeled them back in. "Jack, was it a snap decision to rob the liquor store, or was it more… normal for you to be… bad."

Jack swiped the air at him. "Get outta here. You've had it so easy your whole life. Always been a nice little boy wearing your cute little sweaters and checkered pants. Remember those silly ties your mother made you wear at Christmas, the ones with Rudolph or snowmen?" Jack laughed until he started coughing. When it was under control, he continued. "When all the other cousins were jumping off the garage onto trampolines, you were making mudpies with the neighbor girls." Jack leaned forward. "Look, I wasn't born bad, if that's what you mean, but life certainly serves up enough temptations to turn you bad. And I wasn't smart enough to refuse. Now, if that's all you came her for, why don't you and your little friends go back to the treehouse and play with your dolls."

Jack started to stand when Baxter reached out for him. "NO TOUCHING!" the guard shouted.

"Sorry!" Baxter retrieved his hand immediately, but Jack had stopped, and he loomed over them. "What about your tattoos? Why did you get them?"

Jack looked down at his arms. The hair that had overgrown the tats obscured a large fish swallowing his

Chapter 19

forearm from the fist upwards. "It's something bad guys do, I guess," he said with a sneer and turned away from the trio.

As he walked away, Jack, Murray, and Lisa stood. When the guard escorted Jack towards the rear door, Jack stopped. "Hey, Baxter," he called out.

"Yeah."

"Be a good guy. There's nothing behind bars for you."

The door slammed shut behind him.

"Well, that was interesting," Lisa said as her hands worried in front of her. "I'm not sure we learned anything completely new, but it was certainly eye-opening."

"We learned a few things," Baxter said.

"Like what?"

"People aren't born bad. In fact, I'm not even sure people are bad. They just make really bad choices."

"You sound like my father," Murray said. "He's a high school counselor."

"Huh. We might have to rethink Herb Treadwell a little bit."

The guard returned them down the narrow hallway back to the exit. When the door buzzed open, Baxter frowned when he saw Eris standing by the watercooler chatting (or flirting) with a uniformed guard. He was smiling down at her. His cap was tilted back on his head. Eris was laughing gaily at something witty he had said.

"She really is something, isn't she?" Lisa said.

Baxter sighed. "She is a real piece of work."

Chapter 20

Murray and Lisa marched up the front marble steps of the mansion side by side, but they did not seem to be in step with each other. Lisa carried the umbrella but only half-covered Murray thus ensuring his back was soaked from the droplets off the ribbing. They gave off the vibe that they were, or had been, arguing. Whether it was something Murray said in the car on the way back from the jail, or something they disagreed on, was not immediately apparent. Or, it could have been the fact that Eris cracked a joke about 'young people looking like drowned rats.' Either way, Lisa shook out the umbrella grumpily and Murray shook himself like a dog as Curtis opened the door.

"Just put your things on the table in the living room if you would." Curtis motioned to the right, but the pair was already moving to the left towards the kitchen, whispering animatedly. "Don't worry about your wet shoes..." Curtis mumbled after them.

Curtis turned back toward the door and noticed Baxter's car in the driveway. "Hey, Murray, where's Baxter?"

"Still in the car," Murray shouted from the interior.

As Curtis was about to shut the door, Barbara's car appeared in the circular drive. The wheels crunched as she parked near Baxter. When she opened the door, Curtis was amused to see an assortment of snack boxes in the front passenger seat spilling over onto the armrest. Barbara was on her phone and still chewing something when she acknowledged him with a wave. Even though she was being rained on, she paused briefly to see Baxter and Eris having a

Chapter 20

heated argument in his car. She left them alone to hurry up the steps by herself.

"Hiya," Barbara said to Curtis as she disconnected the line. "Who else is here?"

"Everyone but Baxter. Still in the car."

"I saw that. Weird. I was hoping she wouldn't come."

Curtis raised his eyebrows noncommittally.

As they sat in the car, Eris insisted she would *most certainly* be watching the 'little thing their group was doing.' Eris had taken one look at the mansion, craned her neck to see the apex of the house, and demanded that Baxter begin his financial pursuits to get '*one of those.*' Now that they had advanced beyond the previous relationship, Baxter said she *most certainly* would *not* be positioning herself anywhere near his friends. HIS FRIENDS! He stressed this statement with a particularly emphatic finger.

"You listen to me, and listen to me good, Baxter Burnside. Now that you've allowed me back in your life, you've got everything you want: friends, a job, happiness, and me. Don't mess this up."

His face reddened. She was right. For the first time in years, he felt a spring in his step. Life seemed to be on the upswing even if Eris was trying to throw him from the swingset.

"Look, Eris," he spoke a little more calmly. "I appreciate your desire to come inside and see what we do, but there are so many other things I'm sure you would enjoy more than sitting in a circle with my friends talking about writing books. I could drop you at home, or take you to the movies. Isn't there something else you'd rather be doing?"

"I can't think of anything." She smiled her most winning smile as her finger traced the image of the flowing fountain in the fog of her car window. Eris turned to him.

She saw that twitch, the relenting twitch, and knew she'd won. "Great," she exclaimed with the same smile on her face. "Let's go."

Baxter opened his door and groaned while Eris pulled down the sunshade and checked her teeth in the mirror.

Grabbing the umbrella, Baxter flicked it open sending droplets into the car which landed on Eris' head. She growled at him as he slammed the door, circled the car, and opened hers. "Why do you keep looking at yourself?"

"Habit. Why don't you look at yourself?"

"Because nothing has changed in the last four minutes." Without thought, he checked his reflection in her side mirror. Nope, nothing had changed.

"That's the difference between you and me, Bax. I believe appearances matter very much and you don't care."

"I care."

She snorted as she pulled herself from the car and grabbed the umbrella from his hand. "When did you last get a haircut? A manicure? For heaven's sake, look at the car we're driving?"

Baxter frowned. It was one thing to make fun of his looks but entirely uncalled for to denigrate his wheels. It was almost impossible to find a 1988 Buick Century anymore. It was a classic. "Careful."

While Baxter and Eris argued, Hana joined Curtis in the doorway. "Is everything alright?" she asked.

Curtis shrugged. "Not sure." After a moment, he turned to her. "Are we okay?" he indicated between the two of them.

"I guess so."

"Hana. Just give me some time. There are some painful things in my past that have to be picked at, like a splinter deep down in the skin. It's going to hurt for me. Okay?"

Chapter 20

Without speaking, Hana nodded and leaned her head into his shoulder. Briefly, he put an arm around her shoulder and squeezed. The gesture was intimate, but Hana still felt a distance between them.

Eris and Baxter were not speaking as they climbed the steps. Baxter was one step behind and getting wetter by the moment. They reached the doorway where Hana and Curtis were standing and smiling down at them. Despite Hana and Curtis standing so close to each other, touching, Eris intuitively sensed between Baxter and Hana – something real and redeemable. Eris pressed closely into Baxter's side, ran a hand under his arm and pressed her cheek into his shoulder possessively.

"Hi, you two."

"I'm sorry we're late." Baxter glanced at Eris which spoke more than enough words about the reason. He tried to pull his arm from her grasp, but she held on tight.

"It's not a problem. We haven't really started yet."

They entered the mansion. To the right, the rest of the group sat in a semi-circle in large, cushioned chairs. Murray and Lisa, now clutching mugs of coffee, sat like twin sphynxes near the bay window while Barbara reclined on the chaise lounge.

As their feet echoed across the atrium's wooden floor, Eris leaned further into Baxter's arm and whispered. "Like I said, this is the kind of house we need to be in."

"Shut up, please."

"I'm serious. A home like this," she surveyed the ornate decorations and rich furnishing, "would mark us as a couple who needs to be listened to."

"You think a home like this would help us?"

Eris missed his sarcasm. "Most certainly. Why, I could work with the servants, manage the grounds, host parties…"

"Yeah, that's what I'm really missing." Baxter pulled his arm from Eris' grasp, but she then took his hand.

Curtis broke the tension. "Please, please, come in and sit down. Can I get you anything to drink?"

Before Baxter said 'no thank you,' Eris had demanded a chai latte with soy milk. Curtis nodded and stood.

Standing uncomfortably in the framed archway outside the room, Baxter and Eris looked for a place to sit.

"Baxter, you can sit by us," Murray said. Relieved, Baxter hurried to the spare stool near Lisa and him.

"Sit by me, Eros," Barbara patted the seat next to her.

"It's Eris, with an 'I'."

"Whatever you say," Barbara responded.

While Eris situated herself primly on the sofa next to Barbara and began to make small talk, Murray began his fifth degree. "Why is she here?" he whispered to Baxter. "I thought you were going to drop her off at a coffee shop somewhere. It was bad enough bringing her to the prison and to a Wednesday night class, but it's even worse at Curtis' house." He tacked a rider onto the statement. "*We* don't *want* **her** here!"

"I know. I know!" Baxter whispered back. "But I couldn't just leave her like a dog."

"Why not?"

"Because she's not a dog?"

Murray glanced at her. "Everybody's going to be all tight and fidgety now. I mean, look at Lisa." They turned to find Lisa tucking her legs up tightly underneath her, a fingernail locked firmly between her teeth.

"Look, I'm sorry. I didn't know what else to do. She made me."

As Murray and Baxter whispered, Barbara leaned closer to Eris. "Good God, you are drop-dead gorgeous." It

Chapter 20

was more of an indictment than compliment, but Eris missed it.

"Why, thank you. I barely had time to get ready." She primly flexed her wrist. "Baxter didn't let me know we were coming until it was almost too late," she lied.

"Well, you made it."

"What, exactly, goes on at these little things?" Eris asked.

"The last few times we've done some roleplay. Kind of like what you saw the other night with Curtis."

"He's amazing," Eris said.

"He used to be a professional actor."

"Is that how he came by this house?"

Barbara shrugged. "It's a mystery to all of us."

Hana and Curtis entered the room with two steaming cups of liquid – a black coffee for Barbara (she'd been up all night with a coughing child) and chai latte for Eris.

"Welcome back, everyone," Curtis started as he and Hana stood side by side in front of the group. "Baxter, tell us about the prison."

Barbara and Hana leaned forward on their seats eagerly expecting the recap. "It wasn't what I expected. It was clean and quiet. I didn't hear any clanging doors or riots." Baxter looked back and forth between Murray and Lisa for confirmation. They nodded. Eris checked her cuticles.

"You were expecting a riot while you were there?" Barbara asked.

"I don't know. You see all these things in the movies, and you just assume someone is going to get stabbed, raped, or thrown over the second level railing – probably a guard, or something."

Curtis held up a hand. "What did you *learn*?"

"From our interview with Jack…"

"His cousin is a convict," Eris interrupted, flopping a wrist out to them.

Baxter ground his teeth and continued. "Jack, my cousin, said that badness isn't something you are born with, but something you choose, like options from a menu. When you're hungry for something, you eat anything. It was kind of sad, too."

"Say more."

Murray interrupted. "I think what Baxter is trying to say is: his cousin is doing time for robbing a liquor store and flashing a knife at some clerk. That's sad. We needed to talk to someone who was really bad. You know, like a pedophile or murderer or something."

Lisa slapped his arm. "That's a terrible thing to say, Murray!"

Murray recoiled and rubbed his arm. "I'm just telling it as I see it."

"It is true," Baxter continued. "Jack doesn't seem all that bad."

"A great family trait," Lisa included.

"But apart from the arrest and the genuinely nice surroundings of the prison, and even Jack's faded tattoos, it drew a really different picture of what being bad was like. I couldn't really feel it. Not from him."

"Yeah, me neither," Lisa agreed.

Curtis leaned back in his chair as Baxter finished. "This is why I think it's still best for us to continue with our roleplay. It's one thing to interview a criminal and get the facts, but another to feel it. Right?"

Hana nodded while Curtis spoke. "Tonight, I thought we could try something 'next level.' This time, we're going to brainstorm the next part of our book. To do that, we need to know the trajectory of the characters and narrative. We all

Chapter 20

heard what Professor Mangall said earlier: 'No story is worth more than a bucket of spit if the characters aren't relatable.' It's one thing to have action and another thing to have an interest in the people *doing* the action. But what are we aiming for? In acting, as the character develops, one senses a need for personality adaptation due to unforeseen circumstances. The same holds true for books."

"What in the world are you talking about?" Murray asked.

"We've reached a plateau for the book. Herb Treadwell, feeling betrayed by his employer after the explosion, his watch permanently cracked and stuck on 11:37, is fighting a losing battle with depression and anger. As we've noted, his relationship with Desiree Fenmere is in tatters and now, even as his friendships with other workmates solidifies, Herb still desires retribution against the company he despises. Have I summed things up well enough?"

"Yes," they agreed. Eris looked confused.

Curtis took a deep breath. "Today, we're going to plot what Herb's revenge looks like. Each one of us is going to play one of the characters we've created in the story. As we become these characters, we'll begin to imagine Herb's vengeance."

They all seemed nervous.

"In this bowl are the names of six…"

"Seven," Hana interrupted, nodding at Eris.

Eris held up her hands, the exquisitely long fingers and manicured nails drew attention as she moved them. "What? No, really, that's okay. I'm just here to watch."

"No way," Murray said. "If you're here, you're taking part. No voyeurs. If you can't handle the truth, someone will drive you home."

"Murray!" Lisa and Barbara exclaimed at the same time.

He focussed his outrage on them. "Remember when we had our first roleplay night and everybody felt uncomfortable, but we agreed that we still all had to take part? Remember that little 'step outside our comfort zone?' Who's going to feel like doing this exercise with an outsider watching?"

Baxter was delighted that Murray spoke the things everyone else wanted to say, but couldn't find the intestinal fortitude to say them.

"Fine, fine!" Eris surprisingly responded. "I'll do it. I did some acting in college." It was a commercial for toothpaste. She flashed her teeth; that was it.

"That's settled then," Curtis smiled. "I've also taken the liberty to arrange some props and costumes. You can choose what you think might best suit your character."

"I'm not sure she and I," Barbara flicked her fingers back and forth between her and Eris, "are quite the same size. It's close, but…" It wasn't really close.

"Don't worry," Curtis said. "Just find something your size and then use your imagination for the rest."

Anxious eyes glanced at the paper bags Hana was assembling on the carpet between them.

"For Eris' sake, we'll recap the main characters and their personalities. Who are they?" Curtis glanced around the group.

Lisa raised her hand. "Herb Treadwell."

"Personality and backstory?"

"An average human being who finds himself embroiled in a plot to ruin his employer."

Hana nodded. "And who is his employer?"

Chapter 20

"Harmony Collins," Barbara said. "A smug, self-satisfied jerk who takes pleasure in making life difficult for her subordinates."

"Very good. And who are the subordinates?"

"Gabrielle Snuck, Simeon Oldman and Lowell Chernkov." Murray marked their names with his fingers. "Gabrielle is overbearing and inappropriate; Oldman is literally that - an old man; and Lowell is a brown-noser."

"Outside of work?"

"Herb's mother," Baxter said. "Cromula Treadwell. Oppressive. Manipulative. Yet somehow kind of endearing."

"Lastly?" Hana asked.

"Desiree, of course," Lisa said. "She's Herb's love interest but has obvious personality flaws." She glanced at Murray. "You've written her character really well, Murray."

"Why thank you." He blushed and snuck a glance at Eris.

Curtis stepped forward with a stainless-steel mixing bowl. Each person, including Eris, retrieved a small piece of paper with the name of a character. Lisa began laughing. Curtis smiled bemusedly, while Murray shook his head.

"Remind me again who Desiree is?" Eris asked.

Baxter's heart sank.

He had drawn Herb Treadwell.

After reminding Eris who her character was, Curtis pointed to the bags containing costumes and props. "Take twenty minutes to develop a scenario you'd like to see your character play. If you need others in your scenario, just write their parts in."

Lisa jumped up from her seat first, grabbed some clothes, and raced for the nearest room. The others followed suit. When Baxter reached for his, Eris took hers but also grabbed his arm. "What have you gotten me into?" she hissed.

"You're the one who wanted to come and see what happened at these 'little things'," he retorted. "It's your own fault."

"I don't think I can do this. I can't be this Desiree. I have no idea how to be overbearing and manipulative."

Baxter's eyes darted up to the ceiling beyond her head. "I'm sure you'll think of something.".

"Can I come to your room with you?" she pleaded.

"No."

"I need some help."

"You're the one who said you did some acting in college."

"Commercials. Toothpaste."

"I look forward to your toothy portrayal," Baxter said as he moved away from her and climbed the stairs to find a bedroom. Disconsolately, she stared up at his retreating form and opened her bag of clothes and props. A smile broke across her face.

Maybe it wasn't going to be so bad after all.

Herb Treadwell's prop bag contained a pair of blue jeans, a button-down white shirt, white socks with blue rings around the calves, and a pair of Birkenstock sandals. Baxter had never worn Birkenstock's before, but when he put them on, he suddenly found himself feeling like Dorothy after donning her ruby slippers. The world seemed like a different place, fuller, with more color. He hoped a witch wouldn't appear to drop a house on his head.

Amazingly, the simple act of wearing a costume unfettered his creativity. After pulling up his pants and

Chapter 20

buttoning his shirt all the way to the top, Baxter began to write. Strangely, now that he knew Eris was playing Desiree, there were things that Herb could say which Baxter never could.

While Baxter pondered his dialogue, Murray opened the door where Lisa was preparing her costume.

"Hey!" she called out. "I'm in here!"

"I know," he said, "but I need to talk to you."

"Can't it wait?"

"No."

"But I'm changing," she called out from a bathroom.

"So? What difference does that make?"

"Because I don't want you to see me naked."

"You're getting naked? Why would you do that?"

She poked her head out from the bathroom door. "Because Harmony Collins wears a braless dress."

"To work at a bank?"

Lisa retreated into the bathroom where her voice echoed. "I didn't put these costumes together."

"I got Lowell."

Lisa laughed loudly. "That should be easy for you."

"Shut up. I'm not a brown noser."

"Oh, stop pouting, you big baby. Just get dressed."

Sighing, Murray began to shed his clothes. After he had stepped out of his jeans and t-shirt, Lisa made an appearance from the bathroom. She looked stunning in a black strapless dress. Twirling, she approached Murray whose jaw had dropped. He was so shocked that he paid no attention to the fact he was down to boxer shorts and socks.

"Can you zip me up?"

"Okay."

As he reached out to her, she lifted her hair revealing a shapely neck. He swallowed loudly, certain he had never seen a more beautiful neck. With trembling hands, he found the zipper. She jumped.

"Did I hurt you?"

"No. Your hands are cold."

"Sorry."

Once he finished, she turned and spread her arms. "How do I look?"

"Like a million bucks."

She tapped his cheek. "You say the nicest things."

Murray realized his state of dress. Blushing, he grabbed the brown corduroys. Just as he was pulling his pants up, the door opened, and Barbara stuck her head in.

"I've got a few…" Catching Murray and Lisa in such a state, Murray, looking guilty, made Barbara retreat. "I'm so sorry," she said. "I thought it was just you, Lisa."

Lisa began laughing. "We weren't doing anything, Barbara. You can come in."

"Just let me get dressed first," Murray snarled.

"I think I'll just let you two get presentable."

"Nothing happened!" Murray called out.

"I don't care!" Barbara retreated from the door one hand in the air as an apology.

Shaking his head, Murray finished dressing. "Jeez, that was embarrassing."

"What did you want to talk to me about?" Lisa asked.

"What do you think of Eris?"

Lisa shrugged.

"She gives me the creeps. I mean, I'm unremarkably attracted to her, but there's something… off."

"Are you attracted to me?" Lisa asked.

"When you're wearing that, yes." He checked her out again and blushed.

"But not when I'm in my civvies?"

"You're like my sister."

Chapter 20

"You don't have a sister."

"But if I had a sister, you'd be like her."

Lisa checked herself out in the mirror and spoke to Murray's reflection. "Should I be flattered or offended?"

"Let's go with the first."

"What do you want to do about Eris?"

"What can we do?"

"I guess we have to figure out how to write her out of the story."

Murray grinned. "That's a great idea."

Twenty minutes later, after concocting a few ideas for their roles, Murray and Lisa exited the upstairs bedroom to rejoin the circle. Barbara had returned to her seat on the sofa. Sitting beside her, Eris leaned casually back, one lithe leg crossed over the other. She had reapplied makeup. Although Eris had arrived wearing a beautiful outfit, Desiree's bag contained an upmarket cocktail dress which fit Eris' persona (and person) perfectly. The small spaghetti straps highlighted her thin collarbone and wiry, muscular arms and the fabric appeared smooth, like her skin.

Nervous and uncomfortable, the group appeared like the cast on the cover of the Clue boardgame, circling the living room and wondering who was going to go first.

"From this point on, you are your characters," Curtis said. "I'm Simeon." He hunched over slightly and changed his voice, raising the pitch. "And who are you all?"

```
Lisa = Harmony, the boss
Hana = Gabrielle, the co-worker
Baxter = Herb, Mr. Average
Murray = Lowell, brown-noser extraordinaire
Barbara = Cromula, Herb's mother
Eris = Desiree, annoying ex
```

Simeon continued. "Creativity and originality are of the utmost importance. Hopefully you were able to jot a few notes to give us new perspectives into the story and your character."

More nervous looks.

"Who wants to go first?"

No one met his eyes until Hana's did. "I will."

"Wonderful. Is there anyone else you need as an extra in your scene?"

"Probably you, Curtis."

"Simeon."

"Sorry, Simeon."

Hana primped her floral dress and fluffed the hair on the sides of her head. "We're in the bank where Herb works. I, Gabrielle, an exasperatingly simple teller, have my sights set on Simeon. I've just mentioned to Herb how I feel about Simeon. Herb has shrugged his shoulders and told me I should do what I want to."

Pointing opposite her, she positioned Simeon, straightening him up. "Now, I've entered the bank of tellers and we…"

"Wait. Wait." Simeon said. "Describe the scene, the mood."

"Oh, okay." Taking a deep breath, she gazed up at the ceiling. "It's a Thursday afternoon. It's been a long, tiring day. Clients have been agitated, and Simeon has had a hard day, also. I have been watching him out of the corner of my eye, and hoping he's noticed me, too. I've worn one of my favorite dresses," she spun around once. "It's almost closing time and I'm nervously aroused to tell Simeon how I actually feel about him."

"Good, good," Simeon encouraged.

Chapter 20

Baxter felt his gorge rise. Hana was supposed to be falling for him. Unfortunately, Baxter liked Curtis. That fact made it frustratingly bearable that Hana had fallen for the older man.

"Hello, Simeon."

"Gabrielle." Simeon pretended to be counting money, which made the others snicker. "What can I do for you?"

She placed a hand on his arm to stop his counting. "You can take me out for a drink."

"What kind of drink?"

"One that will make me tipsy."

Smirking, Simeon turned towards her. "Now why would you want to go and do that?"

"Because I want to lose my inhibitions." Taking a step back from him, Hana appeared to hesitate.

"What are you feeling inhibited about?" he asked. Curtis' voice hitched.

"This."

Without forethought, Hana spontaneously moved quickly and took Curtis' face in her hands. Pausing to look into his eyes, she kissed him hard and fierce. The force of her embrace startled both of them. His eyes popped open. Shocked beyond speech, they remained in the kiss for what seemed an eternity. When they breathlessly broke apart, they realized that the rest of the group was staring at them, jaws on their chests.

"What... the... hell... was... **that**?" Murray's voice rose a pitch with each word.

Hana's voice was quick, with a sense of desperation and apology. One hand covered her throat, the other her heart. "I was playing the part of Gabrielle. In the story, I think, as a great alternative parallel to Herb and Desiree's relationship, Gabrielle and Simeon should take theirs to the next level."

Murray asked the group, "Who wrote this? Did someone else think these things this up? I don't remember this part of the thread?"

Hana touched her lips again as if wondering whether the kiss remained. "We were told to come up with something new. Something that might enhance the story."

Eyebrows raised, Murray responded, "How does swallowing his uvula enhance the story?"

"Love interests are good things," Lisa interrupted Murray's interrogation.

"I thought we were writing a bank robbery novella."

"We are," Lisa insisted, "but every good novella needs a good game of tonsil hockey."

He pointed at them. "But they're... they're so... *old.*"

"What does that have to do with anything?" Barbara said.

"Okay, calm down everyone," Curtis said as he broke character. "I think what you've just experienced was an excellent digression from the story into alternative threads for the reader to connect with."

"If that's a digression, I'll order one of those," Barbara said to Eris.

"Now, take ten minutes to write a paragraph – one paragraph only – to describe what you just witnessed. Detail it. Be descriptive, yet brief. At the end of it, we'll share."

Barbara shook her head and murmured, *And then, Simeon and Gabrielle got it on.*

Eris watched the others scribble on their pads of paper. Unsure of what to do, she fidgeted with her beautiful dress. When she had slid it over her head, she had turned back and forth checking herself in the mirror, enjoying how

Chapter 20

the fabric felt against her skin. Pleased that Baxter had noticed, as well as the other two boys, Eris leaned her head back against the cushion emphasizing her slender throat and rounded shoulders. Unfortunately, the boys were too distracted by their little weirdo game. Baxter's tongue poked out between his lips as he wrote. For Eris, the portrayal had been confusing and kind of gross. The guy, although handsome in a lecherous-old-man kind of way, seemed primed for a heart attack when the woman kissed him.

"You write something too," Curtis encouraged her.

"It's not really my gift," Eris responded.

"You've joined the right club," he said. "Give it a shot."

Jaw clenched, she retrieved a pen from her prop bag and began to write.

When the timer buzzed, Curtis stood up in the middle of the circle. "Would anyone like to share what they wrote?"

"Can I just say that what occurred between you two was shockingly weird." Murray's face scrunched up in distaste.

"Yes, you can say that."

"But you did have that planned, didn't you?"

Curtis shook his head. "That's the beauty of stories. Sometimes the characters themselves get startled out of their everyday reverie."

"I'll go first," Barbara said.

"Great!"

Barbara cleared her throat, sat up straight, and read:

Two people caught up in a spiral of passion. It was a perfect storm of pheromones and timing. For Simeon and Gabrielle, this was the tempest they'd been waiting for. Or at least Gabrielle had.

As her heart thundered in her ears, and lightning streaked from her fingers as they connected with his face, Gabrielle wondered if she'd be consumed.

"What are pheromones?" Lisa asked.

"Chemicals which create arousal," Murray responded factually.

"Oh, that makes sense."

Hana's hand was against her face.

"That was an excellent paragraph," Curtis said. "Anyone else?"

No one raised a hand.

"What about you, Eris? You're new to the group. Your reflection would be much welcomed."

She glanced at Baxter whose jaw was clenched and he shook his head slowly.

"Yeah, okay. Why not?"

"Eris," Baxter held out a hand to her, "you don't have to share anything if you feel pressured. You were right – you haven't done any writing. You could sit the reading part out. That's what you wanted, right?"

"He asked me if I wanted to read a paragraph out loud, Baxter. I wrote something, so I'll read it." She stared him down until he retreated.

"Here we go." She sat up and straightened the paper across her knees.

The guy was old. The girl wasn't. When their lips locked, it was gross, like an uncle and his niece's best friend hooking up at a bar. As they connected, the world around them stopped to stare. It was unnatural, to say the least.

Chapter 20

Both Curtis and Hana blushed furiously.

"Well, nothing quite as painful as honest literature," said Barbara.

"Did I write something wrong?" Eris asked.

Barbara was about to respond negatively, but Baxter spoke first. "Yes! Yes! These two are trying to start a relationship and you've basically sawed them off at the knees."

"How was I supposed to know?"

"To be fair, I didn't know either, not until they started sharing saliva," Lisa nodded.

"They're roleplaying," Murray said. "Just because they took the moment to make out in front of the group doesn't mean it was real. Right Curtis? Hana?"

"Yes, of course," Hana's voice shook. At that moment, Hana regretted taking such a public step in front of her peers. They were good people, kind and honest; their time together had been beneficial for her to heal and feel again. It was a rare thing in Hana's life to connect with other humans, people with similar interests and fears; the comfort she had felt with them allowed her to crack open the door of her darkened closet and reveal the skeleton of a woman who wanted new clothes. Unfortunately, Eris' observation had slammed the door shut, and the key fell into the darkened recesses of her emotional closet.

"Thank you for your frank reflection, Eris," Curtis clapped his hands together a little too loudly. For the first time, Curtis seemed discombobulated. "Now, who is going next?"

"We will," Lisa said. "Murray and I are going at the same time. We wrote ours together considering the story calls for us to be at odds."

"Fine."

The two stood up, Harmony in her slinky dress, hair coiffed impressively, skin sensuously young. Across from her, Lowell. The opposite.

Lisa transformed herself unexpectedly.

"WHAT DO YOU THINK YOU WERE DOING?" she shouted at Lowell. "This is a workplace, not a carnival."

Lowell, taken aback by the vehemence of her attack, stammered, "I don't... uh... don't know what... uh... you're talking about."

"The audio! You know what I'm talking about. Don't play stupid!" Harmony shouted.

"What? You mean the audit? The audit? When we look at the books?"

Harmony glanced at her notes. "Yes, that's what I said. The audit!"

"Jeez Pete, Lisa..."

"My name is Harmony, Lowell."

"Of course, of course."

"Now you've got some serious brown-nosing to do."

Lowell frowned. "I... can't even figure out what's happening."

"Well," Harmony said, "when all else fails..." she moved forward and grabbed Lowell by his cheeks and began to kiss him just like Hana did to Curtis.

Murray's face turned a deep scarlet and he attempted to pull away from her. "What the hell...?" he spoke in the middle of the kiss.

Instead of releasing him, Lisa pulled him back in for another round.

"Whoa, whoa, whoa," Baxter said. "What's going on?"

"I'm still in character, Herb," Lisa said. "Back off while I give this employee a good tongue lashing."

Chapter 20

"Stop! Stop! Stop!" Murray pushed her away. "Who are you?"

Lisa frowned. "I thought we were supposed to add some unexpected action to the story."

"That was certainly unexpected," Baxter responded. "But what does that have to do with anything?"

"It has nothing to do with the story, but the surprise worked so well with those two, I thought I'd do a replay." Lisa threw her hands in the air. "I guess it only works for old people."

"Okay, okay," Barbara attempted to calm the group down. "Let's make a rule that there's no more kissing in any of these little roleplays, okay?"

"Holy balls," Murray exclaimed as he wiped his lips with the back of his hand. "We've gone one step past crazy." He glanced at Lisa who winked at him.

"Okay," Curtis exhaled softly, "this was not exactly how I expected the afternoon to go. Do we want to continue?"

"Yes! Yes!" Lisa encouraged.

"I think we should move on to the next roleplay while I spit out Lisa's gum," Murray said as he shook his head and sat down.

"As much as I think it would be interesting for us all to write about the enactment, I think we'll move on. Barbara, would you like to go next?"

Her eyebrows raised, but she nodded. "I'm not sure how I can follow that, but considering I'm Herb's mother, I think I can safely keep my lips firmly away from Baxter."

Heart beating rapidly, Baxter surveyed the circle noting Barbara's encouragement and Eris' condescension. Every fiber of his being wanted to pull out, to revert to Turtle Syndrome, to be the nice guy, the protagonist. Yet

A Miserable Antagonist

Baxter felt deep in his miserable soul, that this might be a turning point. Somehow, whatever would happen in these next moments would shape a distinctive future for him.

Baxter struggled up from his seat. Dressed in his retro clothing, he approached Barbara, who faced him with a glowering countenance. In her, Baxter could see his mother. The disapproval, the guilt, the disappointment. Whatever Barbara might say to him, he would take it as Betty Burnside.

"I am Cromula Treadwell, the aging mother of Herb Treadwell. This is my story." Barbara jutted out her jaw. "My son, Herb, is my everything. Every ounce of my energy has been poured into raising him. But now that he's an adult, I find myself wondering where I went wrong."

Baxter's face reddened. It was the kind of thing his mother would say.

"Mom, I really wish you wouldn't…"

"Herb, hush now. Calm yourself."

"I don't want to be calm, Mother."

"You don't know what you want. Some days you think you're a superhero. On other days you're a superzero. To be honest, I don't know if I can keep up with your mood swings. You're too old to be doing this. To keep doing this to me."

The blood drained from Baxter's face.

"I want you to stand up for yourself, Herb. Sooner or later, your father and I aren't going to be around to support you. We're no spring chickens anymore. If only you could find a girl. A nice young woman to settle down with. You know, make a good man out of you. God knows you struggle." Barbara put her hands on her hips.

"You think by settling down with a woman, somehow things will be all right?" His voice was tinged with bitterness. How dare she think this about him? Why couldn't she love him for who he was, not for the emptiness she felt.

Chapter 20

"It certainly can't hurt. Take, for instance, that girl you used to date. What was her name?"

Baxter was about to say, 'Eris,' but fortunately, Cromula kept him in character. "It was Destiny, wasn't it? Wasn't that her name?"

"No, Mother, it was Desiree. Desiree."

"Really, Herb, it's been so long since you have *had* a woman over to your parents' house. I'm surprised you haven't turned into a monk."

"What a thing to say," Baxter responded as Murray snickered. Baxter cast him an evil glare.

"I don't mean to hurt your feelings, Herb, but you're old enough that you have to hear this."

"There are better ways to express truth than to be nasty about it, Mom."

Barbara's face registered shock. "Don't be that way, Herb. Don't hurt your mother's feelings."

"Don't hurt your feelings? Don't hurt *your* feelings! For Pete's sake, you're the one who's wrecking my life." Baxter gasped as he uttered the words. He'd never expressed his resentment to his mother: the manipulative words, the overwhelming expectations, the insincerity.

"You've finally said it, Baxter," Barbara said quietly. "I mean, Herb."

The room went quiet.

"I think that's probably enough of that scenario," Baxter said quietly.

Without speaking, Barbara touched Baxter's arm and retreated back to her seat beside Eris. Even though Barbara had never met Betty Burnside, she had read Baxter's interpretation of Cromula's character and done an excellent job of encapsulating her.

After a moment's indecision, Curtis cleared his throat. "Okay, take time to write in your own words what just happened to Herb."

At the end of the writing time, Curtis nodded to Lisa. "Perhaps you could share your paragraph? Would you do that too, Murray?"

"Sure," Lisa said slowly, hesitantly.

> Finally, Herb realized he didn't like his mother. Well, that's not exactly true. He didn't like how his mother made him feel: like, insufficient. Now that he was kind of old but also like kind of young, like caught in the middle of a teeter totter, Herb figured he'd have to choose a side. Either let his mother's weight weigh him down, or push off and drop her. He had a big choice to make.

"Wow, Lisa," Barbara said. "That's incredible."

"Thank you so much."

"And you, Murray? What did you reflect on?"

Murray shrugged and flapped the paper in front of his face.

> Herb Treadwell was a real wuss. He tried to pretend he was strong enough to take on the world, but the fact of the matter was, Herb couldn't even walk away from his mother's house without feeling like he was a five-year-old.

Each thing they wrote and spoke was a personal reflection of how Baxter assumed they viewed him. Because

Chapter 20

the scene had been so realistic, their responses were darts to his soul's center.

"I'm not talking about you, Baxter. It's about Herb, remember?" said Murray.

"Yeah, I know," Baxter replied softly. As his eyes lingered on Hana, she dropped hers to her paper. "What did you write?"

"It's nothing. Not very good. I… well, your acting was so good, that I simply felt uncomfortable." She had rolled the paper up into a scroll.

"You're not going to read it out loud?" Baxter asked hopefully.

"I'll read it," Eris said, as she seductively uncrossed her legs and arose from her seat. For what seemed an eternity, she crossed the divide, past Barbara and Baxter, to Hana, and reached out her hand.

It seemed a moment of finality, of transfer, from the future back to the past, if a baton were being passed. Hana glanced at her friends. Barbara's eyebrows were raised. Hana extended the baton and passed it to Eris who, like an ancient Roman preparing for public oration, theatrically unrolled it like a scroll. Eris touched her hair and rotated her head into position for the best possible view of her neck.

Now middle-aged and tied up in knots by his mother's half-truths and manipulative pressure, Herb's will felt compressed into a tiny sphere. Like a radioactive ball of uranium, Herb felt the meltdown coming. Unless something cooled him down, the world around Herb Treadwell would be flattened by fission. When that happened, the fallout would be immense.

Eris' eyebrows knitted. "I don't understand this." The hand which had adjusted her hair was now tapping the paper in front of her. "Why would Herb be so mad about this? I mean, his mother is a pain in the backside, but certainly one person can't ruin all other relationships, right?"

"You'd be surprised," Barbara responded. "One person, over a long period of time, can destroy everything."

"I suppose this is a lot more like you than you first thought, right Baxter?" Eris laughed.

Murray jumped in. "All I can say, Hana, is what you wrote there is the best descriptive writing you've done since we joined the group."

Flabbergasted, Hana blushed. "Thank you, Murray. That was... unexpected."

"Baxter, you can go next." With jaw clenched, Curtis intuitively seemed to know what was about to happen. Baxter, playing the part of Herb Treadwell, needed his Desiree – his horrible desire. Baxter needed to tell her exactly what she'd done to him.

Swallowing deeply, Baxter nodded. Shellshocked, he wasn't sure if he could go through with what he'd written for Herb Treadwell. Summoning courage and fortitude, Baxter rubbed his head with one hand and cracked his neck by leaning his head to one side and then another. "Yeah, all right," he said softly.

The joyful expectation in the room was replaced by strained tension.

"I'll need Eris to help me out," he said quietly. "I mean, Desiree."

Eris' eyes scanned the room for sympathetic encouragement. Slowly, she touched her lips as if covering her words would create a safe space. In that vulnerable moment, Eris surprisingly seemed like a different woman, a young girl who hadn't quite made up her mind about herself.

Chapter 20

"You know, Desiree, I always loved you."

"What?" she whispered.

"From the first time I saw you, you remember where that was?"

"On the trail?"

"You don't remember, do you?"

"It was in the produce aisle of the supermarket," Lisa whispered. "You were testing the firmness of eggplants."

Suddenly, Eris was shaken back to her strange and awkward reality. Quickly, unconsciously, she readjusted her mask, her personality and defense against anything the world might throw at her, and threw her head back haughtily.

"You don't understand anything about us."

"Like what?"

"Like the fact that you work in a bank, that you live by yourself. And even when we did live together, you may as well have been living by yourself. I always felt neglected."

"You felt neglected?" he responded incredulously. "You're so self-absorbed, you don't even see other people."

Now offended, Eris put her hands on her hips. "I'd rather be self-absorbed than self-pathetic."

"That doesn't even make any sense!" Face flushed, Baxter glanced around the circle and pointed towards Eris. "See what I have to put up with? The complaining and the hyper-critical barbs. Every day! 'Do this! Don't do that! Can't you ever do anything right?'"

"I don't do that," Eris responded.

"Yes, you do."

"Then why do you stay with me?" She challenged.

"Because… I'm addicted to the thought of you."

"What the hell does that mean?" Eris sneered.

"We've talked about this before, Er… Desiree. You are my dream."

A Miserable Antagonist

"Am I a dream or a nightmare?"

Baxter paused. In that small space of silence, an entire history was written and retold. Because their relationship was complex, shallow yet vast, Baxter wasn't sure if he could answer the question in any other way than saying… "Yes."

"What? Which is it?"

"Both," he said. "When we met in the supermarket, I imagined a life with you, love, marriage, kids, till death do us part, but…"

"But what?" The frown on Eris' face deepened. "What part of the nightmare am I for you?"

Finally, he spoke the words. "You're the antagonist. You antagonize me. You always have. When I finally begin to feel good about myself, and you, and us, you… you…"

"What, Baxter? What are you telling me?"

"He's not Baxter," Lisa whispered. "His name is Herb…"

"Let's stop the charade, shall we?" Eris spoke loudly, silencing all other voices in the room. "Speak now, Baxter, or forever hold your peace."

His friends seemed a mile away. Baxter's mouth pulled into a tight line before he spoke. "You can be a real pain in the ass."

Murray started clapping, but was silenced by a stiff rebuke from Lisa.

"I think we should probably step away from roleplaying for a while," Barbara said.

Unlistening, Eris and Baxter squared off in the middle of the room, silent, staring at each other, two cowboys in a showdown. "We're not done yet," Baxter said.

"But…" Barbara implored.

"Let us finish."

Chapter 20

Barbara appeared to be swallowed by the sofa. As she did, a cloud passed in front of the sun leaving the room a darker place than before.

"Eris," Baxter said purposefully, "the only thing I ever wanted from you was respect."

"You're lying. You wanted me – my looks and my body."

From the corner of his eye, Baxter could see Murray nodding.

"Okay, three things."

Feeling as if she had scored a point, Eris pressed her advantage. "You loved the way I looked, the way I moved, the way I made you feel about yourself." She pointed a finger at him. "I made *you* look good."

"It's too bad you didn't make me *feel* good about myself. I've been miserable," he said quietly.

Finally, Eris grasped the situation. "What are you saying? That I'm shallow?"

"That's exactly what he's saying," Murray whispered to Lisa.

"Eris… there's a fine line between *wanting* someone and *needing* someone. When I'm with you, I want you, but I don't *need* you."

For the rest of the group, it felt very much like voyeurism. To watch from the outside, to remain passively silent while the dramatic tension played out in the middle of the circle, was both discomfiting and pleasurable.

After Baxter's comment, Eris was surprised at her desire to cry, but she didn't know how. It had been such a long time since she'd felt something, or thought about someone, besides herself. Eris had cultivated her look, built a façade, brick and mortar of favorable comments and likes, cemented by ogling glances, to protect her from a constantly shifting internal world where her inner castle, one of sand and salty tears, where the child who longed to be a princess still lived. It had fallen into a desperate state of disrepair. Baxter's words were a battering ram against her ego making her façade shudder. She shot back.

"That's rich, Baxter, you who are so… so… desperate for attention and acceptance. You sit around with your weird little friends," she waved a hand around the circle, "scribbling in notebooks and pretending you're something you're not. You think you're doing something original by writing. Let's be honest here," Eris knocked the string of her last arrow, the head barbed with the poison of her vitriol, "you're nothing but a middle-aged loser."

With that, Eris, still clad in Desiree's cocktail dress, turned on her heel, retrieved her bag from the sofa, and stomped from the house. Before she reached the front door, she was already on the phone calling for a taxi.

For a brief second, Baxter wondered where she would go. He then realized that he didn't care. He had his life back. His nice, comfortable, orderly life.

When the door slammed, Baxter was still standing in the middle of the circle while everyone stared up at him.

"Well…" he sighed. "I guess Herb Treadwell is braver than I am."

Chapter 21

"**I** just knew that your little group would cause you stress, Baxter."

"It's not causing me stress, Mom."

She peered at him over her bifocals. "That's not what it sounds like to me. Adults getting together, doing whatever it is you do… and all the sudden… whatever it is you do… causes Eris to leave you."

"You don't even like her."

"Of course we do, right, Burnie? We like Eris, don't we?"

Startled from either reverie or sleep, Burnie jumped. "What?"

"Eris. Baxter's girlfriend. You like her, don't you?"

"Sure."

"See? We like her." Betty wheeled back into the kitchen for the drinks. Baxter followed her.

"What *exactly* do you like about her?"

"She's nice. And pretty."

"She's not nice."

"That's not a nice thing to say about your pretty girlfriend."

"She's no longer that, either."

"Not pretty?"

"Not on the inside. Nor is she my girlfriend."

Betty sighed. It was Baxter's least favorite sound. It carried with it a sense of disappointment, exhaustion, and an intentioned prelude to emotional manipulation. "When are you going to find a good girl, Baxter?"

"I don't need a girl, Mother, good or otherwise."

The stirring stopped. "Are you coming out of the cupboard?"

"What?"

"You know…" she raised her eyebrows and spoke softly. "Gay?"

Stupefied by his mother's odd reaction, he shook his head. "No! It's a closet, not a cupboard. And I'm not coming out of the *closet*."

"Oh, yes, closet. I didn't think 'cupboard' sounded right. Why do they call it coming out of the closet? Is there something in the closet that's supposed to stay in there?"

While his mother struggled with verbal diarrhea, what was in her closet – brooms and mops and old rags, a few boxes of old Tupperware and sewing equipment - Baxter wondered how he would ever be able to talk to her about what was really nagging at him. He supposed his own closet was full of invisible skeletons, bones, and blank spaces stashed in the dark. Baxter had never really thought about why he couldn't find a 'good girl' as his mother suggested. Perhaps it was his lack of self-esteem. He was not good looking. He was not fit enough. He couldn't secure a raise or promotion. He wasn't…

"Well?" His mother asked.

"What?"

Another sigh. "Never mind."

"No, tell me," he said.

"I simply asked if you were happy with your life."

"Do I not seem happy?"

"I don't know, Baxter. You don't seem *unhappy*, but I rarely see you smile. It's like…"

"Like what?"

"It's like you're a ghost."

Chapter 21

The truth hit home. Baxter had been floating through life haunting his own reality. He never felt solid or grounded. His transparency allowed others not just to see through him, but to overlook him entirely.

He gritted his teeth. "I'm happy in my own way."

"What is that way?" Betty finished pouring the drinks and set down the orange Tupperware jug. "Tell me, sweetheart, how are you happy?"

"I like my job, the people I work with, my writing group…"

Betty *hhhmed* after each part of the list until she'd listened enough. "Burnie!" she called out shrilly, "It's time to eat. Go wash your hands."

Baxter watched his mother work as she finished with the table. Her hands shook as she adjusted the serving containers. She seemed frail and yet impossibly strong.

"Mom," he asked softly, "do you love me?"

She stopped in mid-plate-shift and looked up at him. Laughing uncomfortably, she shook her head. "What kind of question is that? That's ridiculous. Of course we love you."

It registered that his mother couldn't overtly tell him 'I love you,' but the real question he wanted to know blurted out before he could contain it.

"Are you proud of me?"

Betty Burnside turned towards her son. Searching his eyes, she grabbed his hands and put them under her chin. "You listen to me, Baxter Langfield Burnside, and I want you to hear this very clearly. Your father and I love you very much, and we're proud of who you are – you're a nice, caring, soft-hearted boy who is too quick to give away his strength. We just…" she dropped his hands slowly. "We just want you to be happy, to get married, have kids…"

A Miserable Antagonist

"What do marriage and kids have to do with happiness? Most of the married people I know who have kids are completely miserable."

"Surely that's not true," Betty responded as she pulled out her chair to create a barrier between them.

"It is," he insisted. "Every married adult I know, with children, is so exhausted and frustrated by the demands on their time, all they do is complain. Why, this woman I work with, Carmen, she just had triplets and…"

"Triplets?" Betty interrupted. "I knew this woman who had triplets. Oooh, it must have been back in the seventies. Didn't even know she was having them. Well, she knew there were two, and she said something about hiccups. I remember her telling me about the x-rays… you see, back in those days, they didn't have ultrasounds. I know because when you were inside me…"

It was Baxter's turn to sigh. As his mother's voice faded from high volume to mute in his head, he wondered if she would ever really tell him anything he needed to hear.

Chapter 22

Larry's phone buzzed. "Mr. Spago. Hi. This is Bernadette. I think… well, maybe you should come out here. Um…"

"What is it, Bernadette? I happen to be in the middle of working through some figures." His eyes fell on his swimsuit calendar, May 1984. *What a man.*

"Just come out, Mr. Spago." The phone clicked.

Gritting his teeth, Larry adjusted his shirt and vest to make sure his chest hair was arranged just so, and opened the door behind the booths.

Everything looked normal.

Bernadette waved him over impatiently.

"What's going on?"

"Baxter just got here."

"So?"

"He… he's made a… er… change."

Larry glanced around Baxter's cubicle. It was neatly arranged, just like always. "Where is he?"

"In the bathroom."

Shaking his head, Larry frowned. "I told him to do his business on his personal time."

"I think you need to go talk to him."

"I am not going to interrupt one of my employees while they are going to the bathroom." His raised voice caught the attention of tellers and patrons alike.

"It's not like that," Bernadette continued to whisper. "I think he might…"

"Spit it out, Ms. Welters."

"It's Walters."

"That's what I said."

A Miserable Antagonist

"I think he might have gone crazy."

"Did you suddenly become a shrink?"

"No, but…"

"Then I think you should keep your disrespectful opinions to yourself. Whatever he's done, I'm sure he'll be just fine."

"Mr. Spago, please just go talk to him."

As if he had more pressing meetings, Larry Spago checked his watch. It was 9:15 in the morning. If he didn't come out by 9:30, by God, Larry was going to lay down the law. If Burnside wasn't so good at tellering (and working for less money than anyone else), Larry would be well within his rights to look for a replacement.

"Fine," he replied tersely.

Larry rapped on the door with one knuckle. "Burnside. What are you doing in there?"

Silence.

He knocked again, louder this time. "Burnside. I have a key for the bathroom, and I will use it."

After a moment, there was a shuffling sound and the door unlatched, but Baxter did not come out. When Larry hesitantly pushed the door open, he was surprised by the darkness. Reaching out for the switch, he was stopped by Baxter's voice.

"Don't. Don't turn on the light. Just shut the door behind you."

Suddenly, Larry felt a sense of panic.

"I don't think that's such a good idea, Burnside. If you'll just come out, we can…"

"I'm not coming out."

Larry stepped in but left the door cracked. "You've already been in front of your workmates. Obviously, it can't be that bad."

"Oh, it's bad."

Chapter 22

"Then why did you come to work today? Surely, if you're as crazy as Bernadette says you are, you should have gone to the shrink instead."

"She said I was crazy?"

"I probably shouldn't have told you that."

Pause. "No, no, that's good. That would be the only explanation."

"For what?"

"For what I've done."

Pause. Deep sigh. "Okay, turn on the light."

Larry flipped the switch. As his eyes adjusted, he found a squinting Baxter Burnside staring at his reflection in the mirror above the sink. Baxter was now bald and had a tattoo under his eye.

"What the..."

"It's hideous, I know, but it's only henna. It will come off and my hair will grow back."

"Uh... I'm not sure what to say here." What Larry wanted to say was that Baxter looked like a convict out on bail. His bald head reflected the glare of the overhead lights. Below his left eye was a stylized teardrop tattoo. Even though Baxter was wearing his work uniform, his traditional pleated brown pants and white shirt, tie positioned carefully at mid-throat, Baxter looked like he was on the verge of stealing a car.

"I think maybe I should go home," Baxter shifted his focus to Larry.

"We're short-staffed today, Burnside. I don't have any replacements."

"There are already five tellers out there. Come on, Mr. Spago, I'll take a sick day."

"But you're not sick."

"I think I'm going to be sick. Does that count?"

"No, not really."

"Please. Let me go home."

Finally, Larry closed the door. "Tell me what brought on this radical change. Are you having a mid-life crisis? Did you break up with that fine young… I mean, are you having relationship issues?"

"To be fair, my mental health is none of your business, and my personal life is personal. But what I can tell you is that I've been taking a creative writing class and I thought – absurdly, now that I see the results – if I immersed myself in the main character, I'd be able to write better."

"Your character is in Grand Theft Auto?"

"No, no. I'm writing about a villain. Ultimately, he…" Baxter thought it best not to finish the sentence off with *is going to be an excellent bank robber.*

"He's going to end up in jail?"

"No, actually. That's the point of my story. The bad guy is the good guy. The bad guy finally gets what he deserves."

"And what is that?"

"Fame, fortune and respect."

"And all he needed was a shaved head and a tattoo?"

"You don't understand," Baxter responded.

"You're right. I have no idea why you'd want to look like Eminem."

"I'm sorry," Baxter said ashamedly.

"Apology accepted," Larry said as he clapped his hands. "Now, get back out there and do your job."

"Should I wear a hat? Sunglasses?"

"Of course not. I'm sure our patrons will overlook the slight error in judgment. I can't have tellers wearing hats and sunglasses. It's unprofessional."

Baxter wasn't sure that Larry was the preeminent arbiter on professionalism, especially with his chest hair

Chapter 22

curling out over his collar, but it wasn't the time to say anything. "Just give me a minute, will you?"

A short time later, while the rest of the bank went about their business, Baxter exited the bathroom and went back to his booth. His colleagues tried not to stare, but to no avail. Against Larry's wishes, Baxter donned a stocking cap, but there was nothing he could do about the teardrop, perched like a brown dewdrop, on top of his left cheekbone.

"Who *are* you?" Bernadette asked as he settled in and turned on his computer.

"I made a mistake, okay?"

"Mistake? It looks like you went all gansta."

"I wanted to change things up." Baxter opened his register and made sure he had the correct count of bills and coins.

"Sane people change their cars or their carpets, not shave their heads and get teardrop tattoos." Bernadette nodded at the old woman who paused a little longer to stare at Baxter and his stocking cap before moving away from Bernadette's booth. "You aren't having a mid-life crisis, are you?"

"That's what Larry asked. No. Yes. I don't know. Maybe?"

"You need a vacation is what you need."

At lunchtime, Baxter, Bernadette, Camille and Sheena sat in the cool, sunny air outside Johnny Bing Bings. Behind them, children played on solid plastic playground equipment. They squealed as their small bodies were vomited from the giant hamburger head and dropped onto the wood chips below. One young girl crawled across a bridge created in the shape of a giant pickle. A few mothers picked at their French fries while they studied their phones, biding their time until their children exhausted themselves before their afternoon nap.

"So this is about your writing class. You wanted to… to…," Bernadette spoke and motioned with her hand as she unwrapped her dill pickle and cheeseburger from its plasticky paper.

"I've told you this before. It started out as a desperate attempt to meet a girl. I met her on a walk and one thing led to another. Before I knew it, I was enrolled in night school."

Sheena swallowed before breaking in. "I've been walking lots of times and nobody ever asked me to join a writing class." In her lap, Sheena held the newest version of Fabio-meets-Gandalf.

"Even though the relationship didn't work out, I'm really enjoying the class, which is kind of weird."

"You're a writer? Like an author?" Camille asked.

"No. Well, not in a published sort of way. But I can string together some pretty good sentences now."

"Give us a for instance," Bernadette encouraged.

"I… uh, no… that's probably not a good idea."

"Come on, Baxter," Sheena punched his arm lightly leaving a smear of mayonnaise on his sleeve. "An artist should be proud of his or her work. Just a taste test. See if you can beat this." She raised the book with her non-burger holding hand, and with her mouth partially full, she read from her book. "*Dorentia grasped the wand in her hand, brandishing it like Jesmonica's sword. 'I know you want my love spell. But my wand isn't working right now.'*"

"Are you serious?" Bernadette asked Sheena. "I'm pretty sure Baxter could write laps around…" She squinted to see the author's name on the front cover just above a scantily clad witch. "… Ravisha Lovecotton."

Baxter relented. "Fine. Fine. Just remember, it's a work in progress."

Chapter 22

They leaned in while he unfolded a crinkled piece of paper from his chest pocket. "Chapter 7."

"Oooh," Sheena said, "he's got more than one chapter. Great."

Baxter cleared his throat and repeated,

Chapter 7. In the middle of the night, Herb Treadwell awoke, sweat pouring from his armpits, a sour smell wafting up from the covers.

"I'm eating here, Baxter," Camille said as she paused mid-chew, a partially masticated sandwich visible in her mouth.

"You said you wanted a sample."

"Yeah, but I thought it would contain some spicy dialogue and maybe a racy paragraph about two half-naked gang-bangers washing their car."

"Why in the world would you think that?" Baxter asked.

"By the powers of deduction, my dear Watson," Camille responded. "You've got a gang-banger tear and you've shaved your head."

Baxter sighed deeply. He was thankful that these women were not in his writing group. Baxter scrunched up his sandwich wrapper and stuffed it in the brown paper bag. "Do you want me to finish the paragraph or not?"

"Finish. Finish." Bernadette nodded to the other two to lay off the questions.

He restarted.

The events of the day were imprinted on his subconscious, and in the middle of the night they leaked from his dreams.

"Oh, dear," Sheena said. "He wet the bed?"

"Enough. I'm outta here." Baxter launched the paper bag towards the trash can where it bounced harmlessly on the rim before careening into the gutter. He left it and began to walk back to the bank.

"Aren't you going to pick that up?" Bernadette called after him.

"No," he shook his head. "I'm practicing being bad, remember?"

Later, during a lull in the afternoon, Baxter took off his stocking cap to scratch his head. He caught Bernadette staring at his bald pate. "Do I look bad?"

She snorted and took a sip of water from her gargantuan bottle with a bendy straw. "Well, if you want my honest opinion, you look *bad*, but not BAD, if you catch my drift. Weird, but not evil."

"Gee, thanks."

"Actually," she said as she rotated her stool towards him, "you do kind of look like that bank robber I saw the other day on TV."

"I do?"

"Well, I mean, only in a casual, weakling sort of way. That guy was like, big and muscular, and had more tattoos than just a tear on his cheek."

"Do you think I need more tattoos?"

She held up her hands in front of her. "No, no, I think you have enough. But now that you've got me thinking about it, that guy must have been a complete idiot."

"Because he got caught?"

Bernadette rolled her eyes. "Yeah, I suppose. If you're going to rob a bank, do you really want to do it as a stereotype? You walk in the door and people are immediately

Chapter 22

wary of you. If I was going to rob a bank, I certainly wouldn't get any tattoos. And I wouldn't be big and hulking, either."

"I'm not sure he had a choice about his size."

"I don't know. He looked like he lifted a lot of weights. His bulging muscles and thick chest…" Her voice trailed off.

"Sounds like you fell in love."

She giggled. "Women do like the bad boys." She pointed at his head. "Maybe there's even a girl out there who will be taken with your Captain Stubing."

"I doubt it."

"Don't be such an Eeyore." She leaned closer to him and touched his knee lightly. He jumped, so she withdrew it. "Now, getting back to the bank robber. This guy waltzes in with a gun and a black ski mask – like, so cliché – and threatens everyone in the joint. While the cameras roll, he throws the bag over the bulletproof glass and yells at the tellers to 'Fill it up.' Meanwhile, every last person in the bank is already recording the heist on their phone. Yeesh," she sipped again and the drink burbled empty, "you can't get away with brazen attempts like that anymore. You have to be subtle."

An older woman approached Bernadette's cubicle and opened her brass clasped purse. Bernadette immediately switched gears and chatted amicably with the woman who wanted to withdraw twenty-dollar bills to send to her grandkids for Halloween.

While Bernadette served her, Baxter replaced his hat and thought deeply about his tattoo experience. It had been quite an adventure.

Chapter 23

The sign on the glass door, with neon green letters that read **PHAT TATS**, was surrounded by examples of tattoos: skull and crossbones, roses, butterflies, a few naked ladies, and thorns and knives. When Baxter pushed on the handle, it squeaked as it swung inwards. The room was cold and sterile. With its reclining chairs, head and footrests, polished white floor, it felt and looked like a dentist's office. Baxter had falsely assumed that a tattoo parlor would be a festering, dark, back-alley kind of place with seedy looking characters who were more likely to sell you a revolver than to imprint your girlfriend's face on your thigh. As he let the door swing loudly shut behind him, Baxter was met by the buzzing sound of a needle-gun. It grated his ears almost as much as a dentist's drill and he cringed. To his right, a woman squirmed on a surgical table as a heavily-tattooed, balding man leaned over her lower back. He was imprinting some sort of white rabbit with wide eyes and floppy ears at the base of her spine.

"You've got to hold still, Dana," the tattooist cautioned.

"It's hard," the woman complained as she turned her head towards him. "It feels like you're stabbing me."

The tattooist smirked. "I am, with needles."

"Just finish."

Baxter felt faint as the needle gun worked.

"Can I help you?"

Baxter found himself staring at the most artificial person he'd ever seen. With tattoos covering her skin from cheeks to ankles, at least three dozen piercings glinting in the

Chapter 23

fluorescent overhead lights, and two revoltingly distended earlobes, Baxter shivered with disgust.

She repeated her question, but her eyes narrowed. There weren't many men who opened the door of PHAT TATS wearing brown pants, button-down white shirts and ties, and Hush Puppy shoes.

"I, uh, want to get a tattoo."

She crossed her arms. A red-eyed, green dragon stared at him from a forearm. "You sure?"

"Yeah." Baxter's voice squeaked. Suddenly, he was certain he did *not* want to get a tattoo. He wanted to remain unstained, freakless. If this woman's appearance was any indication of the world he might be stepping into, Baxter's second thoughts were much louder than his high hopes.

"Okay," she responded slowly as his terrified eyes wandered across her skin. "What do you want?"

"A tattoo."

Her eyes rolled to the side. "Yes, but what *kind* of tattoo?"

Baxter couldn't stop looking at the metal posts in the bridge of her nose between her eyes and the one just above her lip. "I hadn't thought that far ahead."

"Are you loaded?"

"What?"

"You know, drunk – or high. Pharmaceutical courage to get inked up."

Frowning, Baxter touched his nose, unconsciously feeling as if he had a dangling booger, and wondered what it would be like to have a nose ring like this woman. "No, not drunk, or high. Just something I've always wanted to do…" His voice trailed off to snuggle into bed with his own lie.

"Right." The unbelieving word stretched out.

"No, really. I've been thinking about a change in my life and getting a tattoo might be just the thing."

"What kind of change do you want?"

"I want to be bad."

"Huh?"

Baxter shook his head quickly. "What I mean is, I want to look bad."

The frown on the woman's face deepened. "Are you saying I look bad?"

"No, that's not what I meant. I... uh... people are always telling me I'm too nice, and that's frustrating. I want to look... evil-bad. Not... ugly-bad."

The woman considered whether this new offensive idea was an upgrade over the last one and decided to let it go. "Well, you've got to make a few decisions: where, what kind, and with what?"

"Excuse me?"

She sighed. "Look, are you sure you want to do this?"

"Yes," he insisted.

"Then *where* do you want to get the tattoo; *what kind* of tattoo do you want; *with what* color do you want it?"

"Aaah." Behind him, the bunny-rabbit woman called out in pain. The big man stepped back to give her a moment. Once again, Baxter felt the blood drain from his face, and he felt woozy. Reaching to the side, he tightly grasped the arm of a chair.

The tattooist waited while the questions processed, then reached for a spiral bound black notebook. "Maybe you need some examples."

"I think that would be best."

"I'll leave this with you." The woman dropped the notebook into his hands and walked behind the counter.

Chapter 23

Baxter sat down and flipped open the book. Most designs were frightening, but a few were a little less intimidating. Finally, near the end of the book, he decided on an intricate dagger. For the forearm. In black.

Swallowing, he nervously stood and handed the book back to the woman who was clicking her tongue-stud against her teeth. "I've made my choice." He pointed to the picture, and she looked up at him.

"You want a dagger."

"Yes. On my forearm."

She studied his frightened eyes. "Are you sure about this? You don't look so good."

He swallowed again. All the swallowing was making him feel queasy. "I'll be fine. Do me."

She snorted. "All right."

After signing a consent form, the woman led him to a spare chair a short distance from the bunny rabbit woman who was still groaning in agony. Baxter started to sweat.

"You'll need to roll up your sleeve."

Baxter couldn't take his eyes off the other woman.

"Hey! Buddy, wake up!"

Startled from his reverie, Baxter, with shaking hands, rolled up his sleeve. "How much is this going to hurt?"

"What's your pain threshold?"

"Pretty low."

"Then this is going to hurt like hell." She began to prep the equipment. Baxter's eyes followed her. As she snapped on her sanitary gloves, she clapped them together once. "You'll have to change the dressing, too. That's not a pretty thing."

"I…"

"And, if I were you, I'd be taking some ibuprofen every few hours. Something stronger, if you have it. Low pain threshold and all." He quailed. "Really, pal, I'm not sure you're ready for a tattoo."

"No, I'm doing this." Baxter leaned back against the headrest.

She studied him with his eyes closed. This was not going to be an easy one. Again, the bunny-rabbit lady cried out. Baxter's eyes widened with terror.

"Stop moving!"

"You're killing me!"

"Dana, you're going to have to suck it up! Come on! You can do this!"

Baxter felt his breath quickening. Hearing the woman's distress, he began to imagine the torture and the permanence of what he intended. As he opened his eyes, the tattooed lady's face appeared in front of his. Like an evil spectre, she grinned. Blackness was consuming her body from her inked thighs all the way to her bluish neck. She was becoming a pinhole of malevolence.

"Are you ready?"

Now hyperventilating, he nodded quickly. "Do it."

Flipping the switch on her machine, it came to life buzzing loudly. Baxter's eyes followed her gloved hands as she grasped the device and held it up in front of her face like an anesthesiologist flicking a needle full of morphine. Lowering it to his wrist, he felt pressure.

Baxter's sight pinpointed.

This feels bad. This feels b…

Baxter emerged from his unconsciousness moments later. Feeling a cold compress on his forehead and neck, the tattooist stood over him smiling kindly.

"Welcome back to the land of the living," she said.

"Is it over?"

"Yes."

He lifted up his arm. "There's no tattoo."

Chapter 23

"You passed out before I could get started."

"I passed out?"

"Yep."

"But I need a tattoo. I've got to look mean, you know?"

"Why, man? Why do you have to?"

"Because the bad guy has to win. Because Herb Treadwell needs to know what it's like to…" His voice fell off when the woman's eyes appeared confused. "Let's just say getting a tattoo is a life altering moment for me."

She sighed. "You feelin' better?"

Glancing to his side, the bunny-woman was now examining her tattoo in a mirror. She was smiling through her tears at the white, very inflamed rabbit munching on a carrot at the base of her back.

"Yeah, I guess so. But what am I going to do?"

The woman patted his cheek. "We're going to get you a tattoo."

"But… I thought you said I'm not going to get one."

"I know this woman. She does tattoos. Henna tattoos. Natural skin dyes. Non-permanent and no needles." She scratched out a phone number. "Call her. It will be a good practice run for you. When you're ready for a real one, come back to me."

Baxter looked at the piece of paper in his hands and immediately felt relieved he hadn't gone through with it. "You're very kind," he said.

"You seem like a really nice guy. Be a shame for you to change."

After a hug from the woman, Baxter left the shop and got the henna tattoo he needed.

And, a haircut.

Chapter 24

"Novella first drafts are due in three weeks, people," Parker Mangall intoned as he stood behind his podium at the front of the classroom. "In case you were worried about falling behind, or worse yet, hoping for an extension, don't even bother. Parker Mangall doesn't do extensions."

Baxter shook his head. *Three weeks.* How had the time gone so quickly? The semester had flown by. Time with his teammates, work at the bank, visiting Jack, ditching Eris. The whirlwind had swept him up so quickly, his head was still spinning.

When Baxter arrived at class the Wednesday night after his shave and tattoo, he left his stocking cap firmly covering the crown of his head. Included in his embarrassment was that he'd had to turn down his mother's invitations for dinner over the last weeks. It would have been one thing for her to attempt to rub the tear from his face by licking a napkin, but another for him to absorb the verbal bombardment about his shaved head.

The group had been shocked by his appearance. When he removed his cap the first time, Murray had burst out with such a guffaw, Lisa had been startled almost out of her seat. Hana had never frowned so deeply.

He explained to them about digging deeper into Herb's character, but Barbara thought he'd dug far enough to reach Herb's bowels.

"I really think we're on the cusp of *the* breakthrough," Baxter said. "If we can just figure out *how* to rob a bank, all the other pieces will fall into place. Right?"

Chapter 24

"You're the banker, Baxter," Murray answered. "Don't they have policies and procedures about how to deal with robberies?"

"Yes, of course," Baxter scratched his head. "But they don't actually give examples of how robberies are planned and how one gets away with it."

"Have you ever had a robbery at your bank?" Lisa asked.

Baxter thought for a moment. "There was one time when a guy came in and demanded some cash, but he was just drugged up. The police came and got him soon afterwards. Chad, the security guard, talked him down. Bernadette poured him a cup of coffee while they waited for the cops to arrive."

"That's your robbery story?" Murray scoffed. "A guy comes in, wants cash and ends up with a cup of coffee?"

"What can I say? It doesn't happen anymore – not in the physical, break-the-bank-and-stuff-the-cash-into-bags sense. It's too easy to get caught. It's all done on computers nowadays."

"What's in the vault, then?" Murray asked.

"There's some cash and other valuables, but Larry is the only one who knows how to get into it."

"So you're saying we need to write about a digital theft?"

Baxter shrugged.

"Wow," Murray said slowly." Our best seller just went down the crapper. Nobody wants to read a book about people tapping away on a computer."

"I didn't say that's what we should write about," Baxter countered. "I'm just saying that figuring out an actual robbery will be very different than how hackers might do it."

"I say Herb Treadwell holds everyone hostage. With a gun." Murray said. "No, a bazooka."

"A bazooka?" Barbara shook her head. "That's stupid."

"What's your idea, then?"

"I think we should tie up the bank manager and hold her for ransom."

"That sounds like fun, Barbara," Lisa countered. "But how does it work? Do you waltz into her office, find her in her desk chair and say, 'Sit still, you.'"

"Take it easy, everyone. This is a brainstorming session," Curtis interrupted. "All ideas are equally valid."

"Or invalid," Murray mumbled. "Look, we don't have writers' block, Baxter. We have writers' wall. Man, I'm so exhausted by this idea. We've literally been thinking about this for three months."

"Yeah, like literally," Lisa copied.

"I don't know about you guys, but I need a break from this topic." Murray searched the faces of his fellow co-authors who looked down guiltily.

"Do you all feel this way?" Baxter asked.

Barbara was the first to speak. "It's nothing personal, Baxter, and I'll be the first one to say how well this has gone, and we've done some great collective work but…"

"But what?"

Barbara blew out her cheeks. "I think we should go have a few drinks."

"I think that's a great idea," Curtis agreed.

"But there's still an hour left of class." Hana noticed Parker Mangall strutting between groups, arms crossed over his chest.

"Screw him," Curtis said as he stood up quickly.

The group was shocked by Curtis' vehemence, and as he took Hana's hand and pulled her to her feet, Murray

Chapter 24

followed by lifting Lisa. Barbara, in turn, held out her hand to Baxter who, after wondering whether his great idea had been hijacked, warmed quickly to the idea of spending a night away from adjectives, adverbs, and bank robbery. Baxter could not remember the last time he had gone out with friends for a few drinks. He accepted Barbara's outstretched hand.

"What's going on back there?" Mangall called out.

"Brain break," Curtis shouted.

"What?"

"We're going to melt our writers' ice block with alcohol," Curtis laughed.

"There is still an hour left of class," Mangall objected and pointed at the wall-mounted clock as the rest of the class jealously watched the group peel off towards the door.

"We're not too worried about it."

"I'll dock your grades," Mangall threatened.

Curtis waved it off with a flick of his wrist. Then, just as he was about to follow his compatriots out the door, he stopped. "If anybody else wants to join us, you are welcome."

A wave of spontaneous excitement passed through the room. Coats were grabbed, bags were shouldered until finally Parker Mangall was left at the front of the room by himself, mouth agape, green whiteboard marker held helplessly in his hand like a decommissioned wizard's wand. Curtis happily held the door for the other members of Creative Writing 102.

As the last class member exited, Curtis studied Mangall.

"You are invited too, if you would like to come."

Mangall hesitated, wrestling with the idea of letting his hair down with his students or standing on his own skewed version of moral superiority. Finally, after a few brief seconds, he held up a finger.

"I'll get my coat."

Chapter 25

The Catamount Bar and Lounge squatted like a troll on the eastern edge of the University of Vermont. It was a large, bulky structure made of sturdy cement blocks and prison-like bars protecting the windows. The Catamount had first been (ironically) commissioned as a bank. The large arched windows on the street front now held neon beer signs instead of stock tickers. Where the tellers' booths used to be was now a thirty-foot, highly polished bar, decorated with brightly colored coasters, plastic olive swords, tip jars, and overshadowed by a wooden structure with dangling wine and beer glasses. A mirror ran the full length behind the bar revealing an assortment of liquors. Behind the bartender's knees were the cheaper, mixer drinks that college students tended towards. The Catamount Bar and Lounge had once been a popular socializing place for upscale professionals who wanted to have a martini after work. Now, almost three-quarters of a century past its heyday in the 1950's, the Catamount would be considered a college dive. On weekends (and Thursday Student Discount Night), the Catamount was a hive of mostly-legal, drinking-age activity.

Dylan Parsons, the resident Wednesday night bartender, glanced up from the beer glass he was polishing when the door opened. As the flood of chattering humanity piled through the door and approached the bar, Dylan glanced at the three locals who were staring morosely at the ancient, mounted television above the bar. Like lichenous rocks, these three men, hunched on their stools, were here every night of the week (except Thursdays and some weekends) to drink in peace and quiet. They, too, watched

A Miserable Antagonist

the horde walk through the doors and cringed at the thought of interrupted drinking. Don, a thin-haired former construction worker, pot-bellied from decades of waistline abuse, nudged Todd with his elbow. In turn, Todd, a grease-handed auto mechanic with a thin moustache and beady eyes, spoke something softly to Dean, a welder and amateur drug dealer, who shook his head.

Dylan watched a young man approach him and raise a finger. "What can I getcha?"

"I'll have a rum and Coke, and she'll have a berry wine cooler." Lisa's head bobbed happily.

"Can we turn the music on, too?" she asked.

Dylan pointed to the corner where an old jukebox sat hunched, squat, like a warthog. "It's a quarter per song."

"What are you pointing at?" she asked.

"The jukebox."

"Huh?"

"That thing. The rounded thing over there." Dylan repeatedly pointed.

"What's it called again?"

"A jukebox. You put a quarter in the slot and then you can choose whatever song you want. It's like old-fashioned Spotify, but analog." Dylan began to pour the rum and Coke while opening the lid on a wine cooler for her.

"You have to *pay* for music?" she asked incredulously. "A whole quarter?"

Dylan rolled his eyes and shook his head then moved on to the next customer.

"Come on," Murray pulled on her arm. "Let's get a look at this thing."

The jukebox was darkened and appeared to be in a serious state of disrepair. Where it used to be lemon yellow, orange, and pink, the ravages of age, mold, and inconsistent

Chapter 25

use had muted the colors. It looked like it was having its own mid-life crisis. "How does it work?" Lisa asked Murray.

"I don't know. I've heard of them before, but I've never actually seen one." He searched the sides for a power button. "I can't see how it turns on."

"You have to plug it in," a voice said behind them. They turned. It was Parker Mangall.

Lisa was shocked to see him. "What are you doing here?"

"Even I remember what it's like to have a life outside the world of academia." He lifted a beer to his mouth and wiped the foam with the back of his hand. "This used to be my hangout when I was in college."

"Really?"

"Yes, and that table right over there was *our* table," he pointed to a dimly lit booth opposite the jukebox.

"Whoa…"

"And every Thursday night, we would walk up here to the Catamount for five-dollar pitchers of beer, play songs on the jukebox, dance, shoot pool, chase girls, and make fools of ourselves. By the time we got home, we were singing *Magic Carpet Ride* at the top of our lungs."

Murray and Lisa looked at him quizzically.

"Magic Carpet Ride – Steppenwolf." He saw that no bells were ringing. "Okay. You're about to have your mind blown." He reached behind the jukebox and plugged it in. Suddenly, the machine came to life. Lights flashed and a wheel of scintillating compact discs spun to the top of the machine. The jukebox perked up like an elderly person being asked about the good old days.

"That's so *cool!*" Lisa set down her drink on a table nearby. "What do I do?"

Mangall chuckled. "Do you have a quarter?"

"No. We never carry any money."

Sighing theatrically, Parker produced some pocket change and sifted through it until he found what he was looking for. He selected four quarters and handed them to Lisa.

"What do I do?"

"Put them in the slot. You should get eight songs for a dollar."

"You know, a Spotify account would give you almost unlimited access to…"

"Just put the dang quarters in the slot, young lady," Parker answered with a laugh.

She did. As the ancient machine worked, it reflected a rainbow of sparkling colors across the room. Beeping and pinging, the jukebox waited for instructions like a panting dog preparing to be taken for a walk.

"Now, read down the list of songs and find eight you really want to hear. Then, very carefully, you're going to punch the disc number and song number into the buttonpad here." He ran his finger down the list and found Steppenwolf. "F-134."

The machine lumbered through the motions inserting the archaic compact disc into the player when suddenly, the magical music burst from the jukebox's front speakers and filled the room with sound.

Lisa was gobsmacked. "OMG!" she shouted. "This music is AWESOME!" Grabbing Murray's hands, she plied him like a marionette to get him to dance. Self-consciously, Murry felt embarrassed by his loose limbs and off-rhythm feet. Eventually, after Lisa's insistence that he 'set his butt on fire', he slugged his rum and Coke and set the empty glass on the table next to Lisa's bottle. Then, without another thought, he let the sound take him away.

Chapter 25

Meanwhile, Hana and Curtis squeezed into a table near the front. Another pair of creative writers asked to sit next to them. The women were young enough to be Hana and Curtis' children.

"Are you two married?" one of the girls asked.

"No, we just met in the class."

The girls shared a look as if saying, *Not married – not yet.* "Your team is writing a collective novella, is that right? What a creative idea."

"It is a creative writing class, isn't it?" Curtis smirked.

"Our group has really struggled, hasn't it Tiffany?" The other blond nodded and leaned in closer to Hana and Curtis. "It seems like every time we get together, we don't try to help each other. We just rip each other to shreds."

"It is human nature," Curtis agreed.

"Do you know how your novella is going to end? Is it a cliffhanger, or does it leave with a promise of a sequel?" Tiffany asked.

"I am not sure how it is going to end," Hana answered. "We are waiting for Baxter's lead."

"That's him, isn't it? The one wearing the stocking cap?" She pointed to where Baxter was leaning backwards, forearms resting on the padded bar. Three locals stared at him from the side, but Baxter failed to notice. His foot kept time with the music and his mouth mumbled the wrong lyrics.

"Yes."

"Has he done a lot of writing before?"

Hana sipped her martini and smiled over the rim. "No, no, I would not say that."

"I wish our group was like yours," Janey sighed. "You guys just sound like, like, you have so much fun…"

Curtis half-smiled and pondered Baxter. Whatever he was thinking was lost in the increasing wall of noise at the Catamount. Lisa continued to select more songs at the jukebox while the conversation level rose with alcohol consumption. After a few more drinks, others moved out onto the dance floor with Lisa, Murray, and Professor Mangall.

When Baxter finally noticed Curtis' gaze, he saluted him with his glass and took a drink. It was good to have something cool to drink. His head was getting hot, but he was loathe to reveal his shaved skull. Finally, believing it dark enough to hide his baldness, he slowly removed the stocking cap. For a few moments, no one noticed. But then, a student pointed at him and began laughing. Baxter reddened and replaced the cap, but not before one of the locals also spotted him. Don nudged Dean who shook his head and muttered something to him. They both motioned to Todd who squinted in Baxter's direction. Just as Todd was about to walk over to Baxter, three students, already at least a sheet and a half to the wind, brushed past the trio of locals and semi-circled in front of Baxter.

"Hi." The young man's voice was high pitched and pinched in a way that made Baxter feel as if he should scrunch up his nose. The young man had a drink with an umbrella in it. "We wanted to thank you for inviting us tonight. This is just so fabulous."

Baxter wasn't quite sure how to respond. "Uh, you're welcome, although it wasn't me that invited you. It was Curtis."

They turned. "Oh, that handsome older man there? The one with his arm around the blonde lady."

"Yes."

"He looks like he would be a good writer."

"What does a good writer look like?" Baxter asked.

Chapter 25

The young man swayed his shoulders. "I don't know. Handsome, or beautiful, I guess. Smart, you know."

According to that definition, the young man was going to fall short of a Pulitzer. "And what about me? Do I look like a writer?"

The young man smiled awkwardly. "If I have a few shots, you might."

"I think I've reached my limit tonight," said Baxter.

"Oh, come on," the young man pretended to slap him on the shoulder. "Live a little."

Then, a short Hispanic girl spoke. "I see you've been in a gang.".

"What?"

"Your tattoo. Which gang were you part of?"

Baxter cleared his throat uncomfortably. "I wasn't in a gang. It's just a little tattoo. I got it the other day."

"For what reason? Who'd you lose?"

"I don't understand what you mean?" Baxter said.

"Leave him alone Bri," the young man said. "He obviously doesn't know what you're talking about."

Bri frowned and moved closer to Baxter to look at his teardrop tattoo. "My *hermano* is in a gang. He's way out west in Pittsburgh. He told me that when someone gets a teardrop under their eye, it means…"

"It means what?"

"You know."

"No, I don't. Tell me."

Bri sneered at Baxter. "Don't be playin' me. I know about this. You betta be careful carryin' that kind of ink."

Suddenly, Baxter felt a nauseous sense of fear flying like a bat in his stomach. It was one thing to think badness was an ideal worth striving for; it was another thing entirely to be confused with someone who actually *was* bad. "It's henna," he said.

"It's what?" she responded.

"Henna. Temporary."

Bri stepped back. "Oh, that ain't good, 'migo. Don't let nobody see that if you ain't intendin' what you mean."

Baxter felt adrenaline surge, and his heart palpitated. "I still have no idea what you're talking about. I went to a henna tattoo artist and asked them for something that would make me look tough. She kind of sized me up and laughed. And when she was done, I had this stupid teardrop under my eye. I thought she was making fun of me!"

"You best be sayin' yo prayers *Malito*," Bri walked away with her friends.

"But what does this tattoo mean? Please!"

Abruptly, with a flick of their wrists, the trio left and were replaced by a very different threesome: Don, Todd and Dean. They, too, blocked off his exit. Don, the eldest, stood in the middle, but it was Todd who seemed the most menacing as he towered over Baxter and his compatriots.

"Hello," Baxter squeaked.

"Who do you think you are?" Todd asked.

"Excuse me?"

"We just heard that guy say you were the one who invited everyone in here tonight to ruin our peace and quiet. Is that true?"

"No! No! It was that old guy over there. Honest!" Baxter pointed at Curtis who was still lolling in the booth with Hana and the two young women. Curtis waved at him. Baxter tried to motion that he was in trouble.

They turned as one to look at Curtis. Curtis waved again. They scowled.

"You mean that skinny little cupcake in the booth with that good looking chick?"

Chapter 25

"Yeah, that's the one."

"Here, we thought you'd be the bad guy 'cause of your shaved head. What are you, some kind of Neo-Nazi?" Dean laughed and ripped the stocking cap from Baxter's hand.

Baxter helplessly backed himself farther against the bar. "Look, I don't know what's happening here, but how about I buy you guys a drink? Would that help smooth over the situation?"

The three conferred soundlessly, then Don nodded. "We'll each have a Three Wisemen," they said.

"Okay," Baxter released his breath, "Three Wisemen it is."

"Four. You're going to have one with us," Dean said.

"Uh, but the only three wisemen I know from the Orient are, bearing gifts they travelled so far," he smiled lamely.

"It's a drink, stupid," Todd responded by putting a hand on Baxter's shoulder and squeezing. "Dylan," Todd yelled out, "set us up with Three Wisemen."

The bartender's frown was telling. It was a drink one started the night with, not finished. "I'm not sure, Todd."

"Our good friend here, Mr. Toughguy," Todd touched the back of Baxter's head, "is buying."

"Are you all right with this?" Dylan asked Baxter questioningly.

He nodded, but it was a definite 'no.'

Dylan lined up three shot glasses and proceeded to pour three different kinds of liquor into them: Jack Daniels, Jim Beam and Jose Cuervo. "We need a fourth for Mr. Toughguy." Baxter tried to back out, but another quick squeeze from Todd's hand on his arm said otherwise.

Once the shots were lined up, the foursome faced each other. "Now, Mr. Toughguy, what are we going to drink to?"

"You know, according to Professor Mangall, you should never end a sentence with a preposition."

"Huh?" Dean's face was an ignorant grimace.

"Never mind."

"Make a toast, Mr. Bad," Don said with an alcoholic's grin on his face. His grizzled, chubby mouth stretched over a set of gappy teeth. Don's breath smelled like an ashtray floating on a beer barrel.

Not one to make toasts, Baxter attempted to find the right words – any words that might ease his way out of the situation and allow him to retreat, gracefully or otherwise. But the words would not come. The only thing he could think of was something his father had taught him once, something from the Vietnam War.

"Open the trap, open the doors, if you aren't ready to fight, up yours!" Baxter lifted the shot glass. Don, Todd, and Dean had no idea what to say, but after thinking about it, they all shouted, 'Up yours!' and laughed raucously over the music.

"That's pretty good, Mr. Toughguy," Don said. "Here, I thought you were going to say something lame like 'Cheers, big ears.'" Don lifted his glass and clinked it against Baxter's causing him to almost lose hold of it. After doing the shots, the three locals slammed their glasses upside down on the bar and waited for Baxter. Carefully, he lifted the glass to his lips, smiled painfully, and sniffed it first.

Baxter cringed. "Mmmm, yummy. Smells so good."

"Come on. Bottoms up." Dean pushed Baxter's drink hand to his mouth forcing him to swallow a sip of the combustible liquid. His eyes began to water. There was so much alcohol in the glass he wondered if he was going to be

Chapter 25

set on fire. "Good heavens," he coughed as he waited for the burning to stop.

"Come on, ya wuss," Dean said. "Down it."

"I'd prefer not to. It's just that, uh… I've got to work tomorrow and…"

"Are these gentlemen bothering you?"

The trio turned to find a staggering, swaggering Professor Mangall standing with Murray.

"Who the hell are you?"

"I'm Peter Mugwell, author and professor. And this is my young protégé, Mortimer."

"It's Murray."

"I know that," Parker corrected with delighted irritation, "but I didn't want these buffoons to know our names until after we retrieve Mr. Burnside from their midst."

"Hey," Dean said. "What did you call us?"

"Buffoons," Parker's 'b' sprayed spittle on Todd. "Dullards, dunderheads, ignoramuses, and…" he pointed a drunken finger in their faces. "…jackasses."

The threesome did know the last word, and pigs would fly before they let some little pissant from the University of Vermont call them names, even if they only understood one of them.

"Why don't you move on, Mr. Dictionary," Don threatened with a slight movement forward into Mangall's face.

"It's Mr. Thesaurus, morons. Synonyms are important." Unexpectedly, Parker Mangall put two hands on the pot-bellied local's chest and shoved him backwards against the bar. This turn of events was a best-and-worst-case scenario for Baxter Burnside as (best case) the rest of his drink spilled out of his glass and (worst case) onto Dean's groin.

A Miserable Antagonist

No one could *possibly* have predicted that Parker Mangall, author of *Be Better Than Great: Be the Best*! would escalate an incident (in the very bar which he'd inhabited thirty years ago) from a verbal confrontation to fisticuffs. No one could *possibly* have foreseen that once Parker had shoved Don backwards that he, Don, only slightly drunk, would take a swing at Mangall and unload on his right ear. As Mangall went down screaming like a stuck pig, Murray retaliated by slapping Don open-handed across the cheek. Shocked by his own action, Murray gasped and stared at his stinging hand, and then back at Don who was beginning to round on him.

The ensuing melee was a sight to behold, something that would be whispered about in the pantheon of the University of Vermont for decades to come. Within seconds, Todd grabbed Murray, put his head in the crook of his arm and pounded the crown of his head. Seeing Murray's distress, Lisa hurried to his defense, and kicked Todd in the crown jewels sending both men to the floor. Dean, unsure of what to do next, knowing that striking a woman would be tantamount to some extended time in jail, decided his best course of action was to throw a surprise punch at Baxter. After landing a right fist in his eye, Dean felt a momentary sense of pleasure.

Baxter Burnside had never been punched before. The worst was an unseemly incident with a fifth-grade girl at Washington Elementary School (Baxter had been in sixth grade) when he tripped her in the lunch line after she had called him Baxter Buttside. After she stumbled to the ground, tater tots rolling hither and yon, the young lady took her spilled coleslaw and stuffed it down his shirt.

Here at the Catamount, though, thirty-one years after the lunchroom debacle, Dean's punch jarred him, and he felt a sharp pain in his cheek and nose. Blood spurted as he reeled away from the big man's fist. Momentarily, Baxter's

Chapter 25

knees quivered, and he felt as if he was going to pass out. But then, suddenly, and unexpectedly, something else emerged from the deep well of his emotions. Whether this was courage, outrage, or simply long-held frustration, he pulled himself upright, ran his finger under his bloody nose and studied the carnage.

"I'm a bad guy," Baxter muttered slowly under his breath as his hand curled into a fist.

Dean's contemptible face filled Baxter with an uncommon fury, a previously unknown rage, bottomless, red and horned, shredding his insides on the way up, and he moved quickly. Just as he was about to land his fist in Dean's face, Bri, the Hispanic student, stepped in front to scream at Dean. Unable to hold the force of his punch entirely, Baxter's fist connected with the back of Bri's head which thumped forward onto Dean's chest. Whirling on Baxter, a mask of fury, she launched into a tirade of mixed English and Spanish. Baxter tried to apologize, but while doing so, Lisa pulled him away from the fray.

"Look what you did!" she shouted with both excitement and fear.

"I didn't do anything! Mangall started it!" They turned around to see Mangall curled up beneath a table holding the side of his head.

"You punched a girl!"

"But I didn't mean to. She just got in the way. I was trying to deck the guy who hit me!"

She laughed with reckless abandon. "Your nose is bloody, and your eye is starting to swell up." He touched his eye and winced. "You know what? You look like what Herb Treadwell should look like."

"Ha ha, very funny."

A Miserable Antagonist

Behind Baxter and Lisa, Murray confronted the oldest member of the trio while Bri rounded on Dean once again. Standing like a prize fighter, Murray bobbed and danced in front of Don. The two of them traded ineffectual blows until Mangall crawled between the two of them to freedom. When Don looked down to take a kick at Mangall, Murray landed a punch in Don's forehead. Shouting in pain, Murray whipped his hand back and forth while Don, seemingly in slow motion, toppled over Parker Mangall.

Though the fight had only lasted for a minute, Dylan shouted at the top of his voice. "THAT'S ENOUGH! KNOCK IT OFF!"

Unfortunately, the pandemonium created by the combination of fighting and background music, (coincidentally appropriate – The Eye of the Tiger) drowned out Dylan's shout. Shaking his head, Dylan called the police.

"Are you going back in?" Lisa asked.

"No," Baxter said. "My face hurts."

"Your tear drop tattoo looks like it's gotten bigger." She reached out but did not quite touch it.

"Gee, that's what I was really hoping for."

The fight lost momentum. Todd, whose painful family jewels prevented him from fully participating with both fists, retreated to a booth where he rocked himself slowly in discomfort. Don couldn't summon the energy to pull himself from the floor. Sitting with his legs splayed, he looked pleased, though. Dean was the only combatant with any energy remaining. As he warded off Bri's blows, he tried to make his way back to Baxter, but Baxter and Lisa were retreating to the front of the bar where Barbara, Hana and Curtis watched while sipping their drinks.

Barbara pointed to the chairs beside her for Baxter. "I didn't see this coming," she laughed.

Chapter 25

"It certainly adds a little bit of spice to our story writing, doesn't it?" Curtis commented.

After a few moments, Murray spotted the quintet from his place at the back of the fight and waved. The five waved back.

Without warning, the front door opened, and a pair of uniformed police officers entered.

"Uh oh," Baxter said.

The officers pulled out their nightsticks and moved quickly towards the fighters. They began pulling people apart by the napes of their necks. When Murray spotted them, he stepped aside while they separated Bri and Dean. Once order had been restored, one of the officers unplugged the jukebox. Joan Baez's voice was cut off mid-lyric.

A tenuous truce ensued. "Okay, okay," the taller police officer said as he posted himself between the combatants. "What happened here?"

"He… he… assaulted me!" Mangall pointed at Don who had now pulled himself from the floor and was sitting on a chair. Mangall's left ear was bright red and swollen.

"He insulted us," Don countered, "and then he shoved me. What was I supposed to do?"

"Back away," the officer suggested. Sighing, he put his hands on his hips. "Now, does anyone need medical treatment?" He stared at Baxter who looked away.

"All right then. We'll have to take you down to the station for the night."

"What?" Dean exclaimed. "We didn't do anything wrong! We were just here to have a drink and these college bullies showed up."

The officer scanned the 'bullies.' A professor with a boxed ear. A quartet of middle-aged people, one with a bloody nose and swollen eye. A dozen other college students in various stages of social media posting. Within seconds of the police arriving, Bri had already Tweeted her side of the story and was waiting for likes and comments of support she knew would be coming: *You go, girl. XX strong, baby!*

Scanning the room, he pointed to the brawlers for his partner to round up. "Looks like we'll take you three," the locals, "and you four," singling out Murray, Mangall, Baxter and Bri.

Mangall attempted to contest the decision, but the officer turned away from him. Nodding to his partner who began to corral the fighters to the front door, Officer Coleman called for another squad car for backup.

After he spoke, Curtis called out to the officer. "I threw a punch, too."

"What?" Coleman was dubious.

"So did I," Hana said.

"Me too," Barbara insisted and swallowed nervously. She hadn't even moved from her seat.

"It's very noble of you to stand up for your friends, but lying to a police officer is not a particularly positive thing to do." He stared them down.

"Okay, okay," Barbara responded. "But I helped instigate the fight."

He waited.

"I… I… called that guy a horse's ass." She waved a finger somewhere between Dean and Todd.

"That's not really an offense which would cause me to take you downtown."

"Nevertheless, to downtown I shall go."

The officer shook his head. "Anyone else want to be arrested?"

The others remained quiet.

As the strange conglomeration of pugilists remained stationary, Baxter felt his face continue to swell further.

Chapter 25

Then, the non-speaking officer piled Dean, Todd and Don into his car while the creative writing class remained.

Once the door shut behind the locals, the officer scanned the motley crew. "Okay, what really happened here?"

Curtis spoke slowly. "This may come as a surprise to you, officer, but we're a university class of writers."

"I'm shocked," Coleman responded sarcastically.

"I think it's best if all of us go together."

For a moment, the officer didn't respond, but when he finally did, he shook his head. "Are you all crazy?"

They stared at each other until Barbara spoke. "I'm not sure crazy is the right word, but maybe inquisitive. None of us have ever been to jail before."

"You're kidding."

"Book us, Dano," she said as she winced.

He raised his eyebrows. "All right."

"Can I just call my babysitter?" Barbara said.

Chapter 26

A few extra hours of babysitting didn't bother Penny, Barbara's neighbor girl. To watch Kelsey and Tommy, while Evelyn did her homework, was easy money. They were good kids, a little precocious, but did as they were told. Penny spent most of her time curled up on the sofa on her phone while they watched television. Her cell phone rang.

"How long?" Penny asked. It wasn't like Barbara to be out so late on a Wednesday night. Generally, after the class was done, she was home by 9:30. But midnight, maybe later? What in the world had happened? "Is everything okay?"

Obviously, Barbara was reluctant to tell Penny exactly what was going on, but Penny could hear raised voices and laughter in the background.

"What time do you want me to put the kids to bed?"

When Barbara told her, she checked her watch. It was 9:00. Tommy was already yawning, but still content to keep watching television. Kelsey could stay up until 10, but Penny had never been with them long enough to encourage Evelyn to go to bed.

"Right, well, I hope everything is okay. Text me if you need me to do anything else." Penny nodded as Barbara signed off.

Dropping the phone into her hand, Penny turned to find Evelyn standing behind her. Though four years younger, Evelyn was two inches taller.

"Was that Mom?"

"Yes."

"Is she coming home?" After Penny hesitated, Evelyn frowned. "It's this writing group."

Chapter 26

"What about it?" Penny asked.

"Forget it," Evelyn turned away from the babysitter.

Penny followed her. "No, really, Ev, what is it? What's going on with your mom and the writing group?"

Ignoring her, Evelyn stalked into her room and plopped down onto her bed. Lying on her belly, lower legs stuck up in the air, she produced her phone and stared at it. Penny sat down in the chair across from her.

"You don't have to tell me, but if it helps…"

Evelyn sighed. "She's turning selfish. Hanging out with her misfit friends, writing stupid stories, staying out. What was she doing?"

"I'm not actually sure. She just said she'd be home late tonight."

"Probably play acting at the millionaire's house. She told me that they roleplay stuff."

"Sounds strange."

"Yeah, but…"

"But what?" Penny asked.

"Like, I wish I had friends to do stuff with. I wish I could, like, go out. I wish…"

"What?"

"I wish life was different."

"Life is hard sometimes."

Evelyn rolled her eyes. "What do you know about a hard life?"

"Not much," she replied truthfully, "but the older you get, the more your eyes are opened."

"Says the eighteen-year-old."

Penny laughed. "I guess so."

"I'm going to text her and figure out what's going on," Evelyn said.

A Miserable Antagonist

"Good idea." Penny pondered the younger girl, hoping the storm would soon pass over.

The jail was surprisingly clean, yet still depressing. Plastic blue chairs, connected at the hip by reinforced metal, lined the walls and ran down the middle of the room. Wads of gum were stuck underneath the seats and on the metal. Some chairs were cracked, but they were comfortable in a temporary-holding-area sort of way. In the back corner, vending machines hummed as they advertised bags of candy, packaged sandwiches, and soft drinks. Posters affixed to the back wall gave notice of various 12 step groups that the newest 'criminals' might be interested in. At the front desk, behind a mesh-and-glass window, stood a tired-looking police officer who was yawning into his hand. He had large bags under his eyes, and the fleshiness around his face told the story of countless, mindless, sedentary hours behind that window.

Around the processing area, an assortment of alleged lawbreakers hunched in the plastic blue chairs and stared morosely above them or at the backs of their eyelids. A prostitute wearing mesh stockings, laddered down the right leg, contemplated the ceiling. In another corner of the room, a hooded young man curled into a ball across three blue chairs attempted to sleep. A despondent, white-whiskered drunk, with his head leaning back against the wall, snored softly while waiting to be given his accommodation for the night.

The room smelled of coffee, body odor, a tinge of alcohol, and desperation. As the Catamount contingent was led through the front doors of the jail, Lisa's face wrinkled with disgust.

Chapter 26

Officer Paul Ryan, after pointing the group to their seats, went into an office where, after talking to a jowly desk jockey, motioned towards the group. He seemed to be laughing.

While they waited, Murray excitedly recapped their night, especially enjoying the part where he punched someone. In slow motion, he pantomimed Baxter absorbing a right hook to the face and Bri taking one in the back of the head.

"This isn't funny, Murray," Baxter's voice slurred. His face throbbed painfully. Even his upper lip looked swollen.

"I know it's not funny, but do you realize what's finally happened? We're BAD!"

"We're also jailbirds," Baxter groaned.

"What do you think is going to happen next?" Lisa asked.

The prostitute, overhearing the conversation, rolled her eyes and strutted over to them. She had long limbs, garishly painted fingernails, and facial makeup. Placing her hands on her hips, she snapped her gum. "What are you in here for?" she asked the group.

"We were in a fight," Barbara said proudly.

The prostitute snorted. "You? Where was the fight? At the convention center? Rebellious accountants?"

Curtis pulled himself up to his full height to tower over the prostitute. "This is none of your business, Doll."

"Don't you 'doll' me, old man. I'll whip you."

"You and me, we got no problems, but if you don't go sit your pretty tush back down on the seat, there will be."

"No disrespect, but the people you're traveling with don't look like… people you would hang out with."

"I am disrespected. Go sit down."

She wheeled and turned back to her seat glowering at them.

"You are a pretty amazing actor," Lisa said.

"Sometimes when you don't know who you are, it's easier to be something you're not."

Lisa wasn't quite sure if she understood what Curtis had just said or what to make of his statement. From her perspective, he never seemed to hesitate about what was the best course of action. He was rich. He was good looking. He could do anything he wanted, and she couldn't imagine him struggling with the same difficulties everyone else did.

"Hey, Baxter," Murray said suggestively, "you could have asked her some tips about being a prostitute."

"Shut up."

The officer returned from the office with paperwork. "I need you all to fill in these forms, and we'll have to fingerprint you."

Lisa oohed. "Fingerprinting!"

Once the forms were filled out, they were marched through a locked door into the back holding area. Lisa was delighted by her blackened fingertips while Baxter asked the jailer for some Tylenol.

As they were paraded by the row of cells, they noticed how much the inmates looked like caged animals. A few heavily tattooed men watched them curiously. The women and the men were separated into cells on opposite sides of the room. There were other women in the cell where Bri, Hana, Barbara and Lisa were placed, large, strong looking women with prominent jaws and a full complement of chips on their shoulders. The women stared contemptuously at the four who were about to enter the cell. When the officer unlocked the door and opened it for them, Hana seemed frightened, but Lisa's adrenaline kicked in. She began

Chapter 26

jabbering to the cellmates who, within seconds, had told her to (in no uncertain terms) keep her mouth shut.

"What are you thinking about?" Hana asked Barbara as they huddled in the front corner of the cell.

"My babysitter wanted to know where we were."

"Did you tell her?"

"Would you?"

Hana reached out and touched her arm. "No, I don't think I would. I don't think I could."

"I suppose I didn't really think this through."

"None of us did," Hana responded.

"I wonder if they'll let us out early?" Barbara asked.

"I'm sure they will."

On the other side of the room, Baxter, Murray, Mangall and Curtis were herded through the cell door. They took seats opposite a few disheveled men. A sotted, grizzled old man slept in the back left corner.

Baxter wasn't sure if he had a concussion, but the threat of vomiting was real. The chaotic aromas of stale alcohol and cigarettes exacerbated his nausea.

As they took seats to await their eventual release, a hulking man with large meaty fists, spoke. He was in his early twenties with chocolate skin, and his face was speckled with dark spots across his cheeks and around his eyes. A scar ran from his left eyebrow up to his hairline. His brilliant white teeth flashed as he spoke. "Who did you lose?" he asked Baxter.

"Nobody. We're all here."

The man pointed to his cheek. "Man or woman."

"Look, I'm sorry, but I don't know what you're talking about."

The man's back went up. "The teardrop. Obviously, you haven't finished the job yet."

A Miserable Antagonist

Baxter sighed, uncomprehending. "No, I haven't."

"My cousin had a tear drop. His sister was killed in a drive by. It took him three years to fill it in, but he did," the man said proudly.

"Let me get this straight," Mangall interjected. "Are you saying the teardrop represents some kind of retribution?".

"You mean he didn't tell you?" the man pointed at Baxter.

"No."

"An empty tear drop means that someone close to him has been killed."

"And when you fill it in?"

The man smirked. "You've finished your revenge."

"You mean m...m...murder?" Mangall swallowed.

"It ain't murder if it's revenge. It's restoring honor."

Baxter touched his painful cheek. He reddened at the thought that these men believed he was a homicidal vigilante seeking justice for the death of someone close to him.

He wasn't *that* bad.

Yet.

"Baxter, I didn't know," Mangall said.

Murray put a hand on Mangall's shoulder and squeezed hard.

"Ouch! What are you doing?"

Murray's eyes widened as he attempted to communicate Mangall's need to stop talking.

"How are you going to do it?" The man asked Baxter.

Baxter shrugged. It hurt to shrug.

"You can tell us. Maybe we can help you plan it." He motioned around to his compatriots who were grinning.

"I don't know yet."

"Who was it?"

Chapter 26

Before Baxter could answer, Curtis stepped forward slowly. "Let's just say the man responsible is a banker."

The other inmates hooted. "What did he do?"

"The guy took his brother's house, his car... his lifestyle... until finally he couldn't take it any more..." Curtis let the silence fill in the blank. Baxter Burnside's non-existent brother had committed non-existent suicide. "It was terrible."

"That's low," the man said. "What kind of name is Baxter? Sounds like a name you'd give to a cat, or a parakeet." The criminals laughed and slapped each other's hands.

"It's not my real name."

"What is it? What's your real name."

Baxter paused. Moment of truth time. "Herb Treadwell." Murray, Mangall and Curtis all shared a look. "Herb Treadwell," he stated louder.

"That ain't much better, bro."

"It's the name my mother gave me."

"What happened to your face?"

Baxter's one functioning eye glared at the big man. "Rough night at the office."

The cellmate smiled. "I like that." He stood and moved closer to Baxter/Herb. "How you plannin' to fill in your tear?"

"For the man of vengeance, retaliation is a bittersweet drink," Mangall said beside them.

Murray and Baxter looked sharply at Mangall who had gone back to holding his head. Murray had recognized the quote immediately. It was one of Herb Treadwell's thoughts regarding the method of revenge for Herb against his boss.

"That's good," the man said. "I'm going to remember that. Now, about your tear..."

A Miserable Antagonist

"I want the man to hurt in places he doesn't even know he has. I want him to know and feel every pain I feel." Even though Baxter's head was throbbing, the words rolled from his tongue, speaking the truth of what he felt about Larry Spago and all people in authority. At that moment, Baxter Burnside wanted a revenge against life itself, to slap its cheek, to scream in its face, urinate on its leg. This, to restore some equilibrium to the fairness scale. "I'm going to rob his bank."

The cellmate was surprised. "Oh, that's good. That's very good. Less likely to get caught, too."

"What do you mean?" Curtis asked.

"People who kill for vengeance almost always do stupid things. But those who steal for vengeance, that takes planning."

Curtis leaned against the cell door. "How would you rob a bank?"

"What, you never done that before?" He laughed loudly.

Smiling, Curtis spread his arms. *If they only knew...* "Let's just assume that for a moment."

"Awright, awright. How big is the bank?"

"Average."

"Security guards?"

"One."

"How well do you know the bank?"

Baxter looked up from his hands again. "I've done quite a bit of surveillance."

"Have you covered your head? Cameras?"

"Of course."

The man, who was about the same height as Curtis but almost twice as heavy, approached Baxter. "How many entrances?"

Chapter 26

"Three. One in the front. One in the back. One in the side."

"Employees?"

"Six tellers, three loan officers and one prick of a boss."

The man rubbed his chin. "Any employees' habits that might help?"

Baxter felt the throb of adrenaline stab the pain of his face with each heartbeat. "A few of the female employees go for lunch at 12:30 every day. The boss doesn't really leave."

Shaking his head, the man studied Murray, Curtis, and Parker Mangall. "Who are these guys."

"We're associates," Murray responded.

"Associates?"

Murray crossed his arms. "Absolutely. We're in this robbery together."

"And you told just a complete stranger what you're going to do?"

Attempting to hold his gaze, Murray swallowed. "We're already in jail. What else can they do to us?"

"What are your names?"

"Murray and Curtis. That's Pro… er… Parker."

He studied them. "Somehow you guys have made it through life with tough guy names."

"What's yours?" Murray asked.

"I'm Rack, this is Q-Bert and that's Diamond." Two other inmates laughed and raised their hands. Q-Bert was not quite as big as Rack, but he possessed similar scars. Diamond, a smallish, young Hispanic man, did not smile.

"Interesting names," Murray said as he raised his eyebrows.

"Almost as good as Murray and Proerparker," Rack responded sarcastically. "Now, what's your play? How much and how?"

"We thought we'd work digitally. You know, through computers. It's too easy to get caught nowadays," Murray started.

Frowning, Rack held his chin in his hand. "I thought you said you wanted revenge."

"I do," Baxter said.

"Then stealing his money is only going to trigger the insurance. You need to hit him where it hurts so he can feel it. You need to take his self-respect as well as his money."

"What do you suggest?" Baxter asked.

Rack motioned for his friends to come nearer. "Everything in life is a diversion. You understand?"

"No," Baxter replied honestly.

"Let's say you want something that makes you happy and there's no way you can buy it. So, what most people figure is bullrush - just take it. But it's always simpler when there's a diversion. I'll show you." He nodded to the man named Q-Bert. Rack switched his attention to Mangall who stood defiantly beside Baxter. "What's your real name?"

"Parker Mangall."

"Okay, P-Mang, I'm gonna let you in on a little secret here." Rack put his hands on Mangall's shoulders.

Without Baxter or his friends noticing, Q-Bert moved to the side and suddenly, without warning called across the hall to the ladies. "Hey, ladies, I got a business proposition for y'all." Q-Bert began to take off his shirt. He was ripped. He had abs on top of abs, and the V from his hips to the magic place below was pronounced. He flexed his arms and then popped his pecs. From his position to the side, Professor Mangall didn't know whether to be offended or disgusted. Across the way, ladies began to wolf whistle.

Chapter 26

When Q-Bert started to unbutton his pants, the noise grew so loud that the officer returned to quiet them down by creating a human obstacle between them and the man on the other side. The officer told Q-Bert to zip his pants and the ladies to zip their lips.

When the officer left, Rack spoke again. "Now, P-Mang, what just happened?"

Mangall moved away from Rack and crossed his arms. "Your muscly friend there started to do a strip tease."

Rack shook his head. "Nope. That was called a 'diversion.'"

"From what?" Parker asked.

Rack held up Mangall's gold chain which had been connected to his neck. "Draw the eyes away from the prize and then pocket the proceedings." His wide smile was disconcerting. Mangall snatched at his chain. Rack let him have it.

Chapter 27

"Okay, I feel like I've been here long enough now," Lisa stated glumly as she sat hunched over on the bench. Checking the wall clock, she noted that it was almost one o'clock in the morning. The euphoria of being jailed had worn off. Her backside was sore, she had a small headache, and she was ready for bed.

"Me too," Hana echoed softly.

"How are we going to get out of here?" Lisa asked.

Barbara shrugged. "I don't know! There's no way I'm going to call my ex-husband. I have to get home to my kids. The babysitter will be freaking out."

"I have no one either," Hana said.

Lisa could relate. "I live by myself." She stood up and gripped the bars. "Hey, Murray. Can you guys call someone to get us out?"

Murray was holding his head. A decent sized hangover had set in. "I could call my parents," he said, "but it would take them a while to get here."

"Where do they live?"

"Buffalo."

"What about you, Professor Mangall. Surely someone from the university would help us out."

He shook his head. "I'm not sure I want anyone to know about this little escapade. Some of my colleagues would find a karmic goodness to what's happened tonight."

"Can you try?" Lisa asked.

Mangall sighed. "All right." He called out for the guard. "I need to make a phone call."

Chapter 27

The burly night guard arose from a desk and strolled to the cell. "Okay. You've got five minutes."

The guard escorted Mangall to the wall-mounted phone. "I don't have the number," Mangall informed the guard. "Can you get my phone so I can find it?"

"What's your name?" Mangall told him. Sighing, the guard took Mangall back to the cell, locked him in it, then left to retrieve the cell phone. When he returned, he handed the phone between the bars.

With shaking hands, Mangall located the number of his 'closest' colleague at UV. Daria was 'close' only in the sense that her office was next door to his. Nervously, Mangall waited for the phone to be answered.

"Daria, I'm so sorry to call you at this time of night. It's an emergency." Mangall shielded the rest of the conversation from others who could overhear. Finally, he disconnected the call and ashamedly turned back to the others.

"Well?" Murray asked.

"She's coming, but…"

"But what?"

"She'll only take me, you and Lisa. The others have to find their own ride."

Baxter lowered his head.

"Why?" Murray asked.

"Because the three of us live here in Burlington while you all," he motioned to the others, "have to drive back to Monty. That's about a two-hour round trip with drop-offs. I think I've stressed our colleagueship enough just to come pick us up on a Thursday morning." They all looked up at the clock. 1:23.

"Curtis? What about one of your servants?"

"No, sorry. I wouldn't put this on them."

"What about your parents, Baxter?"

Baxter rubbed his bristly head. It hurt his hand. It was a thought he'd been dreading. What would his parents say? "Yeah, I guess if it's a last resort, but I'll definitely pay for it."

Curtis touched his shoulder. "If they can get us out, I'll post bail for everyone." He turned to Rack and Associates. "You, also."

"What?"

"It's been a pleasure interacting with you. Thank you."

Rack smiled. "You guys are all right."

Baxter stood and put his face between the bars. "Guard!"

A minute later, the same tired-looking officer entered the room. "I'd like to make my phone call."

"Do you need your phone, too?"

"No, I know the number," Baxter responded. The guard nodded and opened the cell. Leading Baxter out, they approached the wall-mounted phone. Baxter thanked the guard who stood to the side.

Sighing, Baxter cradled the receiver in his shoulder and winced. He was afraid his nose might be broken. Only one eyelid functioned, and he was having a hard time concentrating. He punched in the numbers.

"Hello?" his mother's voice was tired, tinny, and wary.

"Hi, Mom, it's me."

"Baxter?"

"Yes."

"I can't understand you very well. The connection must be bad."

"I've got a swollen jaw."

She gasped. "Have you been in a car accident? Mugged? Are you in the hospital? Dear God! Are you dead?"

Chapter 27

He heard her shoving his father. "Burnie! Burnie! Wake up! Baxter is dying!"

"Mom. Put Dad on the phone."

"Sweetheart, what's happened? Oh, my poor baby Baxter."

"Mom. Hand the phone to Dad."

"But why?"

"Because I want to talk to him."

"I can help you, dear. Just let me know how I can help."

"You can help by putting Dad on the phone."

She handed the phone to Burnie. Baxter heard her stifle a sob.

Finally, his father answered groggily. "Baxter, what happened?"

"I'll tell you when you get here, but you can't say anything to Mom. Not a word. It will be far worse."

"Where am I going?"

"Do not repeat this out loud, Dad. I'm at the jail."

"Jail?"

Baxter swore silently as he heard his mother begin wildly keening that her son had been arrested, and she was going to feel guilty about reacquainting him with Jack. "I told you not to repeat it, Dad."

"Yeah, sorry about that, son. I'm still half asleep."

"Can you come pick me and some friends up here? We've had a tough night."

"Sounds like it. How many am I picking up?"

Baxter swallowed. "Four."

"Four! Were you having an orgy?"

The word 'orgy' sent his mother into histrionics again. *Not only is my son a felon, he's a pervert, too! That darn writing group... that actor... I knew it!*

"Please don't give any more commentary over the phone."

"I forgot."

"I really appreciate this."

"Where are you?" Burnie asked.

"Burlington Jail."

His father was silent. Then, he grunted as he got up from bed. "I'll be there in about sixty minutes."

"Thanks, Dad."

When Burnie Burnside arrived at the police station dressed in pajamas, robe and slippers, the police ushered him to the back where Baxter and crew waited. Burnie took one look at his son's face, winced, saw the lack of hair, and winced again. His eyes were drawn to the teardrop. Burnie squinted but couldn't quite make out what it was. Unconsciously, Burnie rubbed his own cheek, but Baxter did not attempt to wipe off whatever the stain was on his. Despite everything, Burnie did not say anything as the officer released the remaining Creative Writing 102 inmates from the cells.

Once in possession of his wallet, Curtis posted bail for everyone. After a handshake and a goodbye, Rack gave his phone number to Curtis in case he ever needed to get in contact for repaying the debt. Curtis assured him that they were all square.

Burnie drove Curtis, Hana, and Barbara to their respective homes first; then it was just the two of them. The passing streetlights cast their glow on Baxter's bruised face. It had been a night to remember and one he wanted to forget. Though the bruises would remain for a while, the next conversation with his parents would take longer to scab over. Over the years, Baxter had rarely rebelled. His room had been tidy; the friends he had were interested in model cars and stamp collections; he never talked back or

Chapter 27

disobeyed. When he left for college, he returned dutifully for weekend dinners, awkward conversations, and left with twenty dollars in his pocket 'for a little treat,' his mother would have said.

When Baxter got engaged to Eris, neither Betty nor Burnie had said much about it. They simply assumed that their Baxter had chosen a nice girl, even if she did not present as one. When the engagement broke off, they were relieved, but once again said nothing. A pothole. A blip in the road. He would get over it.

Now that they were inexplicably driving home from the jail, neither father nor son knew quite what to say until Burnie broke the ice. "You okay?"

"Yeah."

"You want to talk about it?"

"I suppose it's probably necessary."

Burnie shrugged as his hands gripped the steering wheel. His jaw was set, but not with anger. "If you want, I'm here to listen. You're a grown man. You make your own choices."

"Thanks, Dad."

They drove in silence for just a little longer before Baxter began to explain. "We went to a bar and got in a fight."

"Huh," his father said.

"I got this tattoo."

"Huh," he repeated. "Is that what that is? I thought it was a big zit."

"I wanted to… I don't know how to put it… be…"

"Your own man."

Baxter glanced at his dad through his good eye. "Yeah. I guess I'm just tired of being the same old Baxter Burnside."

A sadness crept into his father's eyes. "You're a good man, Baxter. That's the thing. It's not boring to be good."

"I know."

"But it's also a good thing for you to break out, too," he said with a smirk.

"What?"

"I was wondering how many years it would take for you to throw off your chains, do something a little rebellious."

Surprised, Baxter stared.

"You know, your mother and I used to be pretty rebellious, too."

"You don't have to try to make me feel better."

"I'm not," his father insisted. "One time, we crossed the Canadian border with a bottle of whiskey and didn't declare it."

"Very funny."

"I'm just trying to show some solidarity here."

When they reached Baxter's house, Burnie put the car in park. "In the next few days, give us a call. We'll support you in any way that we can."

"Thanks, Dad."

Burnie stopped him just as he was opening the door. "Baxter, your mother tries hard. She loves you very much."

"I know."

Baxter exited the car and slammed the door shut behind him. The sound hurt his head. After entering the house, he found his way to the mirror, examined the damage, and took three pain pills.

Sleep would still be hard to come by.

Chapter 28

It took the rest of the week for Evelyn to face her mother in any kind of communicative way. Despite the awkward, Monday-morning-silence, and Barbara's hopeful insistence that they talk, Evelyn was resolute in making her mother feel guilty. When Tuesday morning rolled around, Barbara couldn't take it any longer and situated herself across from Evelyn at the breakfast table. A bowl of cereal sat in front of the teenager, an impenetrable barrier of crunchy goodness, with her phone positioned next to it.

"Can we talk?"

Silence.

"I was hoping we could both be mature, you know, speak openly and honestly."

Evelyn rolled her eyes.

"What's that supposed to mean?"

Ignoring her mother, Evelyn picked up her bowl, dropped it in the sink, and wheeled to face Barbara. "Mature? You're really going to use the word 'mature'?"

Barbara's face reddened. She hadn't thought about how her incarceration would look to her children, especially Evelyn. "Look, I'm sorry. I wasn't thinking."

"No kidding."

"You have to understand how important this writing thing has been for me. I feel... alive. More alive than I've felt in a long time. When your father left, I felt like I was floating on top of a sewer. You and your brother and sister were on my raft, but it was leaking. Life is changing fast. You're growing up. Your brother and sister need constant attention. I guess I just wanted a break. Do you know what I mean?"

Evelyn crossed her arms. "Am I supposed to infer that your children suck the life out of you?"

"That's not what I meant. You know that's not what I meant."

"What did you mean, Mom? You say that this writing group, and your roleplaying, and your Wednesday night out on the town and ending up in jail gives you life? I don't know how to take that."

"What would you like to know, Ev?"

"Why is it so important to you?"

Barbara was caught in a vise between the life she wanted and the life she led. When Stanley left her, Barbara battled depression and thoughts of inadequacy, self-doubt, and a niggling sense that life was never going to get any better. Which was why she had enrolled in a creative writing class, just like she and Evelyn talked about. There had always been a deeper creativity burning within her which would give her life hope and meaning. When she was young, Barbara had written short stories about a button which went on adventures around the world. Her kids loved those little stories. Stanley's departure erased any thoughts of writing about a button, and her sense of hope sailed away with him.

Amazingly, after her first trek to the University of Vermont, Barbara felt a peace about the decision to leave the kids at home and do something for herself. When the group started roleplaying, connecting, texting, enjoying the camaraderie, Barbara felt like she was part of another family.

Now, after the fateful night at the bar and subsequent jail time, Barbara felt ashamed that she had somehow let her real family down. Maybe it was time to give up the group.

"I don't know, Ev. Maybe I made it into something bigger than it was. I just…"

"Just what?"

Chapter 28

Barbara stared at her beautiful creation and wondered how someone so lovely could have come from her and him. Evelyn stood before her on the cusp of adulthood, arms fastened securely in front of her, feet splayed, standing strong against whatever might be coming. Barbara approached Evelyn and stood opposite her.

"I want to be young like you again."

Evelyn snorted. "Isn't that ironic."

"I love that song," Barbara said lamely.

"Don't change the subject."

"Sorry. What's ironic?"

"That you want to be my age and I want to be older."

"Why would you want to be my age?"

Evelyn shook her head. "I didn't say your age, I just said 'older,' so I could have some freedom, too. I could find people to hang out with, go to college, go to bars, end up in jail." For the first time, a trace of a smile crossed Evelyn's lips.

"Maybe the first three. Jail is overrated."

"Maybe, but that's the point. You had to get arrested to go to jail. I feel like this house is my jail." She gestured around her. Last night's dirty dishes sat on the sink. The countertop had not been wiped off. A basket of unfolded clothes was perched on the edge of the sofa like a moss-covered rock. "I can't go anywhere. I'm on babysitting duty, or homework duty, or housework duty, or mowing duty." Evelyn noticed the hurt look in her mother's eyes. "I don't want to sound ungrateful, but I'd love to get out of here for a night like you do."

Barbara had not thought about Evelyn's perspective. To be the adult in the family, to work and be responsible, was most important, yet Evelyn was even more lonely than she.

"What do you say we take the day off of school? We'll go for a hike."

Pausing to see if her mother was serious, Evelyn nodded. "I'd like that."

"Go get dressed," Barbara said.

Rushing off, Evelyn raced to her room.

As Barbara watched her go, she found a degree of sadness that her oldest was growing older too quickly. Shaking her head, Barbara called out to the two younger children. "Kelsey! Tommy! Let's go! Time for school!"

Chapter 29

Baxter didn't go to work until Monday. By the time his alarm sounded, he was ready to go. Even though his head didn't ache anymore, his eye had turned a plum-lemon color. At least it opened now. The doctor said his nose was not broken, but he would have some trouble breathing through it for a while.

Larry Spago had been indignant when Baxter called in sick on Thursday and Friday. Baxter was told that he would certainly need a doctor's certificate to miss the two days of work. Even though Baxter reminded Larry that he had never taken a sick day before, the manager remained unmoved.

When Baxter walked through the front door, the entire bank stopped to stare. Bernadette hurried out from behind her booth, buzzed the door open, and rushed to him. "Baxter! What happened to your face? A car accident?"

"No, it's nothing."

"Nothing? It looks like you're growing an eggplant where your nose used to be."

"Thanks."

Bernadette ushered him back to his cubicle and helped him settle in. "Is there anything I can do for you?"

"Maybe a cup of coffee?"

She nodded. When she left, Larry opened the door of his wood panelled office and strode quickly to Baxter. One hand was tucked into the vest pocket.

"Baxter. I need to talk to you."

"I'm just signing in, Mr. Spago."

"Now."

A Miserable Antagonist

Sighing, Baxter dropped his briefcase under his desk and turned to find Bernadette with the coffee mug. She handed it to him and, without thought, hugged him gently. Surprised, but grateful, Baxter unfortunately spilled a few drips of the coffee on the back of her dress, but she didn't notice.

Walking into Spago's office, Baxter found it dimly lit. The calendar, as always was still open to his semi-nude photo. Baxter was surprised to see that all the other pictures were gone.

"What is it, Mr. Spago?"

"I just wanted to see how you were doing?"

"Excuse me?"

"I've been worried about you…"

Shocked and slightly wary, Baxter took a step back. "I must have missed your caring phone calls while I was gone."

"I didn't want to interrupt you."

Hmm. "Thank you for your concern, Mr. Spago. May I go back to work now?"

"Just a minute, Baxter." Spago motioned for Baxter to sit, but he declined. "I know that we haven't had the closest relationship during your years of employment, but I just wanted you to know how much I appreciate your hard work and diligence."

Alarm bells rang like klaxons in Baxter's head.

"I'm sorry for coming down a little hard on you last week, but I was feeling a little extra pressure. Work has been piling up for me."

Baxter surveyed the office and his bare desk. The computer had not been turned on, and he had obviously cleaned since last week. There was something very different about the room, but Baxter couldn't quite place it yet.

"Now that you're back, I think things can return to normal."

Chapter 29

"Is there anything else?"

Spago pretended to think. "No, I guess that's it. Anything that we at Last National can do for you?"

Baxter held Larry's gaze. He was hiding something. "There is one thing," Baxter said.

"Name it."

"I still want to be assistant bank manager."

Larry laughed and coughed at the same time. "Well... I... I'm not sure. That might have to be a Board decision."

"It's not. I checked."

"Well, we'll certainly look into it." Larry's intonation meant the opposite.

"The last time you called me into your office, you seemed to think I had managerial material. You told me to fire Carmen to prove myself."

"Er... you might have... um... misconstrued my words."

"No," Baxter said, feeling unusually confident. "Point blank you said I should go out there and fire her."

"Look, Baxter, if your request has something to do with blackmail, I'm not sure I appreciate the implication."

Baxter inched closer to Spago. The bank manager had never seen Baxter in this state, and it shocked him. Larry felt himself taking a few steps backwards as Baxter's face drew near. "It has nothing to do with blackmail. I took your words to heart, and I feel like I'm ready for the leap. After all these years, I believe I've grown into the role."

"Yes, okay, whatever will make you happy. We'll get some paperwork together." Spago's hasty retreat pounded spikes into Baxter's wariness.

"Why do I get the feeling there's something you're not telling me?"

A Miserable Antagonist

"Please, Baxter," he spread his arms as if about to embrace Baxter. "When have I ever withheld information from you? Now, go out there and knock them dead."

By walking to the office door and holding it open, Larry signaled that the meeting was over. Retreating quickly, Baxter scanned his boss' face searching for any lies he might have missed.

When he reached his cubicle, Bernadette was there waiting for him.

"I thought you were going to get fired," she said.

"For what?"

"For all these changes going on with you. Your hair – or lack thereof, I guess; the tattoo, your general... I don't know... demeanor." She bit her lip as if the assessment would be offensive.

"What do you mean?"

She leaned in towards him and whispered. "Who are you? What's with the tear drop on your cheek? Did you get beat up? Why did you drop that hot girlfriend?"

"How did you know about that?"

Suddenly, Bernadette looked very guilty. "I shouldn't have said anything."

"Come on, Bernadette, tell me. What's going on?"

"We've got to get back to work."

Perplexed and frustrated, Baxter opened his computer and began his morning routine. When the 9:00 bell rang, Baxter waited for patrons to arrive. For one of the first times in his life, Baxter noticed how much people were influenced by appearances. Generally, Baxter assumed his own bias against people like Rack or Q-Bert or even Larry Spago himself was subliminal and his reactions were spontaneous. That people steered away from him because of his looks, and now especially his bruised face, was because of a noticeable 'wrongness' or 'rebelliousness,' even a 'badness.' This last

Chapter 29

thought made Baxter smile. Like Anakin becoming Vadar, or Lex becoming Luthor, Baxter was becoming Treadwell.

Kind of.

"What are you smirking about?" Bernadette asked.

"Just thinking."

"About what?"

"Oh, you know…"

Bernadette swiveled towards him. "Actually, I don't. Come on, tell me."

He faced her. "I'm thinking about the creative writing class." She nodded. "The main gist of the story is that a nice guy turns bad and robs a bank."

She blanched. "Are you thinking about robbing the bank?"

"No!"

She apologized and motioned for him to continue.

"As our team has been developing the plot, I've tried to help them with how it could actually work. Notice Chad over there." They glanced in the direction of the security guard who was yawning into the back of his hand. "Talk about someone who would not be able to stop a robbery. He can't even stop his yawn." Chad checked his watch and scratched his armpit.

"And then there are the tellers. None of them pay much attention to what's going on around them. They count money, sign forms, but are they aware that people could get in behind them?"

Bernadette shivered. "I've seen bank robbery movies where the robbers come in and shoot the ceiling." She looked up at the lights. "And then we'd all have to lie on the floor. I'd be afraid I'd pee my skirt."

Unconsciously, Baxter looked down at her outfit. Red flowers patterned the skirt and blouse. *Had she lost some weight recently?*

Bernadette blushed.

"So anyway…" Baxter continued, "…think about our bank manager and his - how shall we say it diplomatically – shortcomings. We could have a Mardi Gras festival in the staff room, and he would be oblivious because of his moustache grooming."

She giggled.

"All these things are truly helpful when attempting to describe and write it all as a story."

"What about the cameras?" she asked.

"What about them?"

"Like, duh. Cameras record everything. How will you overcome that in your book?"

"I hadn't really thought of that," Baxter responded thoughtfully.

"You need someone on the inside. Someone who knows the system. Someone who can get things done for you."

"That's a great idea!" Baxter exclaimed and Bernadette beamed. "Now, how would a person go about recruiting someone on the inside?"

As the question hung in the air, the front door of the bank opened. Baxter was beyond shocked to see Eris striding towards him. Holding his gaze for a moment, she haughtily tossed her head and made a beeline for the door behind the tellers.

"What in the world…" Baxter intoned as she paused at the door. No one was allowed behind the tellers unless they, or Larry Spago, buzzed them through. As she waited, she looked up towards the camera.

Chapter 29

Pushing himself back from his cubicle, Baxter approached her. "Why are you here, Eris?"

"None of your business, Baxter," she responded snobbishly.

"I told you not to come here. This is my place of work. And... I thought you were still mad at me. I haven't heard from you in over a week."

She sneered at him. "Nice face."

He touched his eye. Her appearance had made him forget about his. She looked stunning. Her blue blazer and skirt were accentuated by navy blue stilettos with white bows on the toes. Her hair and makeup had been done in a way that made her even more alluring, and yet, as Baxter pondered her looks, his attraction to her was irritating.

"I... it's... um..."

The door buzzed and she let herself through. The sound startled Baxter. Who had let her through?

As she opened the door, she tossed a look over her shoulder. "See you later."

Walking past the cubicles where the tellers had turned to watch, she paused briefly at Larry Spago's door. Mouth agape, Baxter watched the door open, and Larry welcome her inside. The last thing Baxter saw as the door swung shut was the two embracing like young lovers, mouths locked, Larry's moustache brushing Eris' nose.

Baxter gagged. "Did you see that?"

"No," she lied.

"Did you know anything about this?"

"Baxter..."

"You did!" he gasped.

"I... well, while you were gone... she came in and they... talked for a while."

"But when did they meet? Jeez, we were together just last week."

"I didn't want to say anything because I thought it might upset you."

"Upset me?" he touched his chest as his voice rose an octave. "Why would this upset me? The woman who's been living with me suddenly shows up at my work and swallows my boss' uvula." He gagged again. "Should that be upsetting?"

"See? This is why I didn't tell you."

Baxter plopped down on his cushioned stool and waited for customers to arrive. Thankfully, they took one look at him and chose other tellers. The break gave Baxter space to fume. Once again, Baxter Burnside was the butt of the joke. Once again, Baxter Burnside had to bear the cruel brunt of others' egos. Once again, Baxter Burnside was miserable.

As he sat there perched on his stool, something small and fragile cracked inside him. At first, the crack allowed the first whistle of pent-up anger and resentment. Thoughts of victimhood and violation swirled inside of him which created a maelstrom of irritation and frustration. As the storm rose in magnitude, Baxter struggled to control it. Instead of stifling the emotions, he allowed them to course through him, and he felt strangely powerful – almost superhuman. When the storm diffused, the winds behind the anger blew an unexpected calm behind them.

Elation.

Finally, Baxter felt free. The restraints of manipulative relationships were carried away, and now, as the fury of the hurricane left, Baxter experienced a hope for a future he'd only dreamed of.

By the time Bernadette returned to him, she found him humming happily.

Chapter 29

"Have you gone crazy?" she whispered.
"No."
"Are you sure?"
"Quite."
"Why are you humming?"
"Hmmm?"
She repeated her question.
"I'm happy that happened. Now I can move on with my life."
"I don't understand," she responded.
"Neither do I."

Chapter 30

Later that afternoon, as Baxter continued humming the same, tuneless song, while simultaneously stroking the stubbly hair growing on his head, the front door of the bank opened. A mother and daughter entered.

At first, Baxter didn't recognize them. When the others had come to visit, they had stuck out like sore thumbs, but Baxter had never met Barbara's daughter. And it was a school day. As they approached his window, he smiled politely, but stopped.

"Barbara?"

"Baxter." She nodded and placed a hand on the shoulder of the teenage girl next to her. "This is Evelyn, my daughter."

"Hi." Baxter's eyes flitted to Evelyn's but then settled on Barbara's.

"You're wondering what we're doing here…"

"Yes."

"Evelyn and I went for a hike."

"Okay," he responded slowly.

"Is there somewhere we could talk privately." Barbara noticed that Bernadette was watching them.

Bernadette peeled her attention away and pretended she wasn't looking. "I… uh… it's not exactly the best time."

"It's important." She nodded at Evelyn who smiled enigmatically. "It's about the future."

Baxter's eyes widened. He had no idea what Barbara meant by that mysterious sentence. "Meet me in that room. I'll be there in a second." He pointed to the empty conference room.

Chapter 30

As they were leaving, Bernadette poked her head around the booth. "Who is *that*?"

"Some friends?"

"Friends? Is that…?"

"What?"

"Is that your love child?"

"Are you joking?" He scoffed. Bernadette shook her head. "No!"

Bernadette glanced towards Spago's office, then answered. "She's pretty, in a motherly kind of way, and the girl looked at you as if you were a matinee idol."

"Please, Bernadette, come back to reality. Barbara is not my lover."

She raised her eyebrows. "It does seem kind of strange that she'd come *here* to introduce you to your illegitimate offspring. By the way you've been acting recently, it's hard to rule anything out."

"Why does it interest you so much?"

She blushed. "I'm naturally nosy."

"Stick your nose back into your own cubicle," he pointed.

"Jeez, don't be so sensitive."

Baxter ground his teeth and made his way to the conference room where Barbara and Evelyn sat next to each other at the table. Evelyn absentmindedly flipped through brochures about IRAs and financial portfolios. As he entered, Baxter noticed the similarities between them: sandy, shoulder-length hair, sharp collarbones, and slender fingers, even the way they sat – slightly hunched, arms outstretched in front of them.

Bernadette's question about paternity had startled him. Was being a father something he was interested in? The thought of rearing a child, changing the diapers of a child, paying for a child, listening to the whining of a child... did not activate his paternal gland. As he pondered the teenage girl sitting next to Barbara, he could appreciate the effort and strength needed to replicate the species, but Baxter felt strangely content not to have another Burnside running around Montpelier, much to his mother's chagrin.

"I'm sorry for interrupting you at your work, Baxter, but we've got something we want to tell you."

As he sat down across from them, Baxter folded his hands on the desk. "That sounds ominous."

"It all depends on how you're going to take it."

"That, also, does not make me feel better."

Barbara's foot bounced nervously, and her eyes darted around the small room. The view through the window was out into the street where SUVs and minivans were parked neatly in diagonal slots. Each car was spotlessly clean. Across the street, turn-of-the-20th-century shopping stores, brick-and-mortar kinds of buildings, were well-kept and gave off the appearance of solidness. Montpelier was a place that wasn't going to change. It was going to remain just as it had for the last two hundred years. Progress, to a point, would be welcomed, but not encouraged, and the people who lived here would be thankful for the steadiness and routine of life.

"I told her." Barbara motioned to Evelyn with her head.

"Told her what?"

"About the book. About the thing."

"I assumed you would. We're all working on it together." Baxter wasn't quite sure why this was such a revelatory thing to necessitate a closed-door meeting.

"I was so afraid you'd be upset," her breath whooshed out and she put her head down. "All this time we've been

Chapter 30

working on your idea, doing our roleplay, getting arrested, and planning for the…"

Baxter held out his hands to stop her. "Don't say it."

"Sorry." Again, she glanced at Evelyn who was smiling broadly. "I've invited Evelyn to be part of it."

"To be part of writing the novella?"

"No, the…" Barbara's head bobbed backwards towards the bank foyer.

"Excuse me. I thought you implied that you invited your daughter to be part of the… final project."

"I did."

Unable to fully understand what was going on, Baxter leaned back in his chair and touched his spiky head.

"Barbara…"

"You don't understand, Baxter. Evelyn has been such a trooper about watching my other two kids, and she's growing up so fast, and she needs something different in her life." The desperation in Barbara's voice irked him.

"So you arbitrarily invite your teenage daughter to be part of *our* thing!"

"Yes. But it's not like that. It's not *our* thing, right? You said it didn't belong to you, it belongs to us. *Us.* So, if it belongs to us, why not make it the gift that keeps on giving."

"Are you even listening to yourself?" Baxter leaned forward. "You've invited a twelve-year-old girl – forget the fact that she's your daughter…"

"I'm almost fourteen," Evelyn corrected.

"Well, that just means you're a couple years closer to getting out of juvenile detention."

Barbara's jaw jumped. "I think Evelyn could be an asset."

A Miserable Antagonist

Snorting, Baxter took a deep breath and blew it out in exasperation. "An asset? This isn't the CIA, or... or... even basic accounting. This is real life!"

"No, it's not, Baxter. This is fiction. This is a book. This is what you're writing, and what we're doing is creating something different. So people can connect with normal authors."

"But you invited an outsider."

Finally, Barbara lost her cool. "Look who's talking! You invited your bimbo along to our group meetings and look what happened. She now knows what's going on, and unlike my *daughter*, Eris could -and would, if given her druthers - ruin everything."

Confronted with this inconvenient truth, Baxter was speechless. Eris' insertion into the equation, unintentional though it was, was a monkey wrench in the entire plan. He hadn't had the guts to stand up to her, to protect what they were growing; he hadn't cared enough for the group to be courageous enough to deny Eris. Now if Evelyn, a minor, for Pete's sake, was in on the bank robbery, the pressure and risk would be turned up ten notches.

"You do realize that if we're caught, you could lose your kids."

Barbara and Evelyn shared a look. "I was losing Evelyn anyway."

"Jeez, I don't know. I don't know! This has all taken a turn for the whacko. Maybe we don't do the thing and we just write as best as we can. Finish the story, collect our grades, and move on with life." His voice petered out as he peered over their heads to see Larry Spago tapping his watch and pointing to Baxter's cubicle. Eris was standing in his doorway checking her appearance in a compact mirror.

"And then what, Baxter?" Barbara questioned. "Then what will you do? Go back out there, open a few more bank

Chapter 30

accounts, go home at night and pretend that life is going to get better and more meaningful? And what about us? We'll just swallow our chance for something new and exciting, risky, most assuredly, but a way for my family to move out of the doldrums. We can do this."

"Are you going to bring your other children, too?"

"Do you want me to?" Her eyes lit up.

"NO! Of course not." Rubbing his forehead and then his non-bruised eye, he grunted as he stood. "Look, I don't know what you're expecting to happen here, but whatever does happen with your *asset*," he pointed frustratedly at Evelyn, "is on you."

"Agreed." Barbara reached her hand out to shake as if finalizing a transaction. Baxter paused, but then shook. Evelyn copied her mother.

As they left the room, Baxter felt the weight of the world suddenly become even greater on his very narrow shoulders.

Chapter 31

The mid-afternoon sun streamed through the skylight above them and settled onto the coffee table. In the next room, the chef was preparing a delicious lunch of chicken and rice. Anna patrolled the grounds outside giving orders to the gardeners about the hedges and preparing the estate for the winter. Meanwhile, Curtis sat nervously across from Hana who held an old book, *Arsene Lupin, Gentleman-Thief*. Her mouth was twisted into a wry grin. She was unaware that Curtis was watching her.

"Are you enjoying the book?"

"It's amusing, yes."

Curtis leaned forward over his knees. "Hana."

She didn't look up. "Hmmm?"

"I need to tell you something."

Slowly, Hana inserted a bookmark and set the book on the table. "Those words are never a great way to start a conversation."

Curtis rubbed his temples. "I need to show you something."

"What is it?"

Curtis handed her an envelope and she took it from him. There was no return address. "Algonaut? What's that?"

"It was the name of my company."

She raised an eyebrow as she turned the envelope over and opened it. "Do you want me to read this?"

"It will initiate a very difficult conversation."

Feeling panicked, Hana laid the envelope on her leg. "Should I really read this? You are scaring me. I don't want to be scared."

Chapter 31

"Please, read it."

Hana did not like the pained look in his eye. Never before had he seemed frightened, or even disturbed: not in class, not in jail, not once. His composure was one of the things she had grown to love. Love – that word – that most difficult, scary word which meant so many things and implied so many others. Hana knew she loved him and believed it was reciprocated, but people who loved each other didn't hand envelopes to each other.

The paper rustled as she opened it. A cloud blocked the sun momentarily through the skylight. As she scanned the letter, her pulse raced.

It was a suicide note.

"Curtis?"

"Please, finish it first before we talk."

The last line shook her to her core.

Your greed is the source of my death. Know this, your actions will haunt you the rest of your life. I hope you rot in hell with me.

"I don't understand."

Curtis placed his head in his hands. "It was something I didn't want to reveal."

She shook her head, not understanding.

He took a deep breath and blew it out slowly. "When I graduated from college, I had a degree in computer science and finance. As an impressionable, upper-middle-class young man, wealthy by no effort of my own, I had disposable income as I entered the work force. I never lacked for anything. Not growing up. Not during college. Never. To my great detriment, I didn't struggle. I had no appreciation for the small things."

"That seems like a small thing."

Curtis reached out for the letter which she returned to him. He pondered it for a moment before restarting his narrative. "Unfortunately, it was a large thing, and I had no perspective outside of myself. My needs. My desires. My greed." He carefully put the letter back in the envelope. "My company, Algonaut, invested in stocks, but on a scale that the average investor can't even imagine. We're talking tens of millions of dollars."

Her eyes widened and she subtly glanced around the house.

"Through a convoluted computerized process, my company developed software which would buy and sell stocks in fractions of a second. Instead of depending on a financial advisor to buy and sell which could take hours or days, Algo-Trading removed that time frame. In the first two years after graduation, with the money I inherited from my ancestors, I multiplied it one hundred-fold. My net worth, by the time I was twenty-four – and I'm not telling you to boast – was seventy-nine million dollars."

Hana's mouth dropped.

"Like any cocky, opinionated rich boy, I pushed the limits of ethics. Although Algo-Trading is technically legal, there are questionable, unethical opportunities that are tempting and dangerous. As you can see with this letter," he tapped it on his leg, "I went one step too far."

"What happened?"

His eyes fastened on the letter. "One of my biggest competitors was a man named Edwin Casterfield who owned Casterfield Financial. Through one of my corporate spies, I found out that Edwin was going to short a specific tech stock."

"Short?"

Chapter 31

He waved the question aside. "Forgive me if I don't go into the specifics of terminology. It won't help you to understand what happened." She nodded. "Instead of jumping on Casterfield's information, I decided to see if I could program my software to ambush his algorithm. I only wanted to see what was possible." There was immense guilt in his eyes. "You have to believe me."

"I believe you."

"The software worked to perfection. To my great shame, I made hundreds of millions of dollars by ruining him. Edwin Casterfield lost his entire fortune in less time than it takes to warm up your coffee."

"How much?"

"Almost half a billion dollars."

"What? Half a b… Curtis, oh my…!" Her shock was as painful for him as recalling the memory.

"Hana, the money could have been replaced. I could have given him my earnings. I should have, but I didn't. I stole everything from him."

Hana was silent. Her heart was in tatters while her mind was on fire. How could this good and decent man have pushed another to suicide? Was everything he owned, everything that surrounded them now, blood money?

"As we've been working on our creative writing novella, as much as I've enjoyed it, part of me cringes every time we speak of the 'bad guy' as the 'good guy.' I'm the bad guy, Hana." He tapped his chest and repeated the sentence. "I'm the bad guy."

Overcome by emotion, Hana stood. She covered her mouth and walked to one of the large windows on the east side of the house, to the right of the bookshelves. The wind was blowing leaves off trees to the ground leaving a blanket of brown. What was once alive was no longer. Hana's mind whirled furiously. How could she trust him? If he was really broken up, why did he live like this? If she stayed with him, would she become infected by the same kind of greed?

Hana spotted movement in one of the elm trees. A squirrel furiously chewed on a nut and packed it into its cheeks. Hund would have had a field day with…

"Hana?" Curtis had moved behind her.

"I don't know what to say."

"Say something. Anything."

She couldn't turn around. Not yet. "I… It feels like I'm standing next to a different person."

"This is why I didn't want to tell you."

"I'm glad you did."

"How can you say that? I've changed the direction of our relationship. How will you ever be able to trust me?"

Slowly she turned to him. They did not touch. "That was the question I was asking myself."

"Ask me anything and I'll do my best to answer."

"How rich are you?"

"I'll never want for anything. It would take a hundred years to spend it all."

"Do you feel guilty?"

"Every day. Every single day I wish I could take it back."

"But you can't."

"But I can't."

Hana crossed her arms and moved around him. "You made us believe you were so good, so pure. The way you bailed out all the inmates. Did you do that out of the goodness of your heart, or were you just trying to impress us? Impress *me*?"

He threw his arm in the air. "I don't know. If I'm being honest, I suppose I wanted you to be impressed so

Chapter 31

that you'd stay with me. Consequently, as my psychologist says, I'm paying the interest off on my shame."

"He knows?"

"*She* does, yes."

Hana turned towards him again. "How do you live with yourself?"

"That's why I live alone. And I was going to die alone, until I met you."

"Curtis…"

"The first time I saw you, the first time you entered the classroom, my heart started beating again. I convinced myself that this," he motioned around at the richness of his house, "would overcome any reservations regarding the fact that I'm so much older than you are. To my utter shame.

But then, I realized I would give it all up for you. Every dime. Every book. Every nook and cranny in this house, because I suddenly knew that none of life was worth living without you."

A tear dripped down her cheek. She didn't want to be manipulated, but he seemed so sincere. Was he acting?

"Hana, I'm asking you to forgive me. I need someone to forgive me."

"What you are asking is impossible. I can't forgive you for a dead man."

"No, but you can forgive me for deceiving you."

Torn, Hana pondered her options. If she left now, not only would she lose the man she was falling in love with, but she would lose the creative writing group. If she stayed, she would always wonder if he was hiding things from her.

"I don't know," she said honestly.

He sighed. "It is not my place to convince you, but I must tell you, everything about our writing group has been a sheer joy. Even the arrest. The acting, the roleplay, kissing you. Even if I died tomorrow, I would be happier than I have been since I received that letter in the mail." He pointed at the coffee table.

"Curtis, I…"

"Yes?"

"I forgive you." The words poured out of her heart as much as rolled off her tongue. Her husband would never have admitted guilt much less sought forgiveness. She had seen Curtis' kindness and beauty. The past was the past. If she could be part of his present, she would, for as long as it would last.

"Are you sure?" He closed the distance between them.

She nodded and wiped the tear from her eye. "You stole Edwin's life from him, but you won't steal mine. I know that because you told me the truth. Lies are the greatest robbery because they steal our hope and our courage to lead exceptional lives." Reaching out for him, she grabbed his face in her hands. "I love you."

Their love was sealed with a second, first kiss.

Chapter 32

Murray's eyes narrowed as he pondered the teenage girl sitting in *their* circle. Although Curtis' house was lit up like Christmas, the mood inside was far from festive.

"No offense, Barbara, but you should have consulted us before inviting your offspring into the circle of trust."

"She has a name, Murray. It's Evelyn."

"I'm just saying that involving a minor complicates things immensely." He pointed at Baxter. "You have to agree with me there, right?"

"While I agree in principle, I also had my eyes opened to the scope of what we're doing and how it has influenced all our lives. Including Evelyn's."

"What are you talking about?"

Baxter stood and found his attention momentarily captured by the painting of Curtis' grandparents, stern faced, judgemental, full of dark determination and condemnation, yet imperceptibly marked by the minutest, impish grins, as if they had gotten away with something of which only the painter knew. "No one, save Barbara, has other people who rely on them. Curtis, other than your servants, has no family to speak of. Hana, you're a widow. Lisa and Murray, you've got parents or siblings and long-lost relatives stashed away somewhere, but you never really talk about them. I have parents, but I'm a middle-aged bank teller with no real attachments. Except now, with you guys."

The others acknowledged this, but remained silent, waiting for him to finish. "Barbara's got kids, and she's decided that this opportunity will help her family, not harm it. So, I'm willing to concede the risk and continue with our planning." He paused and turned slightly as if trying to figure out how to tell them the worst news.

"It's not Evelyn's appearance that will lower the percentage of success for our mission, it's someone else…"

Concerned looks turned up towards him.

"Who?" Hana asked.

"Eris."

"What about her? You broke up with her, which was a good thing, I thought."

Shamefacedly, he nodded. "It's a very good thing for me, but not for us."

"That doesn't make any sense," Murray said.

"I'm sorry, you guys, but when I spurned Eris, she retaliated. As of last week, Eris began a relationship with Larry Spago. My boss."

The room erupted in noise. Murray threw up his hands in disgust. Lisa grabbed the hair at the sides of her head and then released it to work off the last bit of her fingernails on her right hand. Hana covered her mouth as she murmured to Curtis. Strangely, Curtis was the only member of the group who seemed unmoved by Baxter's revelation.

Baxter nodded at him.

"Okay," Curtis said emphatically, "now that we've got it out of your system, it's time to move forward."

"But Eris has seen all of us. She'll probably guess what we're doing. If she happens to be at the bank when this is all going down, we're in deep sh…" Lisa punched Murray in the arm and nodded at Evelyn.

"Deep schnapps."

Evelyn wrinkled up her face. "I'm almost fourteen. I'm not a baby. I have heard profanity before."

"From her father, of course."

Chapter 32

Curtis motioned for Baxter to sit down. "Let's regroup and think this through. We can still go ahead."

"How?"

"I wrote some things down." Reaching to his side, he pulled out a sheaf of paper and distributed the pages to the circle. "Let's talk through this."

Herb Treadwell stared at himself in the bathroom mirror. Although he had done this many times before, the backlit reflection revealed someone who had been stifled for far too many years. Reaching out to touch his own image, Herb wondered if the person in the mirror was his true self – the Herb who was strong and confident, the Herb who could make things happen and learn from mistakes.

Outside the bathroom door, the bank's usual noises continued to hum. People shuffled in with their money and shuffled out with their false sense of security. Herb felt sorry for them. It wasn't their fault that they had put their trust in this bank, in this institution led by a heartless and arrogant jerk.

But Harmony had to pay. There is always a reckoning for sins.

As the reflection's face shifted to the plan, the timing and execution, Herb thought deeply about misdirection and its necessity for success. Harmony need only take her eyes off the wheel for just a few moments and her life would go up in smoke.

"That's all well and good," Lisa said, "but what does this writing have to do with finishing the book?"

A Miserable Antagonist

Baxter tapped the set of papers. "When we were in jail, Rack said that the best way to cheat someone was by misdirection. Take their eyes off the thing they were supposed to be watching and replace it with something more distracting. When Q-Bert removed his shirt, everybody watched – even Mangall – which led to Mangall getting his necklace stolen. Now, on a much grander scale, we're going to have a different set of misdirections so that Herb Treadwell can make off with Harmony's treasure."

"What misdirections?" Lisa asked.

"Remember when we were doing roleplay and each of us had a character to portray? We'll do it again – this time, for keeps."

"I don't understand."

Baxter smiled. "We're actually going to roleplay robbing the bank. In my bank."

They stared at him dumbfoundedly. Baxter Burnside had lost his mind.

"There's no way the bank would ever let us do that." Hana's voice quavered as she spoke.

"They'll never know."

"What?" The rest of the group asked the question at the same time.

"One night, we'll go in and pretend to 'rob the bank,'" he used quote fingers, "but I'll have all the cameras turned off, so it's just us."

"Do you have access to the cameras?" Murray asked.

"Not yet."

"And how do you plan on getting access?"

"I start as assistant manager as of tomorrow."

"Really? Congratulations!" Lisa clapped lightly. "How did you do it?"

Chapter 32

"I twisted Spago's arm by telling him that what he was doing with my former girlfriend was highly unethical and that I'd mention it in a letter to the Board of Directors."

"Uh, that's blackmail," Barbara countered.

"What's good for the goose is good for the goblin."

"That's not a correct use of that phrase, Baxter," Murray said. "What's good for the goose is good…"

"NOT the point," Baxter interrupted. "The point *is* that we all will do the roleplay and then write about it. Isn't that what we've been aiming for this entire time? We need to finish the book. The roleplay will be icing on the cake."

"What are you suggesting?" Barbara asked.

"The end goal is that Herb Treadwell steals something Harmony Collins can't afford to lose. Ultimately, Herb not only robs the bank blind, but steals Harmony's self-respect also."

"And what does that look like?" Murray was exasperated.

Baxter opened the door to the vault of his brain.

Chapter 33

Larry Spago reclined in his desk chair, feet up in front of him, studying the fingernails on his left hand while holding his phone in the other. Even though this discussion took place during office hours, 3:27 in the afternoon, to be exact, Larry felt no compunction about chatting with his new girlfriend, Eris Cromwell. When Baxter knocked quickly and trespassed into his office, Larry felt a surge of irritation. He was already regretting Baxter's promotion.

Spago frowned as Baxter neared his desk and waited with arms crossed. To show his superiority, he covered the phone with one hand. "I'll be right with you."

"I'll wait."

Voice lowered, Larry mumbled the words, 'Me, too,' and then, after a second, turned beet red. "Not right now," he said. Finally, he turned slightly away from Baxter and whispered, "Yes, you're very sexy."

Baxter did not respond.

"What do you want, Burnside?"

"I need you to sign these forms, initial here and here, accept these loan applications, and read these documents."

Frustrated, Larry took his feet off the desk and leaned forward. "I assume you've read the documents and verified the loans?"

"Yes."

"Then why aren't you signing them? I made you assistant bank manager so I wouldn't have to do all these things. Can't you see I'm overworked the way it is?"

"Of course, Mr. Spago. But I know you're testing me. I know as well as you do that by specific board directive,

Chapter 33

loans of more than $10,000, and security procedures have to be signed by the manager, not *assistant* manager." Baxter re-thrust the documents to Larry who snatched at them angrily.

"Well, you passed the test," Larry said irascibly as he signed them without reading them. "Is there anything else I can assist you with?" he asked sarcastically.

Don't end your sentences with prepositions, Baxter thought. Before leaving, Baxter paused, not because he needed Larry to do anything more, but he noticed the number of photos of Eris taking up prominent positions of maximum visibility in Larry's office. Baxter supposed he should have felt uncomfortable, but he didn't. But he needed to act as if he did.

"Nice pictures."

"Yes, well… that's the way life goes sometimes…" Larry responded lamely as his eyes landed on a photo of Larry and Eris climbing a rock wall. Their spandex outfits matched nicely.

"I'll leave you to your work." Baxter's sarcasm was lost on Larry whose first move was to grab a few random pieces of paper and stack them straight.

"You too."

As the door shut behind him, Baxter was pleased that his deception had gone unnoticed. One of the papers Mr. Spago had signed was an innocuous document giving Baxter the authority to access all security devices in the bank. Including video cameras. In five days, the team would use the bank as the staging scene for the novella.

"Did you get what you needed?" Bernadette asked him when he returned to his station.

"Yes. He seemed quite willing to sign away his life…" The double meaning made him smile.

Chapter 34

"Tell me again what the dare was and how you got that smudge on your face?" Betty was washing dishes and handing them to Baxter who wiped them with a towel to be placed in their respective cupboards and drawers.

"I've been experimenting with a few things to make me look a little different, Mom. No big deal."

"If you ask me, I think you're having a mid-life crazy."

"If I go out and buy a Ferrari, you'll know it's true."

"You can't afford a Ferrari," she said dismissively.

"Did someone say 'Ferrari?' His dad called out from his chair. "Glorified dune buggies, if you ask me. What you need is a good Chevy."

"Did you and Dad ever have mid-life crazies?" He accepted a carving knife carefully from his mother.

"No, not that I know of. We just kind of gradually got old, you know? We worked hard, married young, had you and retired. That's how we did it in my day. Although there was that one time…"

"What? What did you do?"

She giggled. "One time when you were little, maybe four or five, this must have been back in the 80's, such a long time ago. I think we were living in that house over on Manchester Street. Wasn't that right, Burnie?" He didn't answer. "Burnie?"

"Is the address important to the story?" Baxter asked.

"No, I suppose not. Now where was I?"

"Back in the 80's."

"Ah, yes." She pushed her glasses up with a rubber gloved forefinger knuckle causing a drop of dishwater to fall

Chapter 34

onto her nose. She rubbed it with the squeaky back of her hand. "For once, we decided to go on a date. That was unheard of for us, with your father's small salary and saving for the future. Anyhow, we dropped you off at Aunt Debbie's house and your father and I went to the *casino*." She enunciated each syllable of the word as if it was profane. "We told Debbie we were going to the park." She snickered. "Your father and I, we each had ten dollars, so I went to the dime slot machines while your father played Blackjack. With about ninety cents to go, I struck it rich and won $150. Oh, Baxter, you should have seen me. I started screaming." He stared at her dubiously. "I know, I know, you can't imagine it now, but I was a little less reserved back then."

"Your father heard me yelling and came running. He thought something had happened to me, like I'd been groped by all those perverts running around in casinos. Anyways, when he saw all those shimmery coins lying in the bottom of the slot, he kissed me hard, right then and there. It was our lucky night because your father had just won seventy-five dollars, too."

"What did you do then?"

Betty dipped the last pot in the very dirty dishwater. There were only a few bubbles left and the water was greasy. "We called Aunt Debbie and asked if you could stay the night because we'd decided to rent a hotel room. Aunt Debbie said, 'Are you working on a little brother or sister for Baxter?'" Betty smiled. "So, we found a hotel, oh, what was it called? Burnie? What was that hotel called that we stayed in back in the 80's? Do you remember?"

Because the question had nothing to do with cars, racing, or circuits, Burnie ignored Betty's plea for memory.

"I think it was something like Max's Economy Cabins. Cost us almost forty dollars, too. We bought a bottle of cheap wine, sat on the back porch, and got slightly tipsy while the moon rose over our heads."

"That's it? Your mid-life crazy was to go to the casino and hotel for the night?"

"We haven't done it since," she said as she dropped the pot in his hands. It was noticeably greasy, but he dried it with the towel anyway.

"But why not? Why didn't you do anything spontaneous? Why not give in to some unexpected craziness and startle yourselves?"

"What for? You were unexpectedly enough for us. You startled us with your beauty. We had our home and our family. Burnie had his job and I had you. We were happy with normal."

Baxter felt frustrated that his parents' happy normal had become his unconscious normal. For so long he had wandered through life letting each day pass with a morning yawn and a nightly sigh. Now clearing what seemed to be the mid-hurdle of his life, when he looked back, he couldn't tell one day from the next.

"I guess that's why I got a tattoo, Mom. I wanted something considerably different than normal."

"And your purple eye? Was it a fight?"

"If I tell you this, will you let it go?"

"Of course."

Baxter knew that once he told her, it would be indelibly recorded, etched in the stone fortress of his mother's memory. She would bring it up and replay his confession like someone else bringing out slides from their trip to Disneyworld.

He proceeded to tell her (almost) every detail of the fated night at the bar. Starting with the book, Mangall's interaction, Curtis' invitation, the locals, and a fist to the cheek (he didn't include his own inadvertent handiwork on

Chapter 34

the back of Bri's skull), to their momentous time in the jail cell. After each successive part, her eyes widened further.

"Then, not long before we were about to be released, these two other guys in our cell talked to us about criminal activity." Betty gasped. "It was because of my tattoo that they talked to us in the first place."

Betty took in the whole story before she pulled the plug in the sink, yanked off her rubber gloves, and turned them upside down on the counter. They looked like twin rooster combs.

"Why didn't you want to tell me?" she asked softly.

Without warning, Burnie appeared behind them. Slowly, he approached, and as Betty fell silent, he put his hands on her shoulders and smiled. "It was our turn to protect you, sweetheart. At that moment, you didn't need to know because it would have only caused you grief."

"But the not knowing was even harder. He's my son, for criminy sakes."

"He's also his own man, and doing a pretty good job of it, too."

Surprisingly, Baxter felt tears in the corners of his eyes. In the most awkward of three-person hugs, they embraced and began to laugh. Releasing each other, they backed away.

"Now, tell me about this book. I want to know how it's coming."

"Novella, remember? We've decided that we're going to rob a bank."

"WHAT?" Betty's face blanched.

"Not really, Mom. We're going to act it out so that all of us can write about it. That way, we can take the best description and add it in."

A Miserable Antagonist

"You're going to act it out?" Her face was incredulous.

"At Last National."

Betty looked at Burnie who was grinning.

"Sounds like fun, doesn't it?" Burnie said.

"I suppose so," she said. "But you're not actually robbing the bank, right?"

"Why would we do that?"

"Because you're having a mid-life crazy."

Baxter laughed nervously.

"Can we be involved?" she pointed from her chest to Burnie's who looked inordinately surprised.

"Uh… in what way?"

"We could do something, right Burnie? Maybe we could hold a camera or something. Or, we could play a part?" Betty seemed to have startled herself.

"You want to be part of the bank robbery."

"You said it was fake bank robbery. Maybe it's time for our second mid-life crazy."

Baxter raised his eyebrows. "I'll talk to the others, but maybe we can slot you in for something."

"We'll do anything, won't we, Burnie?"

Burnie Burnside was no longer grinning. It was one thing for his son to step out of said comfort zone; it was another for Burnie to do it. Acting had never been Burnie's thing. He was a responsible, this-is-how-it-is kind of person. But if his wife wanted to do it, well, now would be the time to do it.

Chapter 35

No one, not Baxter, nor any of the other conspirators, expected Eris to hold court at Last National Bank, Montepelier, on Monday, the day before the fake 'heist.' As the other conspirators went about their daily business, Baxter shook his head as Eris waltzed through the tellers' gate in a particularly fetching number: cream business suit, matching shoes and a net-like hat that drew attention to her perfectly coiffed hair.

"She's still really hot," Bernadette stated as her eyes followed Eris waltzing across the front of the bank. It was blatantly obvious that Chad the Security Guard agreed with Bernadette's assessment.

"More like she's *in* heat," Baxter muttered.

"Look at her legs. Holy Mojo. I wish I had legs like that."

Baxter had had enough of Bernadette's physical appraisal of his former girlfriend. "You've got lots of things going for you that she doesn't."

"Like what?"

"You've got interesting hair."

She stared at him.

"That's a compliment."

"No, it's not. It's like if someone asked you if they were fast and you said, 'Well, you're wearing some nice shoes.' Not exactly a ringing endorsement for speed."

Baxter studied Bernadette attempting to come up with anything that might compare favorably with Eris. Indeed, Bernadette had interesting hair. It was so springy it looked as if she weaved tiny Slinkys into them. Although some would have considered her pudgy, Bernadette had a lovely face and nice eyes. He told her so.

She blushed. "I think that's the nicest thing you've ever said to me, Baxter."

"I'll have to do it more often."

"Still, I think I'd trade my interesting hair, oblong face and friendly eyes for that smokin' hot body."

"You also have a very nice person…"

"Don't say it!" she held up a hand and stopped him. "It's the kiss of death. Whenever someone tells me I have a nice personality, that means I come across like a puppy. I'd rather you tell me I'm a witch with a capital 'B.'"

"Alright, you're a b…"

"Baxter," she warned, "I was sharing it as a figure of speech. Don't even think about it."

"Duly noted," he said.

The morning passed slowly. Because of the anticipation for tomorrow, Baxter checked the wall clock five or six times per hour.

Around 11:00, Eris and Larry exited his office. Larry followed like a puppy. Eris left the area behind the tellers. Larry finished watching her walk toward the front door. Chad tipped his cap to her.

"Burnside. My office. Now."

Baxter and Bernadette shared a look. *Now what did you do?* She mouthed. He shrugged. After locking his till, Baxter followed Larry to his office where he held the door open for him just like he did Eris. The comparison made him shiver with distaste.

"What can I do for you, Larry?"

"Don't you Larry me."

"You seem upset." Baxter's eyes fell on the calendar hanging on the wall. Beside it was now a recent photo of him

Chapter 35

and Eris. She had taken a selfie of them in a small café. Larry was smiling; Eris was licking her lips.

"And damn well I should be. I just found out that you've been doing some things on the side that might be considered detritus for the bank."

"I think the word you're searching for is 'detrimental.'"

"I don't give a flying fig newton about your vocabulary. What in the world are you doing?"

"You'll have to give me a little more to go on, Larry."

"Sit down!" Larry pointed at the chair. Baxter did so while Larry tried to bully him by looming above.

"Now, it's come to my attention that you've been planning to rob the bank."

Baxter's heart leapt into his throat.

Eris.

Attempting to hide his dismay, Baxter waved a hand in the air. "That's absurd. Where did you get this information?"

"It doesn't matter where I got it, Burnside. Is it true?"

"Why in the world would I want to rob the bank?"

"She said it was for your silly creative writing group."

Baxter swallowed. "Who is 'she,' Larry? Is this Eris you've been listening to?"

"As I said, it doesn't matter."

"Actually, in this case it does. Don't you think there might be a conflict of interest between the three of us? Maybe she's upset with me for dumping her?"

Larry scoffed. "*You* dumped *her*? That's ridiculous. There's no way someone like *you* would do that."

"It would be the second time."

Frowning, Larry sat down in his desk chair and leaned forward.

A Miserable Antagonist

"That's right," Baxter continued, "We were engaged to be married, but in the end, I pulled the pin. She's incredibly difficult to live with. I hope you don't have to find out."

His face turned red. "I'll let you know that Eris and I are nearing phase II of the relationship."

Baxter rolled his eyes. Eris never changed. Phase I was establishing her physical superiority and Phase II was always just out of reach. Always around the next corner. *Maybe if you're a good boy, I'll let you show me off to your friends.* "Sure. Whatever you say."

"Now, back to the real issue at hand. Are you, or are you not, planning to rob the bank?"

"Not."

"How can I trust you?"

"Look, Larry, you made me assistant bank manager because you wanted me to help you with your workload. That was one week ago. Suddenly, you start making out with my ex-girlfriend, and you can't trust *me*? Sounds like you've got it backwards."

"Do not insult my intelligence!" Larry shouted.

"I'm not. There is no possible way I would do anything to jeopardize my job here. I've invested far too many years of life to throw it away on something so stupid as robbing it."

"I'll still be watching you, mister."

As Larry Spago continued his frontal assault to intimidate him, Baxter felt a surge of power. Somehow, he could read fear in Larry's eyes. Baxter was breaking his boss' hold on him and thrusting himself into a brighter world. Larry could feel his power waning.

"Your vigilance is noted."

Larry appeared as if he wanted to respond, but decided not to. "You're free to go do your job."

Chapter 35

"Thank you."

When Baxter returned to his cubicle, Bernadette leaned over to him. "What was that about?"

"Larry has erectile dysfunction."

A bray of laughter erupted from her lips, and she covered her mouth quickly. "Are you serious?" she whispered.

"No, of course not."

"So then what was it about?"

"Doesn't matter, Bernadette. Time will reveal all."

Chapter 36

On the way to the Schachman residence, Evelyn studied her mother's expression. Although wrinkles were rapidly appearing around the corners of her eyes, as if her face had been soaked in salt water far too long, she seemed happy.

Fortunately, Penny had been willing to babysit the two youngest again for 'an emergency night out.' Monday nights were usually a no-go for nocturnal activities, but when questioned why and where they were going, Barbara announced to Penny that they were doing some mother/daughter bonding.

"You look excited," Evelyn said. It was mostly dark in the car, but she could still see her mother's expression in the dusking sun.

"I am. It's going to be a fun night."

"What do you think is going to happen?"

Barbara tapped in rhythm on the steering wheel. *Smells Like Teen Spirit*. "Last minute planning. Hopefully we can do a walk through so that we won't have too many takes tomorrow."

"Are you nervous?"

"About what? About the fake robbery?"

Evelyn shook her head, but her mother didn't see her. "No, about finishing."

Casting a glance sideways. "Finishing the book?"

"No. Finishing the class. The get-togethers. You know, the friendship."

Frowning, Barbara flicked her blinker and turned right. Tired commuters honked and streamed around them. The glow of the business signs reflected through the

Chapter 36

windshield onto their faces illuminating them in a ghostly, bluish light.

"Why do the friendships have to stop?"

Evelyn sniffed. "They always do, right? You graduate from first grade - you graduate from first grade friends. You graduate from elementary school - you graduate from childish relationships. Maybe every stage in life, you graduate from people. Take the next step up."

"That's pretty deep for a teenager."

"I'm being serious. What's going to happen to you when you graduate from your writing group? What's the next stage beyond? Who is going to bring this kind of excitement to your life?"

Barbara had been worrying about that exact question for weeks. When the last 'The End' was written, what would happen to their relationships? Would they slowly float away with false promises of continued connection, or would they grab their final assessments and give a flick of the wrist: 'See ya later, alligators?' Barbara hadn't come to fully internalize how much emotional capital she'd invested in the class, but now that the end was in sight, she felt a sense of dread.

"I guess I don't know the answer to that yet. I hope that we can still get together. Maybe we've got more than one novella in us." Unfortunately, the odds were against it.

As she pondered her mother's words, Evelyn instinctively knew the demand to accompany her mother was to protect her from the pain of losing them. "Yeah, okay."

"What do you think is going to happen tonight?" Barbara asked.

"Honestly, I have no idea. But if you guys dress up in costumes and play act, I'll be so embarrassed."

"We haven't done that for a while."

"I'm just saying."

Barbara turned left and entered the long, graveled lane which led to Curtis' residence. Now that the dark had fallen over them, the trees were ghostly apparitions illuminated by the headlights. They seemed to be reaching out to grab them, to pull them back to reality.

"Whatever happens tonight, Ev, just be yourself."

"It's pretty hard to be someone else, isn't it?"

Barbara sighed. "You'd be surprised."

Betty Burnside was beyond nervous. As she and Burnie were ushered to their cushioned chairs, Betty proceeded to wriggle in her seat until Baxter settled them.

"I apologize for calling this emergency meeting," Baxter started, "but something's happened."

"You're getting cold feet?" Murray asked. "I knew you would."

"No. In fact, my feet are getting warmer, actually."

"What's that supposed to mean?"

Baxter held up his hands. "First things first. Informally, you've all met my parents. Betty and Burnie Burnside - these are the people I've been talking about." The group welcomed them warmly, yet with curiosity. "You would be wondering why they are here." He took a deep breath. "For much of my adult life, I have been the epitome of boring. But over the last months of our creative writing class and our collective literary genius," they snickered about this, "I've found purpose in life. I've brought my parents here because I think they can help. They have been helping me for many years." Betty covered her smiling mouth and then blew him a kiss.

Chapter 36

"That being said, I wanted my parents to meet you, and you, them. The other night, as I was telling them about what we do for our creative writing group, they asked if they could be included in the final project. Our fake bank robbery and subsequent completion of the manuscript."

Murray impatiently waited for Baxter to finish before jumping in. "I think I can speak for all of us when I say, it's nice to meet you, Betty and Burnie, but I would have felt better if we would have discussed their addition ahead of time."

Betty's face reddened and she touched her cheek.

"No offense, Mrs. Burnside."

"Maybe we should go," Betty tapped Burnie's arm.

"No. Please," Hana said, "you will be great additions to the team."

"I just don't understand what part they're going to play," Murray insisted. "Are they going to hold the camera, or…?"

Baxter stopped him. "We're getting to that now. This morning, Eris let the bomb drop to my boss, Larry, that we're attempting to rob the bank."

Gasps.

Betty frowned. "I thought this was going to be a little play, or video, or something like that. You aren't really planning on robbing the bank, are you?"

"No, Mom. But now that Larry is watching out for me, we have to change tactics and…" he paused, "…timing."

"What do you mean?" Barbara asked.

"Before you all arrived, I spoke with Curtis and Hana about it, and they've agreed. We need to push our re-enactment to tomorrow morning instead of tomorrow night."

"But... but... there will be customers there. Real live people," Lisa spluttered. "How can we do that? I thought we were just doing this for the cameras. I'm not prepared for that. I don't know..."

"I'm sorry, Lisa, but I now think we'll have to do it live. It's the only way that we'll experience the *true* feeling of robbing a bank and, if I can be so honest, to feel the full weight of revenge that Herb Treadwell needs. It will accentuate everything and help us immensely with the final project."

Murray appeared distrustful. "This isn't just about revenge, is it, Baxter? It's one thing to write about stiffing your boss, but your ex-girlfriend seems a little more personal. Are we risking our futures for you to stick it to her?"

"I assure you," Baxter responded, "that my motivations are centered exclusively on us – this class."

Barbara glanced nervously at Evelyn. Evelyn appeared excited by the prospect of doing something dangerous.

"But we could get caught! Last time we were in jail, but this time it could be prison!" Lisa had brought her legs up to her chest, knees under her chin.

"We need to go tomorrow," Baxter stressed. "Trust me. Thankfully, there is less chance of Eris showing up in the morning as the afternoon. She usually has some kind of beauty treatment done in the mornings."

"What's the plan, then?" Murray asked.

Before Baxter launched, Curtis leaned forward in his chair and folded his hands between his knees to speak. "We've been working towards this moment for months. From the very first time we roleplayed crimes, we've learned to be adaptable, flexible, and spontaneous. Each one of you," he pointed around the circle towards the Creative Writing 102 group, "has grown in the way you write and the

Chapter 36

way you speak. Remember how Baxter started his first assignment?"

Laughing, Barbara started the sentence and then they all joined in. "Once upon a time there was a bad guy…"

"Now, think of the last paragraphs Baxter has written. Look at how he's changed – not just the tattoo and the shaved head, but the way he carries himself. He's self-assured, confident, persuasive. All this because we helped him along the path of Mr. Nice Guy to Mr. Bad Guy."

As they applauded, Baxter's face flushed with happiness. Betty clasped her hands in front of her chest, so proud that her son was the bad guy.

Curtis continued. "Here we are at the apex of Baxter Burnside's transformation. He has embraced his alter ego – Herb Treadwell. Although Herb won't make an appearance tomorrow, two more people will."

The group pondered Curtis quizzically. "I called in a marker, not that it was necessary," he raised his hands as if an apology, "and invited them to join us for our adventure tomorrow morning. And it will be glorious."

At this appropriate juncture, the door to the sitting room opened theatrically and two very large African American men stepped behind the circle.

"Betty and Burnie, Evelyn – this is Rack and Q-Bert, and they have very special roles to play tomorrow."

Rack and Q-Bert greeted them almost shyly.

"As Rack showed us when we were so fortuitously jailed, misdirection is everything." Curtis reached for the side table and gathered up a small sheaf of papers. "Here are your roles. Study them. Learn them. Tonight, though, while we're here, we'll work out staging. Even though we won't be able to have a dress rehearsal at the bank, I've replicated, as lifelike as I can, what the bank looks like – in my garage. In a moment, we'll go there, but for now, let's look at the parts."

Greedily, each person snatched their role from Curtis' hands and scanned it. Barbara snorted when she saw her part. Betty was confused as to why she and Burnie were playing themselves, but secretly she was happy. Murray and Lisa high-fived each other.

"Where is your role?" Murray asked Curtis.

"Every good production needs a director. I'll be making sure things go as planned."

"But you're our best actor by far."

"Not anymore," he said. "Are you ready for a read-through?"

Eagerly, they nodded.

"All right. Prepare for a long night. It's time to show you the bank..."

Chapter 37

What constituted Curtis' garage would have been luxurious accommodation for most people. Styled as a storage space for his small fleet of vehicles, but more accurately could be described as a home for priceless things, the garage was two levels of decadence. On the lower level, various collectible cars were parked side by side. A Ferrari sat next to an Aston Martin; across from them was an early model Mustang partnered with a Corvette Stingray. As the spotlights flashed, magnifying the sparkling shine of the beautiful cars, the group entered as if it was a shrine.

Burnie had never seen such automotive extravagance. His deep, intense love affair with car racing made him gasp with holy amazement. Like a child who had just had the door opened to backstage of heaven, Burnie rushed to each of the cars reverently touching the hood of each.

"You've got a '61 Jaguar!"

Curtis nodded.

"And a…" he gasped in spectral wonder, "… a 1964 Pontiac GTO."

The others stared at Curtis until Barbara broke the silence. "All right, Curtis, give. Where in the hell did you get all the money to afford these frickin' cars."

Except for Burnie, Rack and Q-Bert, who wandered with drop-jawed amazement among the cars, the team waited expectantly for Curtis to reveal the source of his immense wealth. Even Barbara's daughter Evelyn seemed dazzled by the surroundings and the mild-mannered man – the actor – her mother had told her about.

"Let's just say family money takes you a little farther in the world than one could possibly expect."

"That doesn't tell us anything," Murray said.

Curtis took a deep breath, put one hand on his hip and the other as a plow through his hair. "We don't have much time, so I'll give you the Readers' Digest version."

"What's a Readers' Digest version?" Lisa asked.

Murray patted her arm. "Don't worry about it. I think what Curtis means is that we're going to get the short version, and the long version will come later, right?"

Curtis nodded. "In 1920, my great grandparents owned a bar in downtown Montpelier called Speak Easy Street. They did an extraordinary business. Life was electric. People were making money hand over fist. Socialites were out and about spending their cash and dancing the night away. Especially at places like Speak Easy Street."

"Then, a small group of people thought Temperance was a good idea." Lisa was about to insert her question, but Curtis headed her off at the pass. "Temperance was a movement to get rid of alcohol in the 20's. No sales. Close the bars. Get rid of the alcoholic 'evil' in our country brought about by drunkenness. As you would expect, Speak Easy Street lost its business."

"What happened?" Evelyn asked.

"My great grandfather, angry as a hornet, barred the doors shut, but he kept the recipe for his famous rye whiskey. Into the hills he went, and he began to distill it by the gallon. In secrecy, people from all over New England would show up at the farm and purchase his whiskey. He made a killing."

"And then…?" Evelyn couldn't help herself.

"They earned enough money…"

"Illegally," Murray inserted.

Chapter 37

"Granted, yes, it wasn't on the up and up, but they made enough money to buy the house we meet in tonight."

"Okay, your grandparents gave you the house, but you can't make that much money from rum-running to buy cars like these," Murray said.

"No." Curtis' face darkened. "Because I have a certain financial acumen, I made some investments that paid off."

"I'll say," said Lisa.

"But in everything, there are trade-offs. Some of my investments, shall we say, were not as ethically sound, something like those of my great grandparents'."

"What do you mean by that?" Barbara asked.

"I would prefer not to go into all the details, but the ramifications of the last deal, though it netted me a lot of money, caused me to sell my business and retire."

"Some people have all the luck," Barbara muttered.

Curtis smiled sadly at her.

"So what you're saying is, you're a bad guy!" Murray's face lit up and he pointed at him. "You're a bad guy!"

"That's enough, Murray. He's a good guy now. The best." Hana wrapped her arm around Curtis' waist.

"I guess you could say I have been rehabilitated. Even if we were robbing Last National Bank in reality, it wouldn't be the worst thing I've ever done."

Silence settled over the group.

Lisa placed a hand to her mouth. "But… how could you… so is this, what we're doing here, one of your roleplays? Are we just another diversion?"

He spread his hands. "This is the real Curtis Schachman, and I've revealed the bones in my closet to you. I probably don't deserve a second chance, but I would beg for one. Since I've met you all, I realized I've been missing out on the most important thing – human connection. I'd give all of this up just to spend more time with you."

"I wouldn't give up the Corvette," Burnie mumbled.

"So, Murray, I guess you're right. I'm a bad guy." Surrounded by all the accoutrements of wealth, Curtis' revelation was an open forum for the others to back out.

"Phew," Murray said, "if you only stole money from rich people, who cares? I thought you were going to tell us you were a Ponzi Scheme magician."

The group's relieved laughter echoed in the room.

"It's all right, Curtis. We're all bad guys." Baxter spoke on behalf of the others. "We all have our dirty little secrets."

Burnie's hand still stroked the hood of the GTO as if it were a thoroughbred horse. "I don't care what you've done, Curtis. Anybody who has a stable of cars like this is all right in my book."

"Would you like to take the GTO for a drive, Burnie?"

"Are you serious?"

"Of course. They're cars. They have to be driven."

"Oh, man, oh man, Curtis. Let's not get arrested so we can drive all your cars!" Burnie's face lit up like a Christmas tree.

Rack moved forward to the Corvette. "Can I drive this one?"

"Yes."

Lisa nudged Murray. "Which one are you going to take?"

Murray shrugged and pointed at the Jaguar. "I like that one."

"Me too," she said. "Good choice. Maybe Curtis will let us take it to the drive-in." Curtis smiled in acceptance.

"All right," Curtis chuckled. "How about we head upstairs for our practice?"

Chapter 37

"Good idea," Baxter said.

Curtis ushered the group away from the automobiles towards a central staircase leading to the second floor. Reluctantly, Burnie and Rack pulled themselves away from their respective dream cars.

Once upstairs, Curtis flipped the switch. The lights blinked and illuminated a room eerily laid out, down to infinite detail, a replicate Last National Bank. Six tellers' booths sat side by side in the middle. To the left of the front door was a fake ATM in an alcove. He even found similar aluminum waste baskets. To the right, the bathroom doors.

"How did you do all this?" Lisa asked as she walked through the large room noticing his exceptional eye for detail.

"I still have a few friends from the theater who are always up for a challenge. When Hana and I went there to see Baxter, I surreptitiously took a few pictures."

"But all the stuff – booths, glass panels, computers, even the sofas…"

"What can I say? I'm retired. And rich." He smiled and led them to the center of the room where they circled up.

As they gawked at the layout, Curtis continued. "Tomorrow, as we enter Last National Bank, the setup should be almost identical to this. I haven't included the meeting rooms as they are unnecessary, and those doors over there are where the bathrooms would be located are only for show."

"Ultimately, the goal of this exercise is to experience all the emotions and senses of a realistic bank robbery so we can finish our novella in an exciting and memorable way. Doing this as a mock set up, like a stage play, albeit fun and entertaining, would not present us with the option of danger and adrenaline. Right?"

Evelyn raised her hand.

"Yes, Evelyn?"

"I know I'm new to the group and all, but isn't this going overboard? Just to write a book? Who's going to read it anyway?"

Faces lowered. Lisa pulled at her cuticles. Hana unconsciously stroked the hair on the side of her head. Murray's foot tapped unconsciously.

"You're absolutely right, Evelyn." Baxter answered. "This is so far overboard it's comical. But then again, who in this circle has done anything so outlandish, so… not-themselves…, so not-play-it-safe that they can feel something different. You know, electricity? A surge of fear and adrenaline?"

The only people who raised their hands were Rack and Q-Bert. Murray started to raise his hand but thought better of it.

"What about you, Evelyn? Have you done anything that caused your heart to race? You know, that if you got caught, there were going to be some serious consequences at home, but if you got away with it, you've got a story to last a lifetime?"

She looked guiltily at her mother. "I thought about it. There was a boy in my class. He was very attractive." Barbara's jaw dropped. "Don't worry, Mom. I didn't do it."

"We've all *thought* about things like that. Called the bully a name. Gone somewhere we weren't invited. Fell in love with someone out of our league. Now, here is our chance to actually go through with it."

"Nobody goes to jail for calling a bully a name, Baxter." Murray's voice was pinched.

Chapter 37

"Regardless… Now, let's go through the roles and do a walk through. Is that okay?"

Lisa went first reading from her notes. "Murray and I are a young married couple who have come to the bank to empty out our savings so we can go on a spontaneous holiday. According to the script, we'll be at the cash machine." She pointed to the fake ATM hunched in an alcove of the room.

"Good. You'll be our first line of misdirection. We want to draw all eyes away from the real action."

"Where is that happening?" Barbara asked.

"We'll get to that in a second," Curtis interjected as his eyes fell on Rack and Q-Bert. "Now, Burnsides, how about you?"

Betty cleared her throat and read slowly from the script underlining their parts with her finger. "We are an old couple who wants to talk to someone important about the foreclosure on our house." She looked up from the paper. "Do we have to act old?"

"As old as you can," Curtis said.

"Did you hear that, Burnie? You have to act old!"

"What?"

"YOU HAVE TO ACT OLD!" she shouted.

"What?"

"Perfect," Curtis smiled.

"Then, after we get really upset – I'm going to start crying and Burnie," she touched his arm, "is going to pretend to have a heart attack."

"That's right. While his angina takes him to the floor, a crowd will gather around him."

Barbara jumped in. "That's where I, Dr. Barbara, will enter the confusion and proclaim loudly, 'Everyone stand back, I'm a doctor.'"

"Yes, but a little more natural," Curtis said gently.

"Natural. More natural." Barbara muttered her lines again. *Everyone stand back… I'm a doctor. I'm a doctor.*

"And you're with your daughter who has anger issues." Curtis winked at Evelyn. "Do you think you could do that?"

"Oh, shut up, Boomer."

They laughed nervously.

"Now, as the crowd gathers around you two, Hana and I will stand on the fringe alerting people when Larry Spago makes his appearance. When he does, that's when Rack and Q-Bert make their entrance."

Murray flipped his sheets back and forth. "I don't see their lines in here."

Curtis eased his worry with his hands. "Their role will be a surprise to you. And we want it to be a surprise, so your responses are as real as possible."

"That's not exactly a comforting thing," Murray said.

"Don't worry," Rack responded, "everything will go just as planned."

"So we're all part of this diversion," Murray rubbed his chin, "but what *is* our focus? Who's going to rob the bank?"

Curtis held up his hands. "While all the commotion is happening at the front, Baxter will stealthily buzz me through. I'll make my way to Larry Spago's office and voila! Larry Spago loses."

"How much are we stealing? How are we going to divide the spoils?" Murray asked.

"Never fear, Murray. We'll divide everything equally after it's accomplished. Now," Curtis said and looked around the circle, "let's step this out."

"Wait a minute," Lisa stopped them. "What part does Baxter play? This is his story, right?"

Chapter 37

With a Cheshire-Cat grin on his face, Curtis glanced at the man of the hour. "Baxter's role begins earlier in the day. As the employee/central figure of the robbery, Baxter's task is the most crucial."

"What is it?"

Baxter felt his heart pound wildly in his throat. "You'll see."

Chapter 38

Baxter Burnside studied his eyes in the mirror. Dark, heavy pouches, like old medical bags, hung beneath his lower lids, and his eyebrows were pinched. He'd slept very little during the night, and what sleep did come was embroiled in dreams of cataclysmic failure, jail time, and emergency heart surgery for his father. At 3:00 in the morning, he bolted upright in his bed aware that they had missed one extraordinarily important detail.

Unable to control his panic, Baxter called Curtis who answered groggily.

"Yes, Baxter?"

"What if Eris is there? She knows all of us! She knows my parents! She knows the creative writing group!"

Curtis was silent momentarily. In the background, Baxter heard another voice, a woman's voice asking who the caller was.

Hana.

Surprisingly, Baxter no longer felt jealousy.

"Relax, Baxter. Remember, my theater connections? We've got countless costumes down there. I'll call in a favor for a friend who is a makeup artist. Don't worry about it, Baxter. I'll take care of everything. Even if she shows up, you won't even be able to recognize your parents. You just focus on what you have to do."

Baxter flopped back in his bed and heaved a sigh of relief. "Thanks, Curtis."

"Go back to sleep."

Yeah, right. He tried counting sheep. He tried shooting sheep. He tried eating lamb chops, but to no avail. After he

Chapter 38

pulled himself from bed at 6:00, showered and shaved, hand trembling so badly that he nicked himself three times, he made his way to the bank at 8:30. Twenty minutes earlier than normal.

Bernadette frowned at him. "You look terrible, Baxter. Are you sick?"

This question sent Baxter directly to the bathroom where he stared at his reflection in the mirror.

Maybe you're having a mid-life crazy?

Have you really considered what this might do to your friends' lives if you're caught? Your parents'?

What about your own? There's every chance you will end up in jail.

It's not 'if' you get caught, it's 'when.' This is insane! What are you thinking? You should abort this insanity right now!

Without warning, though, Baxter felt a surge of adrenaline. Something changed in his eyes – a transformation. The fear swirled and morphed at a dramatic depth. Whether channeling his inner Herb Treadwell, or simply experiencing the thrill of the chase, Baxter felt stronger and more confident. He splashed water on his face and prepared to open the door.

This was the moment you were born for. Everything will be fine. Curtis has taken care of it. People know their roles. Relax. Like a free diver preparing for an underwater cave, he took four deep breaths and exited the bathroom.

It was 8:55 a.m.

He needed to be in Larry Spago's office at 10:17.

As nonchalantly as possible, Baxter whistled as he strolled back to his cubicle.

"Well, you certainly seem to have perked up," Bernadette said.

"Sometimes you just have to go to the bathroom."

"What great morning wisdom."

He sorted his desk and then took a deep breath. "Hey, can you do me a favor?"

"Sure. What is it?"

"In about an hour, I'm going back to Mr. Spago's office for a short 'managers' meeting. Basically, he'll give me all the things that he doesn't want to do."

"And…"

"I need you to interrupt the meeting. Get him out somehow."

"What are you going to do in there?"

"I'm going to write him a little note. It's his, uh, birthday soon."

Bernadette frowned. "I thought his birthday was in March. I'm sure it is. He announces it over the loudspeaker."

Baxter's face turned red. "I meant his dog's birthday. I wanted to do something nice for him."

"That's our Baxter. Always the nicest guy in the room." She touched his arm and then her face as if she'd done something wrong. There was a tinge of red, a heat that immediately bloomed red-rose over her collarbone and climbed her neck like a red vine.

Unable (or unwilling) to notice the symbolism of her blush, Baxter felt guilty to involve her in the plan, but he needed to be alone in Larry's office. "Can you do that?"

"Anything, obviously."

Fifty minutes later, Baxter's shirt had soaked up pools of sweat under his arms and his forehead was beaded with perspiration. Bernadette once again asked him about his health, but he brushed it aside.

With heart pounding furiously, he checked his watch, then the wall clock, then his phone.

It was 10:15 exactly.

Chapter 38

Nervously, Baxter approached Larry's door and glanced up at the video camera in the upper right corner of the room. *They were always watching.*

After knocking, Baxter heard Larry's voice through the door telling him to enter.

The décor had subtly changed again. Where there used to be more masculine effects, there were now a few more feminine touches. A vase in the corner. A small black statuette of a naked woman in repose on the edge of his desk. Anyone else save Baxter would have assumed nothing, but Baxter knew firsthand Eris' *modus operandi*. If unchecked, Larry's clothing would begin to change. And if they were all lucky enough, the moustache would come off. Eris detested facial hair. It was obvious already that he'd had his chest waxed. Baxter hoped it was painful. As Baxter approached, the smiling face of Larry's Speedo modeling calendar caught his eye. Baxter swallowed, and his thoughts snagged on the fact that Larry's personal safe was located directly behind the calendar.

Larry, wearing a three-piece suit with a chain fob hanging from the pocket of his vest, stood arrogantly behind his desk, one fist planted on his hip pushing back his jacket. It appeared staged as if he had practiced standing like that.

"Take a seat."

Baxter did.

"Anything I should know about?" Larry asked.

Gritting his teeth, Baxter shook his head. From a purely managerial perspective, Larry should never have had to ask the question. "No."

"Are you sick?"

"Why do you ask?"

"You're all sweaty." Larry grimaced.

"Just warm."

"Now, about yesterday. I have to..." Baxter thought that, for the first time, Larry Spago was about to apologize, "... clarify my comments from yesterday. Eris and I had a talk about it last night over dinner, and I think we've come to a conclusion. I believe you've earned enough trust for me to give you a little leeway on this."

"How magnanimous," Baxter said. It was a word he had learned from Curtis, and it seemed like the perfect opportunity to unleash it.

"Excuse me?"

"That's very kind of you."

"It's the least I could do – to... to be manganese."

Baxter stared at him.

"We need to go through some loan applications. There are a few clients I want you to take care of. I've got some pressing things needing urgent attention."

While Larry spoke, Baxter checked his watch. *Come on, Bernadette!*

"Do you have somewhere else you need to be?" Larry asked.

"No, I..."

Before he could finish, there was a knock at the door. Baxter breathed a sigh of relief.

Irritated, Larry checked his own watch. "Who could that be? They should know better than to interrupt meetings."

"It must be important," Baxter said.

"Get the door."

Baxter arose from his chair while Larry reset his pose. He opened the door. Bernadette's face appeared in the crack.

"Hi, Baxter." She looked past him towards Larry. "Mr. Spago, I think you should come out here. I'm having some problems with an account."

Chapter 38

"Get one of the other tellers to help you," he responded testily.

"It's a sensitive matter, sir." She never called him that and Baxter was afraid she'd overstepped. But the opposite happened. The respectful title moved Larry from his pose. With an exasperated, dramatic sigh, he threw up his arms and hustled across the room before stopping opposite Baxter. "Don't go anywhere. Don't touch anything," he said as he held a finger in front of Baxter's nose.

"Aye, aye."

As Larry departed, Baxter leaned toward Bernadette's face. "I need three minutes," he whispered. "Can you do that for me?" She winked at him.

After shutting the door, Baxter nearly tripped over a chair leg as he raced around to Spago's computer. Baxter quickly logged on.

What Larry Spago did not know was that when Larry recently signed unread documents, he had handed over access to the security network of Last National Bank. Within a day, Baxter had received the passcodes to turn off the cameras and alarm systems. Now, no matter what happened, there would be no footage, and the police would not be alerted regardless of how many times someone pushed the silent alarm.

At the same time, Baxter shut off Larry Spago's office camera. Hurrying back to his seat, he was dropping back into the chair when Larry opened the door and let himself back in.

Slowly, Larry strolled back to the desk and resumed his position.

"You sure are sweaty today."

Baxter touched his forehead with his palm. "What did Bernadette need?"

A Miserable Antagonist

"Any imbecile could have solved that problem, but she needed my expertise with a particularly tricky transaction."

"What was it?"

"It doesn't matter."

It definitely did not matter anymore. Everything was ready for 11:30.

Just as Baxter and Larry were about to finish their meeting, the office door opened, and Eris appeared.

"Come in," Larry waved her inside.

"I'll go," Baxter said. He felt a surge of dread. She wasn't supposed to be in the bank. Eris' presence could possibly ruin everything. Everything they'd prepared, studied, practiced – it all could come to nought if Eris smelled something fishy beforehand. Baxter felt like swearing.

"We're all adults here," Larry responded.

"Hello, Baxter," Eris said with a knowing smile on her face. "It's good to see you. Are you feeling okay?"

"Yes."

"I just want you to know, Baxter, that I have no bad feelings towards you. Our history is in the past and we'll just let things go. Is that fair?"

"That's very manganese of you, dear," Larry said.

"What?"

"It's very kind of you to forgive Baxter like that after all he's put you through."

Baxter frowned. "What in the world are you talking about?"

Eris moved to Larry's side, grabbed his arm, and spoke. "The emotional manipulation. The endless sarcasm. And, of course, you were only interested in my looks."

Baxter leaned his head back and sighed. "Well, at least you got the last part right."

Chapter 38

"Do you see what I mean, sweetheart?" she said to Larry.

"I'm so sorry that he put you through that, Pumpkin."

"Can I go now?" Baxter asked without looking at them.

Larry checked with Eris for permission before waving him onwards and outwards.

Baxter slammed the door shut behind him when he left.

"What happened?" Bernadette asked.

"Nothing."

"Did he like your note?"

"What?"

"Your note about his dog's birthday."

"It's hard to tell," Baxter responded.

"Especially once *she* entered."

"Yes. It's hard to find happiness when she enters a room."

Bernadette shrugged as she turned to her computer where a young man was waiting for her. "Let's hope for an uneventful day," she said.

Chapter 39

Baxter couldn't focus. 11:26 - In four minutes, the first actors would arrive. Baxter hoped Larry would stay in his dang office until the commotion began. His greater hope was that Eris would remain ignorant of the whole thing. She was the linchpin. If she saw through the costumes and makeup, the Chittendon Correctional Center might have return visitors. But not as guests.

"What are you doing for lunch today?" Bernadette asked him.

"What?"

"I asked you what you're doing for lunch."

"No idea," he replied quickly.

"Do you want to have lunch with me?"

"Hmmm?"

Bernadette grabbed the partition between them and scowled at him behind it. "What's wrong with you? You're so preoccupied. Has that bimbo really got you all bent out of shape?"

"I'm just thinking."

The front door opened. Chad the Security Guard did not flinch. He barely glanced in the direction of the young couple who had moved into the lobby. Baxter squinted, then gasped softly in amazement. Whoever worked their magic on Murray and Lisa's costumes and makeup had done an extraordinary job. Murray was wearing glasses, a moustache, and a brown wig while Lisa wore a tight skirt, flowing blouse and three-inch pumps. Large hoopy earrings dangled just above her shoulders and the bright lipstick was wildly overdone.

Chapter 39

A true diversion.

Even though she towered over Murray with her shoes, she clung to his arm. They looked as if they were about to step onto a cruise ship.

"Excuse me," Lisa said to Chad. "Can you point us to the ATM Machine?"

Chad appraised her and then pointed.

"We're here to get some money," she said loudly and robotically.

Shrugging, Chad half-smiled. "Well, it is a bank..."

RELAX! Baxter wanted to yell at them. *Just be normal. Remember the roleplay!*

They sauntered over to the ATM where Murray produced his card.

A moment later, Baxter saw an elderly couple enter. If he hadn't known what time his parents were supposed to come in, he never would have picked them. His father had been given an incredibly realistic combover, and he was using a cane to walk. His mother wore a floral-print dress. A curly white wig hid her normally dyed hair. A pillbox hat covered the wig, and she carried a cream-colored handbag. Hunched over and shuffling, the elderly couple approached Carmen who had been specifically chosen because of her propensity for emotional overreaction.

As they planted themselves in front of Carmen, who welcomed them cheerfully, Hana and Curtis walked in. Hana's transformation was as complete as the others. Instead of her normal trim physique, she had been filled out in all the wrong places. Given a set of false teeth, Hana had been changed into the plainest of Janes. Standing next to her, Curtis, in brown pants and a tan sweater, squinted through thick glasses.

Curtis caught Baxter's eye. Baxter nodded imperceptibly to let him know that the cameras and security system had been disengaged.

The door opened again. Evelyn and Barbara entered. Dressed in a smart business suit and expensive shoes, Barbara had shed every bit of her housewife image and looked the part of a professional medical practitioner. Touching the corners of her mouth to wipe away lipstick, she stood at the front bench with the dangling chained pens and pulled out an envelope from her purse. Evelyn stood next to her fidgeting, yet simultaneously appearing bored. Her lips were pulled down into a frown. She had darkened her eyes and appeared vampirish. Evelyn spotted Baxter behind the glass and sneered at him.

She was a good actress for her age.

At the ATM, Murray suddenly pounded on it. "This isn't right! We had at least one hundred dollars in here!" All eyes turned towards him while Lisa held onto his arm for dear life.

"Calm down!" She said woodenly. "We'll get it figured out." She glanced around and caught Sheena's eye. "Can you help us with this machine?"

Sheena left her computer and slowly made the passage behind the bank of tellers and out the gate to the frustrated young adults. As she crossed the lobby, Betty began her story to Carmen. Baxter craned his neck to hear.

"Hello, Miss," she said. "I was hoping you could help us."

"Of course. What can I do for you?"

"My husband, Bob, and I, well, we've been living in our house for fifty years. That's right, isn't it Bob?"

"What?"

"FIFTY YEARS!"

"Fifty beers? Is it that time already?"

Chapter 39

"NEVER MIND!" She leaned into the glass towards Carmen. "He's lost some of his hearing…" she explained.

"I never would have guessed."

"But now, the bank is telling us that they're going to overdose on our house simply because we used our home as collateral to help our son buy his house. They can't do that to us, can they?"

"I don't understand. What do you mean 'overdose on your house?'"

"You know, take it from us, because we can't make all the payments on time."

"Aah," Carmen raised a finger. "Foreclose."

"WHAT DID SHE SAY?" Burnie asked.

"FORECLOSE!"

"WHAT?"

"I'LL TELL YOU LATER!" Betty's voice was very loud. Perfect.

Other bank patrons stopped to watch the aural drama, the second diversion, occurring at the teller's booth. Chad attempted to cover his chuckle with his hand.

"All righty, do you have your account number? Let's just have a little look at your account." Carmen typed madly and then waited for Betty to give her the information.

"WHAT DID SHE SAY?"

"SHE'S HAVING A LOOK!"

"SHE'S HAVING A BOOK?"

Betty neared his ear. "I'LL TAKE CARE OF THIS!" Burnie nodded.

"Excuse me," Curtis said to Bernadette in a strained, elderly voice. His teeth were a disgusting brown, as if he'd been smoking three packs a day and using melted chocolate as toothpaste. "I was wondering if you had a bathroom. I've got to…" He smiled embarrassedly.

"Of course, sir. Right over there." She pointed and grimaced, attempting to hide her revulsion.

As Curtis ambled to the bathroom, Hana took up position by a potted plant near the conference room. This placement had been particularly important for when…

Rack and Q-Bert entered the bank. As they strutted in, pants at half mast, hoodies and sunglasses, they spoke loudly with generous flourishes of mild profanity.

"Yo, check this out," Rack said as he pointed at Bernadette. "I just won me some cash in the lottery." He placed a stub in front of her. "That's two hundred big ones right there." He slapped the stub on the desk.

"I'm sorry, sir," Bernadette responded, "we don't cash lottery tickets here."

He stared her down. "What you're saying is, 'We don't cash lottery tickets for people like me?'"

"No, sir, that's not what I'm saying. What I mean is, the bank doesn't…" Bernadette looked to Baxter for help. He moved into her booth.

"Can I help you, sir?"

"I just told this… lady… that I won the lottery. We make the trade. Lottery ticket for two hundred dollars." He pushed it forward again.

"This lady is correct. You'll need to take the ticket to the store where you purchased it. They will…"

"I AIN'T TAKIN' THE …. TICKET ANYWHERE. YOU… WILL PAY ME!"

"Sir, if you can't control yourself, we'll have to ask you to leave." Baxter looked over his shoulder at Chad the Security Guard who had turned green. Betty and Burnie, along with Barbara and Evelyn, had paused their rehearsed scenes to watch. Betty looked frightened.

Chapter 39

Rack and Q-Bert leaned forward. "Are you telling me you're going to escort me out? Get outta here." They started laughing and exchanging handshakes.

"Chad," Baxter called out waving.

Uncertainly, Chad pulled himself from his stool and walked towards Rack and Q-Bert. "Gentlemen, you've been asked to leave," he said with a quavering voice.

"We ain't leavin' until we... get... our ... money." Rack moved directly into Chad's whitening face.

Chad withdrew a phone from his belt. "I'm going to have to call the police."

"For what? For demanding my rights?" Rack said.

Baxter had to admit: these guys were doing a pretty good job at their role.

Chad began to punch a few numbers into the phone, but before he could finish, Q-Bert knocked the phone out of his hand. It clattered across the room. Chad reached for his taser but was too slow. He'd never drawn it before, and, if quizzed about how it worked, he would have failed the test.

"Don't even try that, boy," Rack said.

Chad had had enough. In what seemed like slow motion, Chad reared back and punched Rack in the stomach. Rack easily could have dodged it, but he absorbed the blow and fell to the floor, unhurt, but acted as if Mike Tyson had hit him. Q Bert stood back. "Did everyone see that? That's assault. Someone had to have recorded that." He pointed at Evelyn. "You saw that, right?"

Evelyn's mouth was agape. She nodded, but like Lisa and Murray, who were standing wide-eyed in front of the ATM, Evelyn was too shocked to do anything. "We just want our money."

"ME TOO!" Q-Bert shouted. "I want some money too." The tone of his voice bordered on anger.

A Miserable Antagonist

Rack recovered and stood up quickly to wrestle with Chad the Security Guard. It was obvious that Rack could have taken him down at any point, but it was equally obvious they were waiting for something.

At that moment, Curtis exited the bathroom. After noticing the commotion, he said to Bernadette, "You need to get the manager. Right now!"

Eyes full of terror, Bernadette fled to the office where she burst in. Without apologizing for the interruption, she explained the emergency. Larry Spago appeared in the doorway and surveyed the situation.

"You need to get out there, Mr. Spago! This is your bank!"

"Chad looks like he's handling the job quite well. Has anyone pushed the silent alarms?"

"We all have, sir."

"Then we'll just wait."

As the wrestling match continued, Burnie suddenly held his chest. "I'm having a coronary!" Ensuing was the most theatrical, fall-to-the-floor-pretend-heart-attack in acting history. As he reeled sideways, then the other way, then down to one knee (*That would have been hard for him,* Baxter thought) and finally onto his back, Burnie Burnside divided the attention from the fight to his angina.

"Mr. Spago!" Carmen shouted. "We have to get an ambulance!"

It was then that Barbara made her acting debut. Holding up both hands she exclaimed at the top of her voice, "I'm a doctor. I've been trained for this sort of thing. Please, give this man some air!" Barbara glanced up at Evelyn. "Call the paramedics!" The fear in Evelyn's face was not feigned. With trembling hands, she held her phone and punched in numbers. Then, pretending to talk to the 911 operator, she mumbled into the phone the location.

Chapter 39

"Get out there!" Bernadette pleaded with Larry.

Larry glanced back at Eris. She nodded.

Quickly, but unsurely, Larry strode from his office and entered the melee. As he attempted to make his way over to Burnie, Betty, and Dr. Barbara, Larry gave the fight a wide berth. Rack saw him coming and caught Q-Bert's eye. Suddenly, Rack gave Chad the Security Guard an enormous shove which caused Chad to crash into Larry sending them both to the floor. When Chad rolled off Larry, Q-Bert lifted Larry off the floor by the underarms.

"Don't touch me!"

Q-Bert dropped him to the floor again. When Q-Bert backed up, he moved directly next to Curtis. At that moment, Barbara shouted, "He's got a pulse!"

Betty began to wail loudly. It was comically fake, but loud enough for all eyes in the room to turn towards the fake heart attack drama.

This three-pronged distraction Larry's eyes to narrow. "We will have order, right now! This is a bank, not a boxing match." He flattened his suit coat. "Sirs, I'm going to have to ask you to leave," he said to Rack and Q-Bert.

"Man, this ain't worth it. Your security guard tried to kill me. I just want you to know that all these people saw that, and you'll be hearing from my lawyers. And it won't be for no... two hundred dollars. It's gonna be two MILLION!" With that, Rack and Q-Bert adjusted their hoodies and strutted back out into the street.

Blanching at the thought of a lawsuit, Larry tried to think of what to do next. He glanced at Eris who was still behind the counter. Then, turning to Barbara he asked, "Doctor, how is he?"

"He's stable. The paramedics should be here any second."

"Where are the police?" He searched his teller staff. "You all pushed the alarms, didn't you?"

They nodded rapidly, together.

"All right, let's get back to order here."

Curtis and Hana's eyes were wide. The one wild card in this whole scenario had been Eris who was positioned in front of the closed door to Larry's office. Now, she was standing as the bridge between success and failure. For the plan to succeed, Curtis needed to get into the office. Once Chad and Larry had tumbled to the ground, Q-Bert surreptitiously had lifted Larry's keys from his pocket and handed them to Curtis who, when all the commotion was going on, was to slip into the office.

Something had to be done about Eris.

Everyone knew it. Especially Baxter.

The night before, after everyone had left, Curtis had briefed Baxter on what needed to happen. They'd practiced everything multiple times, but no one expected Eris to be guarding Larry's door. If nothing transpired in the next moments, the operation was finished. And they very well could be arrested.

Taking a deep breath, Baxter turned from his cubicle and approached Eris. Taking her by the arm, he led her to the vacant space to the far left of the tellers' stations. "Eris," he said with quivering voice, "I... just wanted you to know that despite all the things that have happened between us, from our first unexpected meeting, to living together, to our failed engagement, to living together again, to breaking up for the second time. I've... I've..." He was struggling to say these words, these great lies, "I've never stopped loving you." He couldn't look at her and he bit his lip.

"What?" she demanded incredulously.

"In these moments of chaos, I feel like my life flashed before my eyes, and I wanted to take it all back. I want you

Chapter 39

to know that I would do anything for you. And… I want to get back together."

"Baxter," she frowned, "I don't know what to say. I'm sorry if you feel like I've led you on again…"

"I just assumed you were using Larry to get back at me." He moved closer to her. "Truly, what could you possibly see in him? The chest hair. His posturing. And that moustache. I know how much you hate facial hair. I know everything about you."

Eris glanced out through the glass booth at Larry who was watching her quizzically. "It is pretty disgusting, isn't it?"

Surprised, Baxter pushed his advantage. "Will you have me back, Eris?"

Flustered, she touched her hair and then her neck. Baxter had changed so much. He was so confident, and the way he carried himself. Even that disappearing tattoo… Baldness was kind of becoming on him. Why couldn't he have been like this when they were engaged?

"I need some time to think," she said.

"Don't think. Kiss."

With that, he reached out for her cheeks and in his best Ryan-Gosling-pulling-Rachel-McAdams-to-him-Notebook moment, Baxter Burnside kissed the heck out of his ex-girlfriend. So engrossed was he (and she) in the kiss that Baxter did not hear Larry Spago running for him. Suddenly, Baxter and Eris were separated by Larry's enraged face.

"What in the hell are you doing?"

"I'm being liberated," Baxter responded as Larry gripped his upper arm tighter.

"From what?"

"From you. From this place. From life. I'm finally free." Baxter's face carried a dopey smile. "And you'd better let go of me. That's assault."

Larry dropped his arm like a hot potato. "Are you on drugs?"

"Just glucosamine and chondroitin."

Face full of confusion, Larry's brow furrowed deeply. "I want a full explanation!"

Behind Larry, Baxter saw Curtis sneaking into Larry's office. It was now or never. "I feel like Luke Skywalker and my transformation will only be complete when I do it."

"Do what?" Larry demanded.

"This."

In the most unexpected move of the morning. At exactly 11:49 a.m., Baxter Burnside channeled Herbert Treadwell and punched Larry Spago somewhere between the nose and forehead. It was not an Oscar-winning punch, but it was accompanied by a completely satisfactory thud. No one in the room was more shocked than Larry. Except, that is, Eris who covered her mouth. Her gasps, mingled with a sense of respect and arousal, echoed those in the room. As Larry recovered from the strike to the face, his eyes wide and his mouth agape, blood beginning to stream from his nose, the words formed.

"Baxter Burnside. You're fired." Larry touched his nostrils. Blood stained his fingers.

After hearing those blessed words, Baxter sighed with intense relief. Just then, Curtis finished closing the door behind him and left Larry's office.

Last National Bank of Montpelier settled into a strange silence. As the assembly of onlookers, six tellers, a faux-angina affected old man, two strange couples, a fake doctor and her excited daughter, Larry Spago himself, waited

Chapter 39

for something to happen, the front door burst open, and a paramedic rushed in with a gurney.

"Where is the victim?" he shouted.

"Down here," Barbara called out. "I'm a doctor."

The paramedic struggled to lower the wheeled gurney. As he wrestled with the mechanism, Curtis came over to help. When they finally collapsed it, Curtis, Barbara and Hana helped the paramedic lift Burnie Burnside onto it. Once prone, Curtis tapped the old man on the chest and the paramedic hurried Burnie and Betty out the door.

It was only when the paramedic glanced at Lisa and Murray that Baxter recognized him.

In some kind of purgative way, Parker Mangall atoned for his past.

Chapter 40

The novella release party took place two months later.

Curtis invited the Creative Writing 102 group (with Barbara's kids) to his house, as well as the Burnsides, Rack and Q-Bert, and Parker Mangall. As the drinks flowed and food was consumed, the conspirators reveled in their success.

When the class had wrapped up, each member of the group submitted their own chapters of *The Bad Guy* and compiled them into a novella. During the editing process, they wrestled with descriptions and adjectives. Ultimately, though, it wasn't until Baxter reminded them with his words, 'It doesn't really matter how it reads, but how we lived it,' that they truly understood.

Eris appeared at Baxter's house the day after the robbery. He had to explain to her that there really was no future for them. She begged and pleaded with him, but Baxter said he already had his eye on someone else. 'The kiss was just a spur of the moment thing,' he said.

After his rejection, Eris got a facial and had her nails done.

Larry Spago held true to his word to fire Baxter, but it didn't go on his record. Baxter reminded Mr. Spago about his lapses in managerial judgement and that if he ever received a bad reference from him, Baxter was not beneath blackmail. It only took three days for Baxter Burnside to be hired at a small accounting firm for much more money and more happiness than he had found the last twenty years.

And he took with him his new girlfriend, Bernadette Walters.

Chapter 40

Once Baxter let her in on the secret of their 'bank robbery,' she laughed harder than she had ever laughed before. Instead of being angry, Bernadette had impulsively kissed him. And that was that.

A ringing sound broke out over the festivities. It was Curtis holding his champagne glass in one hand and a spoon in the other.

"Thanks for coming tonight," he said with a broad smile. "I'm sure you wouldn't have missed it for the world." Cheers of approval.

"No way I'd miss out on the spoils," Murray said as he rubbed his hands together. They had all agreed not to divide the take until after the class was done. In fact, no one but Curtis and Baxter knew how much had been stolen from Larry Spago.

"I think we should have a toast, first," Curtis said. "Baxter, would you like to do the honors?"

Baxter nodded and felt Bernadette grasping his arm with immense pride. Many things about Baxter Burnside had changed, but one of the most noticeable things was the new tattoo he had on his cheek.

And it was filled in.

Still henna, though.

"Who would have thought that less than six months ago we'd be standing in a mansion, surrounded by a new family, enjoying fine wine and great food?" The others laughed and lifted their glasses. Betty and Burnie shouted happily with the younger people.

"There are many things which seemed inconceivable a year ago. For me, taking a creative writing class, writing a novella, starting a new job, finding love…" Bernadette squeezed his arm with a giggle.

"Punching Larry Spago in the face!" Bernadette's face flushed with glee as she spoke. They cheered again.

"But life doesn't have to be fiction. We don't have to be confined by routine, or passivity, or the rules of someone else's narrative. This is my life. This is our life. We can do whatever we want! We're the authors of our destiny!" The group drank.

"Thank you, friends, for helping me on this journey. Rack and Q-Bert, thank you for being an amazing part of the story. Murray and Lisa, for helping me relax. Barbara and Evelyn, for encouraging me to enjoy the moment. For you, Curtis, and your exorbitant hospitality and immense talent and hidden dark secrets." Curtis toasted him individually. "And for you, Hana, who went out of your way to invite me. That took courage, also."

"But tonight, I think, I'll save my best and largest thank you to my parents, Betty and Burnie Burnside, who raised me to be a nice guy. You helped me see that in the brevity of life, a few mid-life crazies are certainly important. But being kind is the craziest mid-life of all."

While the stern faces of Curtis' great grandparents looked on, a few more *Cheers!* echoed in the room.

"So, are you ready for the big reveal? Our take? Our spoils? What we absconded with?"

A rousing *Yes!*

Parker Mangall, to a chorus of cheers, left the room and returned pushing the same gurney on which he had wheeled Burnie out of the bank. There was a mound with a sheet over it.

Baxter took up a position beside the gurney and placed a hand on the sheet. "When Q-Bert lifted Larry's keys and gave them to Curtis, Curtis snuck into the office to take Larry Spago's most prized possession."

Chapter 40

Baxter theatrically gripped the sheet and grinned. With one quick motion, he ripped the sheet away revealing only one object.

A calendar from 1984.

"As Rack said, it's not enough to make them hurt financially, you have to hit them where it hurts most!"

Exultant laughter erupted. After a time, Baxter shushed them with his champagne hand spilling it on his shirt. Bernadette patted it and hugged him.

Lifting the calendar, they all booed seeing Larry's face. "As I said, each one of us will receive an equal share of the loot." With that, he ripped off a month of Larry Spago for each conspirator. "If you don't mind, I'll keep May!" The laughter continued. "Do with it as you wish, but as for me… Tonight, I'll be setting Larry Spago's memory on fire."

He pointed to the fireplace where a small blaze was burning in the hearth. Under the watchful eye of Curtis' rum-running forebearers, Baxter downed his champagne and strolled to the fire. With one last look at Larry Spago's face, he threw it in.

The rest of the team did the same.

It was the baddest thing Baxter Burnside could think to do.

Chapter 1

Once upon a time, there was a bad guy named Herb Treadwell.

This is the story about Herb and a bank robbery.

And how he wrote a book about it.

www.ingramcontent.com/pod-product-compliance
Lightning Source LLC
Chambersburg PA
CBHW071953290426
44109CB00018B/2004